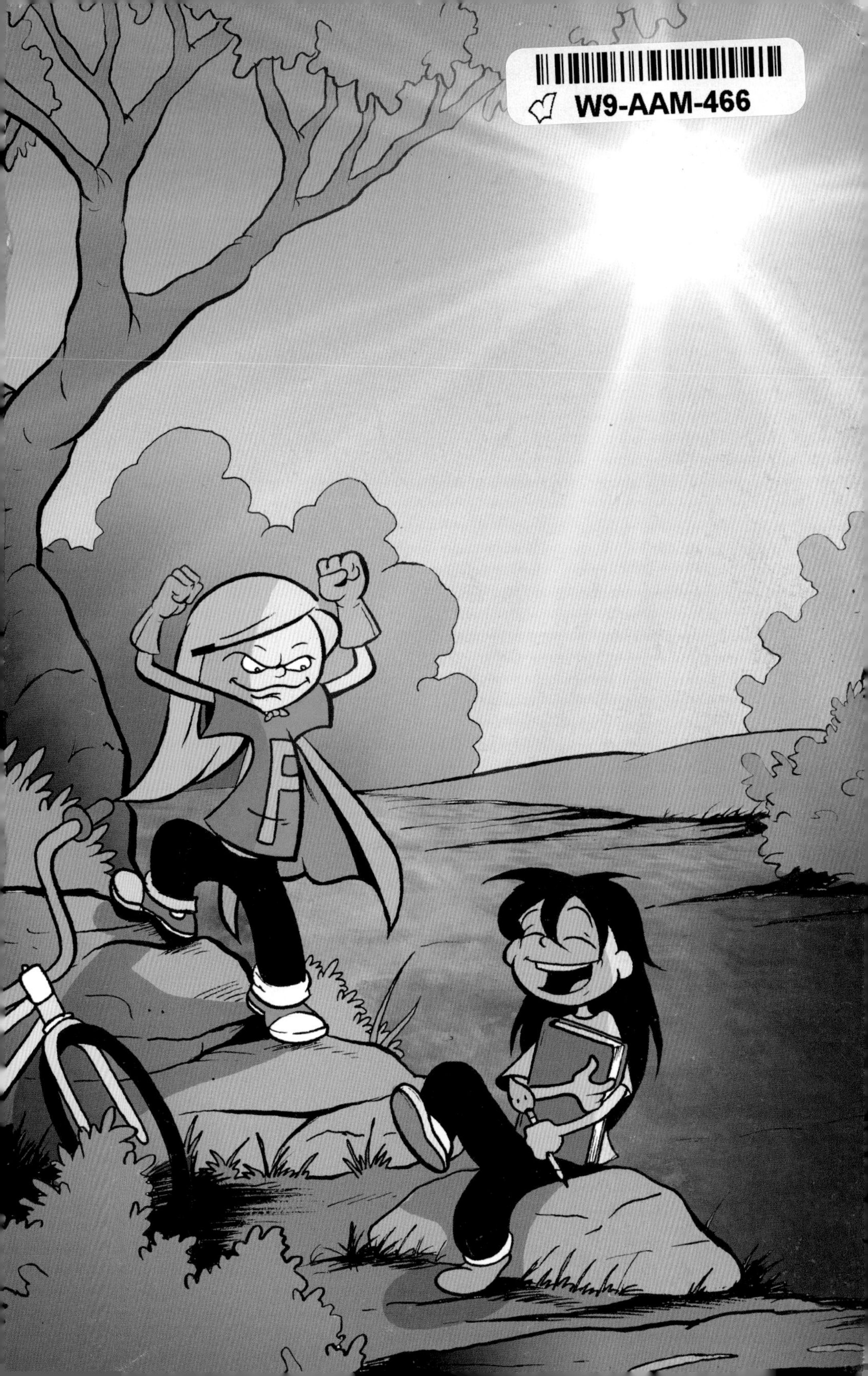

A Publication of **Renaissance Press**

Amelia Rules! Volume Three:
Superheroes

Renaissance Press
PO Box 5060
Harrisburg, PA 17110

www.ameliarules.com

ISBN 0-9712169-6-7 (softcover)
ISBN 0-9712169-7-5 (hardcover)

First edition 2006
10 9 8 7 6 5 4 3 2 1

Editor: **Michael Cohen**
Marketing and Promotion: **Karen Gownley**
Director of Publishing and Operations: **Harold Buchholz**
Brand Manager: Ben Haber

Special Thanks to Rich Thomas and Ben Doyle

Printed in Korea

Other Books in This Series:

Amelia Rules! The Whole World's Crazy
ISBN 0971269-2-4 (softcover)
ISBN 0971269-3-2 (hardcover)
Amelia Rules! What Makes You Happy
ISBN 0-9712169-4-0 (softcover)
ISBN 0-9712169-5-9 (hardcover)

To order additional volumes from Renaissance Press, visit us at ameliarules.com
or to find the comic shop nearest you call 1-888-comicbook

AMELIA Rules!

SuperHeroes

By **JIMMY GOWNLEY**

Renaissance PRESS

·a Renaissance Press book·

Dedication:

To Major Stephen M. Murphy, who will
first read these words while serving the
United States of America in Iraq.

Come home soon.

INTRODUCTION

If you have never read *Amelia Rules!* before, you have been missing out on something special. There is nothing else like it out there. Sure, other creators have explored the world of childhood. But we've never seen any other piece of entertainment that does the "Amelia" thing. Where else can you get a hilarious bit on the rigors of freeze tag and a heartbreaking glimpse at the pain of divorce in the same issue?

A word of warning, though–this stuff is addictive. You will want more. Correction, you will need more. Amelia's family and friends will take up permanent residence in your heart. That's how you know you're dealing with great characters–when the audience wants to spend time with them again and again. You feel like you know them and can't help but love them.

That's how it went for us. The more we read of Amelia, Tanner, Reggie, Rhonda, and Pajamaman, the more we got tugged into their world. A world that was funny, poignant and true.

Then it hit us. This Jimmy Gownley was good. Too good. Who needs competition like him out there? Our path seemed clear...we had to deal with Gownley...totally take him out of action...there was only one thing to do–

Nail him with a sneeze barf!

But then where would we turn for the future adventures of Amelia? Curse you, Gownley! You win...for now.

Bob Schooley & Mark McCorkle
Creators of *Kim Possible*
2006

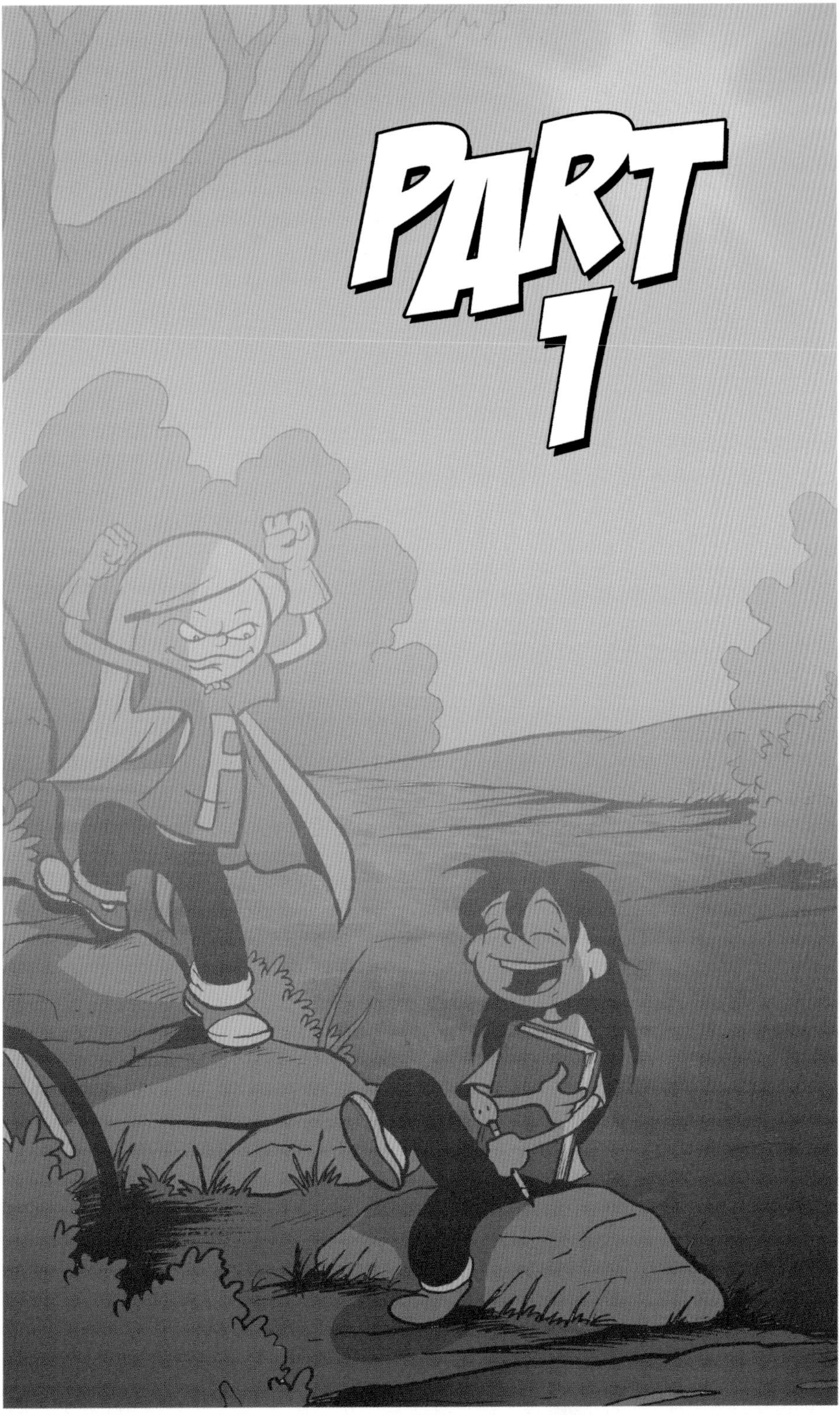
PART
1

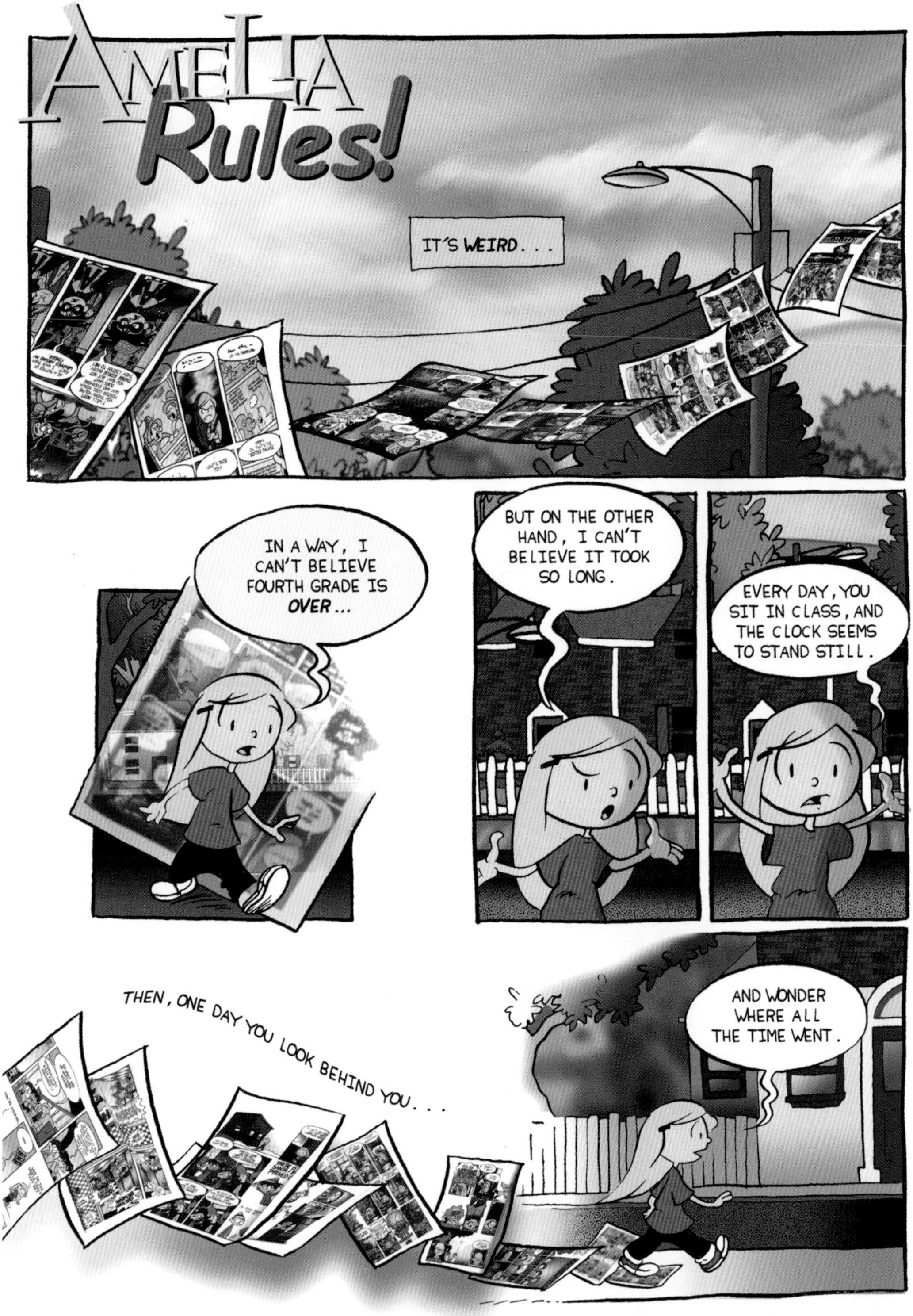
Amelia Rules!
IT'S WEIRD...
IN A WAY, I CAN'T BELIEVE FOURTH GRADE IS OVER...
BUT ON THE OTHER HAND, I CAN'T BELIEVE IT TOOK SO LONG.
EVERY DAY, YOU SIT IN CLASS, AND THE CLOCK SEEMS TO STAND STILL.
THEN, ONE DAY YOU LOOK BEHIND YOU...
AND WONDER WHERE ALL THE TIME WENT.

SUPERHEROES

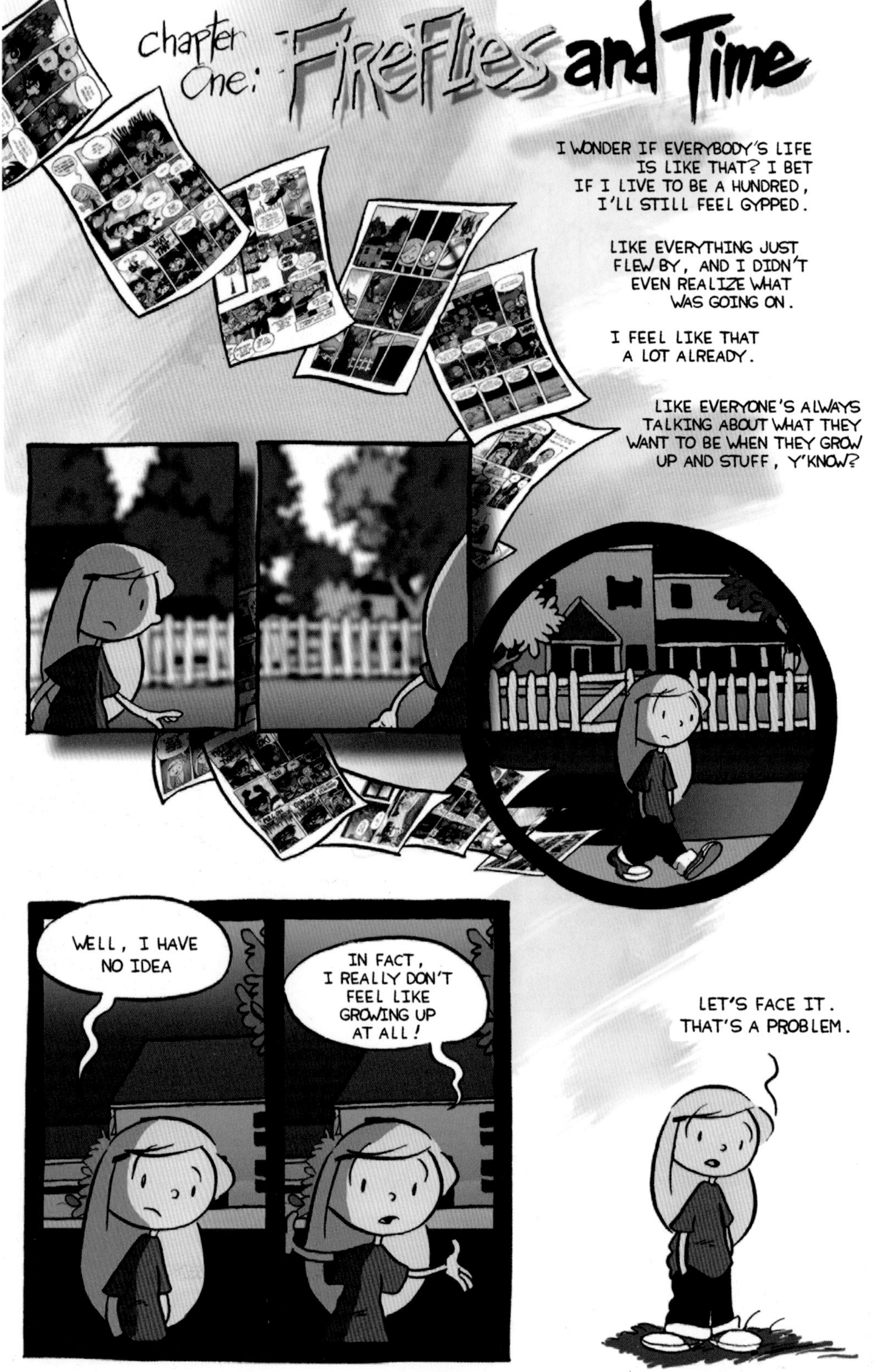
Chapter One: FireFlies and Time
I WONDER IF EVERYBODY'S LIFE IS LIKE THAT? I BET IF I LIVE TO BE A HUNDRED, I'LL STILL FEEL GYPPED.
LIKE EVERYTHING JUST FLEW BY, AND I DIDN'T EVEN REALIZE WHAT WAS GOING ON.
I FEEL LIKE THAT A LOT ALREADY.
LIKE EVERYONE'S ALWAYS TALKING ABOUT WHAT THEY WANT TO BE WHEN THEY GROW UP AND STUFF, Y'KNOW?
WELL, I HAVE NO IDEA
IN FACT, I REALLY DON'T FEEL LIKE GROWING UP AT ALL!
LET'S FACE IT. THAT'S A PROBLEM.

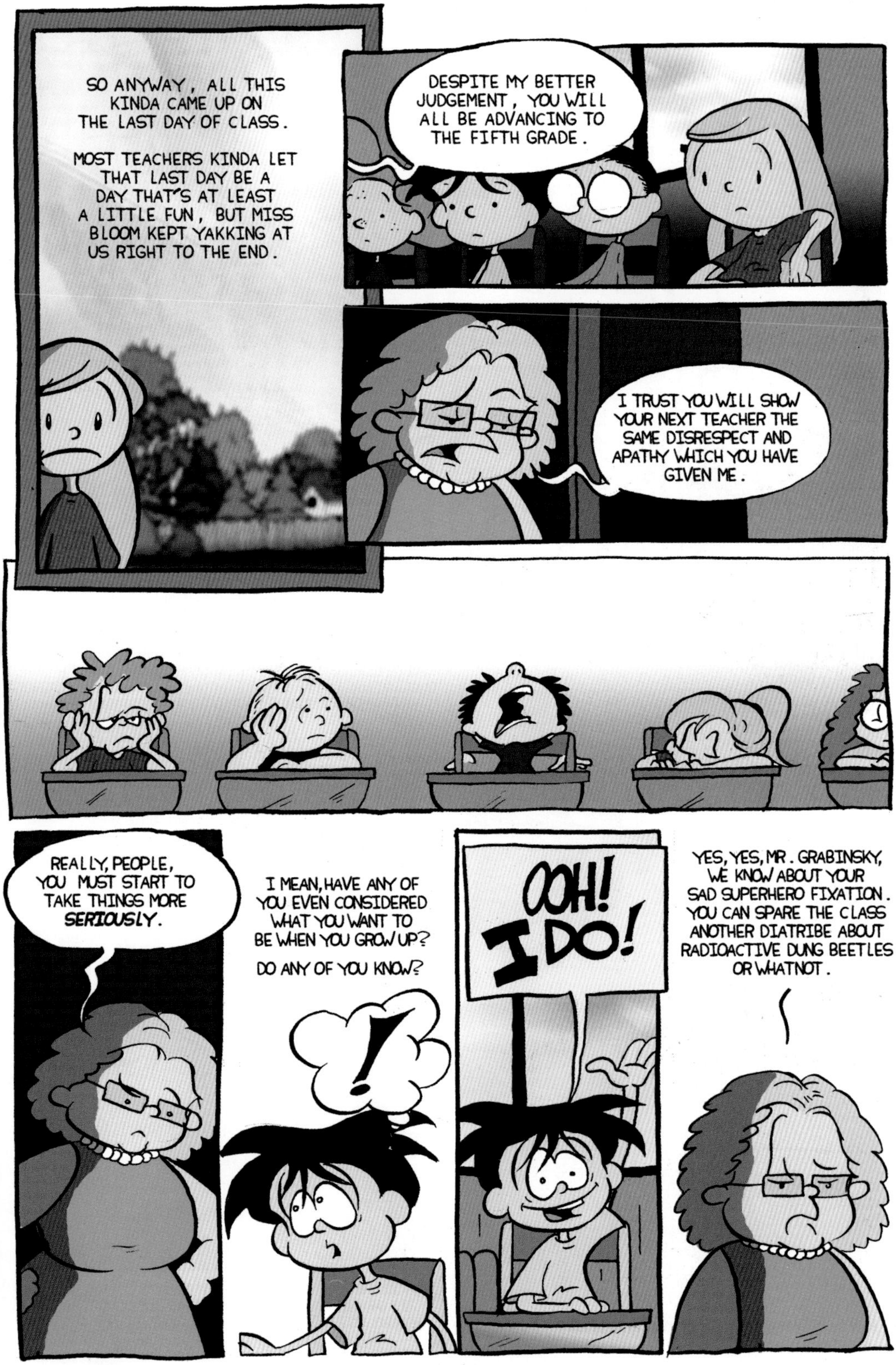
SO ANYWAY, ALL THIS KINDA CAME UP ON THE LAST DAY OF CLASS.
MOST TEACHERS KINDA LET THAT LAST DAY BE A DAY THAT'S AT LEAST A LITTLE FUN, BUT MISS BLOOM KEPT YAKKING AT US RIGHT TO THE END.
DESPITE MY BETTER JUDGEMENT, YOU WILL ALL BE ADVANCING TO THE FIFTH GRADE.
I TRUST YOU WILL SHOW YOUR NEXT TEACHER THE SAME DISRESPECT AND APATHY WHICH YOU HAVE GIVEN ME.
REALLY, PEOPLE, YOU MUST START TO TAKE THINGS MORE SERIOUSLY.
I MEAN, HAVE ANY OF YOU EVEN CONSIDERED WHAT YOU WANT TO BE WHEN YOU GROW UP?
DO ANY OF YOU KNOW?
!
OOH! I DO!
YES, YES, MR. GRABINSKY, WE KNOW ABOUT YOUR SAD SUPERHERO FIXATION. YOU CAN SPARE THE CLASS ANOTHER DIATRIBE ABOUT RADIOACTIVE DUNG BEETLES OR WHATNOT.

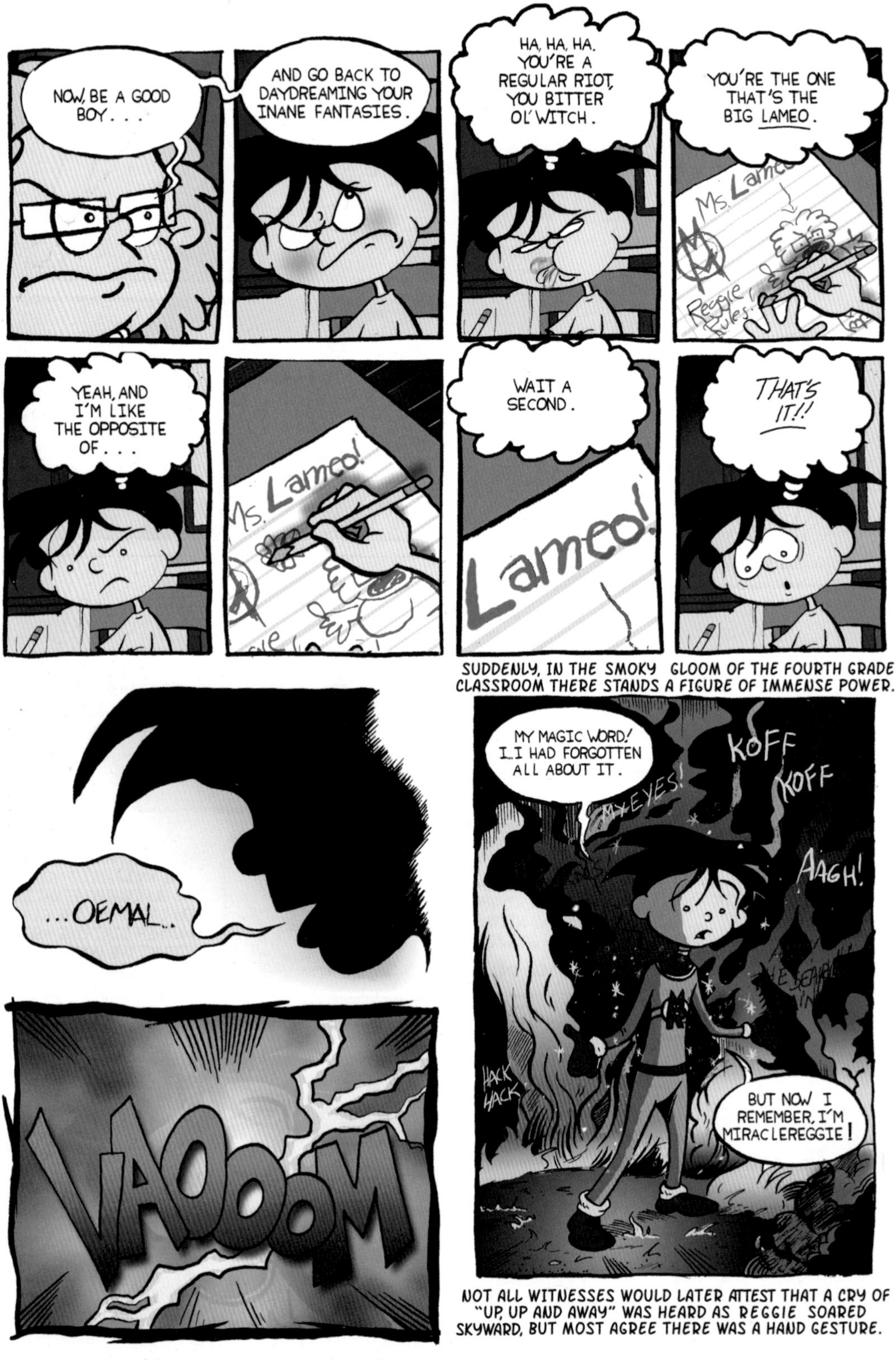
NOW, BE A GOOD BOY . . .
AND GO BACK TO DAYDREAMING YOUR INANE FANTASIES.
HA, HA, HA. YOU'RE A REGULAR RIOT, YOU BITTER OL' WITCH.
YOU'RE THE ONE THAT'S THE BIG LAMEO.
Ms. Lameo
Reggie Rules
YEAH, AND I'M LIKE THE OPPOSITE OF . . .
Ms. Lameo!
WAIT A SECOND.
Lameo!
THAT'S IT!!
SUDDENLY, IN THE SMOKY GLOOM OF THE FOURTH GRADE CLASSROOM THERE STANDS A FIGURE OF IMMENSE POWER.
. . . OEMAL . . .
VAOOOOM
MY MAGIC WORD! I..I HAD FORGOTTEN ALL ABOUT IT.
KOFF
KOFF
MY EYES!
AAGH!
HACK HACK
BUT NOW I REMEMBER, I'M MIRACLEREGGIE!
NOT ALL WITNESSES WOULD LATER ATTEST THAT A CRY OF "UP, UP AND AWAY" WAS HEARD AS REGGIE SOARED SKYWARD, BUT MOST AGREE THERE WAS A HAND GESTURE.

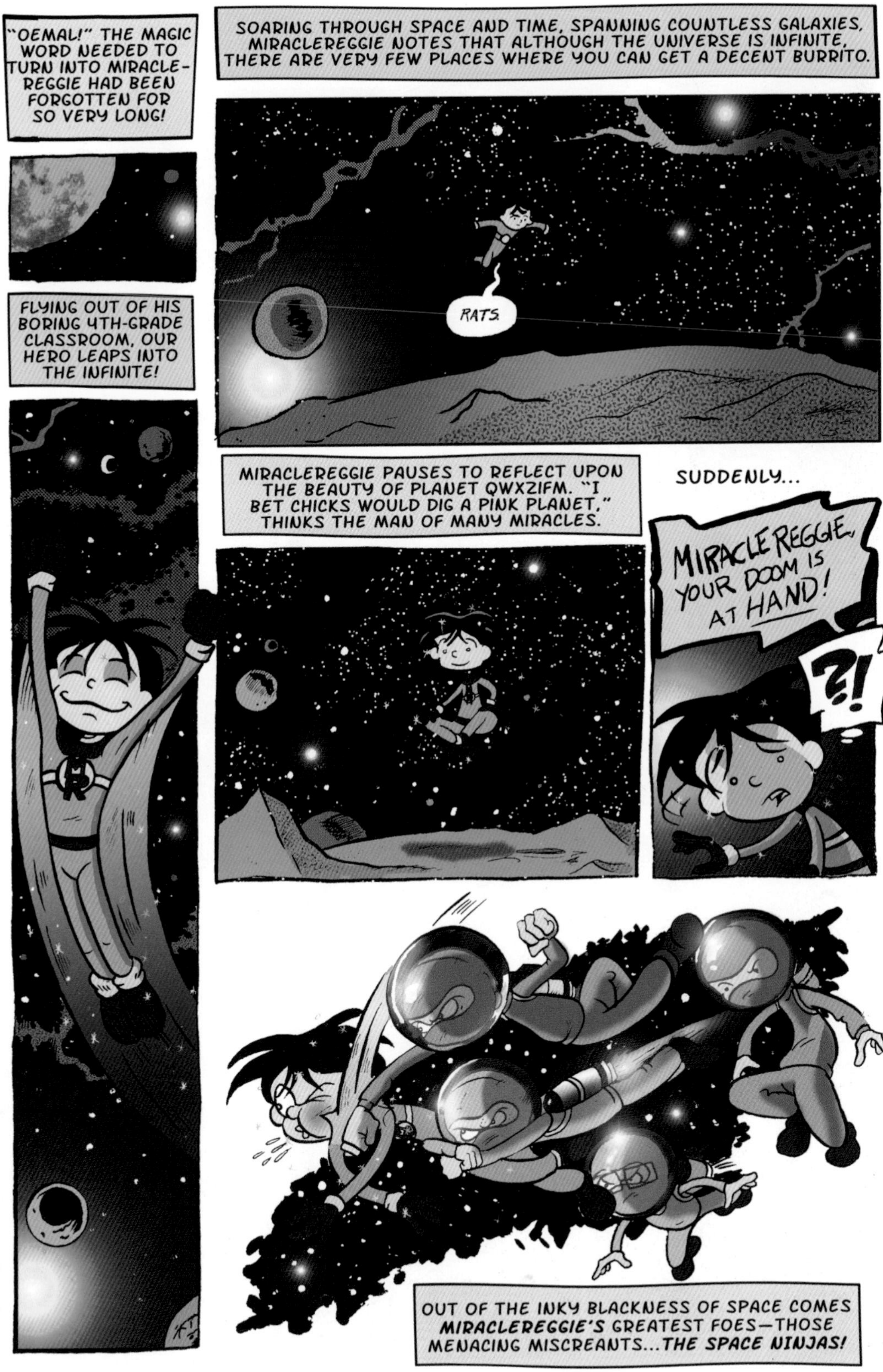
"OEMAL!" THE MAGIC WORD NEEDED TO TURN INTO MIRACLE-REGGIE HAD BEEN FORGOTTEN FOR SO VERY LONG!
FLYING OUT OF HIS BORING 4TH-GRADE CLASSROOM, OUR HERO LEAPS INTO THE INFINITE!
SOARING THROUGH SPACE AND TIME, SPANNING COUNTLESS GALAXIES, MIRACLEREGGIE NOTES THAT ALTHOUGH THE UNIVERSE IS INFINITE, THERE ARE VERY FEW PLACES WHERE YOU CAN GET A DECENT BURRITO.
RATS.
MIRACLEREGGIE PAUSES TO REFLECT UPON THE BEAUTY OF PLANET QWXZIFM. "I BET CHICKS WOULD DIG A PINK PLANET," THINKS THE MAN OF MANY MIRACLES.
SUDDENLY...
MIRACLEREGGIE, YOUR DOOM IS AT HAND!
?!
OUT OF THE INKY BLACKNESS OF SPACE COMES MIRACLEREGGIE'S GREATEST FOES—THOSE MENACING MISCREANTS...THE SPACE NINJAS!

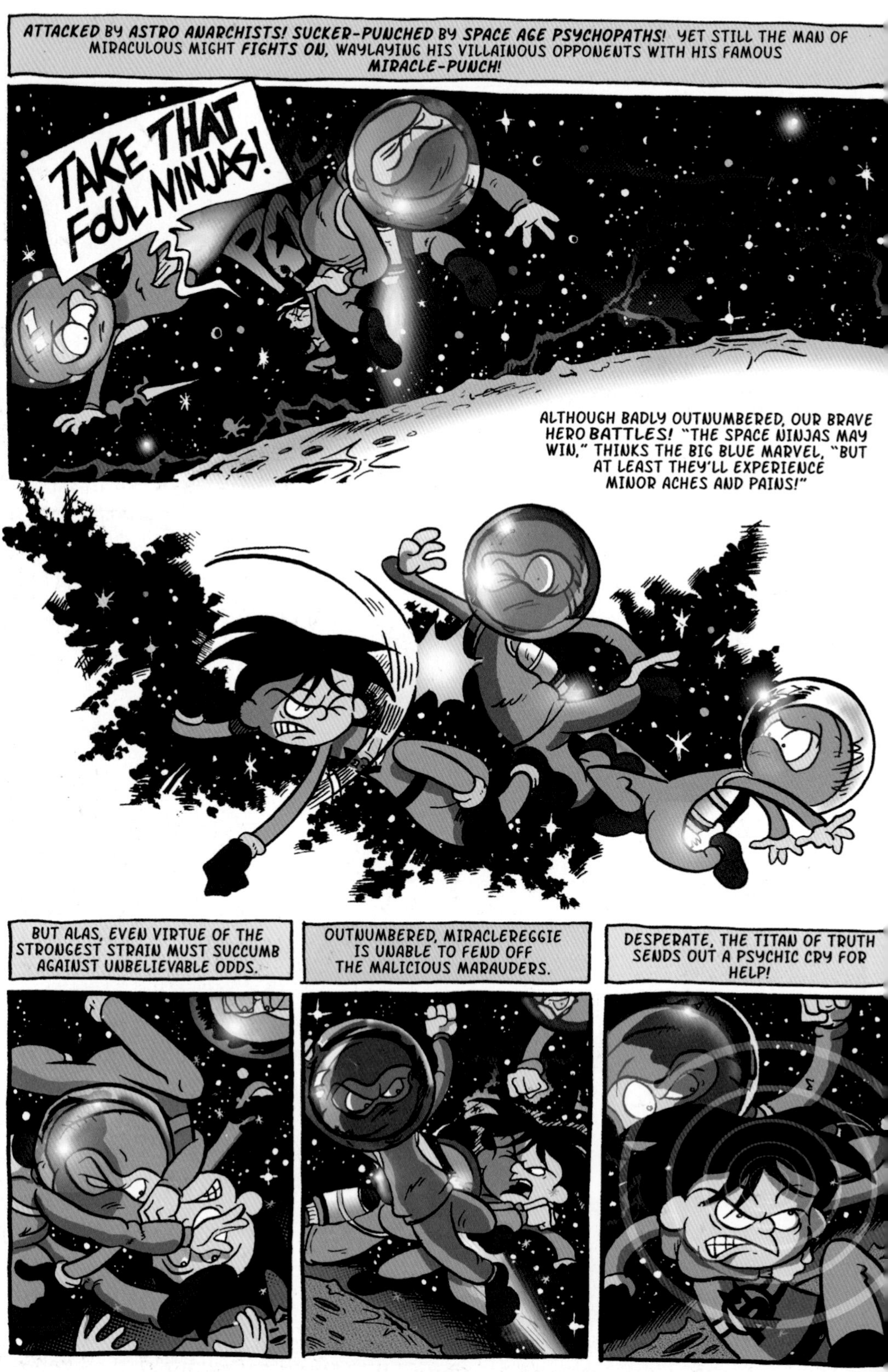
ATTACKED BY ASTRO ANARCHISTS! SUCKER-PUNCHED BY SPACE AGE PSYCHOPATHS! YET STILL THE MAN OF MIRACULOUS MIGHT FIGHTS ON, WAYLAYING HIS VILLAINOUS OPPONENTS WITH HIS FAMOUS MIRACLE-PUNCH!
TAKE THAT FOUL NINJAS!
ALTHOUGH BADLY OUTNUMBERED, OUR BRAVE HERO BATTLES! "THE SPACE NINJAS MAY WIN," THINKS THE BIG BLUE MARVEL, "BUT AT LEAST THEY'LL EXPERIENCE MINOR ACHES AND PAINS!"
BUT ALAS, EVEN VIRTUE OF THE STRONGEST STRAIN MUST SUCCUMB AGAINST UNBELIEVABLE ODDS.
OUTNUMBERED, MIRACLEREGGIE IS UNABLE TO FEND OFF THE MALICIOUS MARAUDERS.
DESPERATE, THE TITAN OF TRUTH SENDS OUT A PSYCHIC CRY FOR HELP!

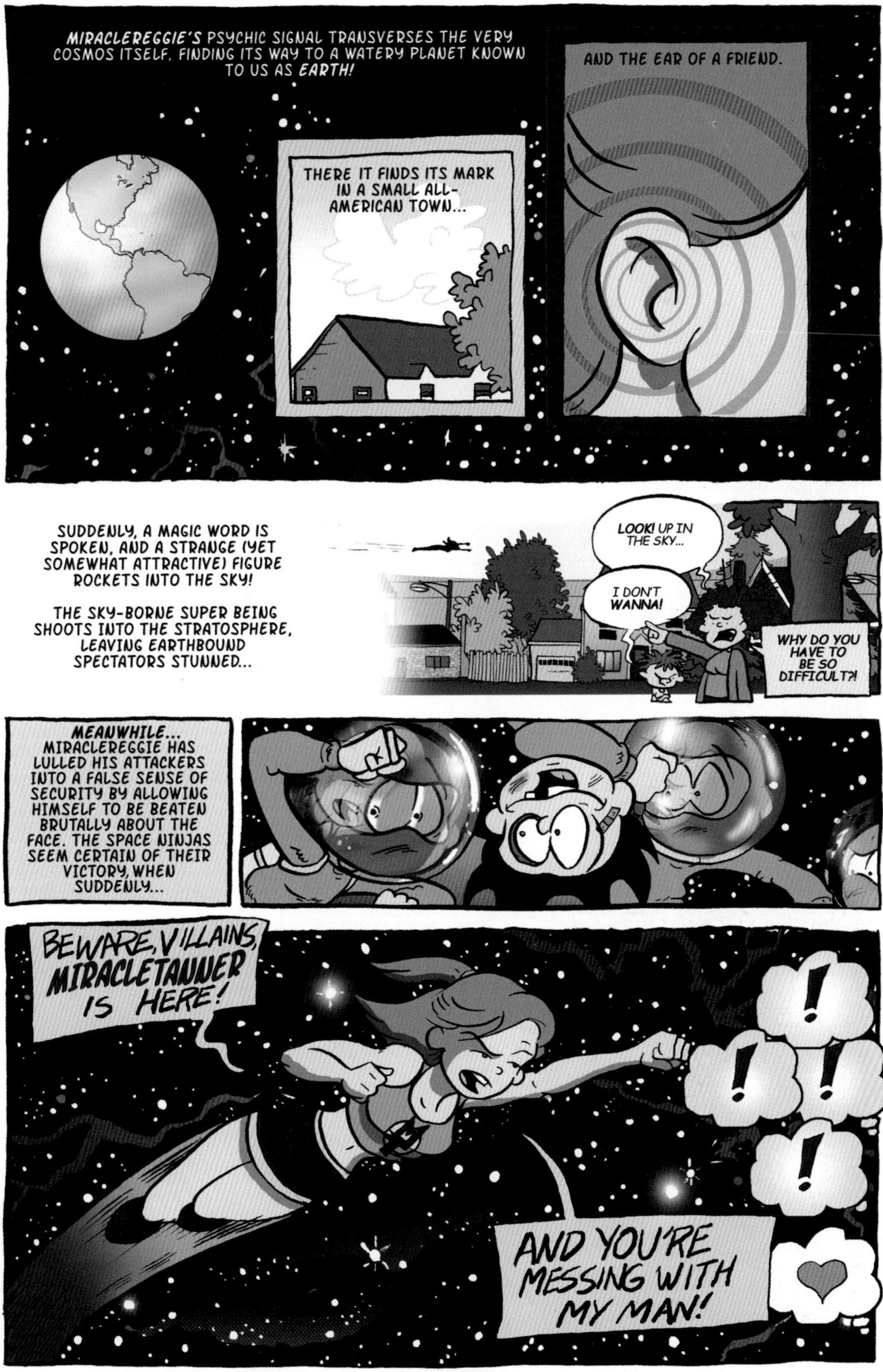
MIRACLEREGGIE'S PSYCHIC SIGNAL TRANSVERSES THE VERY COSMOS ITSELF, FINDING ITS WAY TO A WATERY PLANET KNOWN TO US AS EARTH!
THERE IT FINDS ITS MARK IN A SMALL ALL-AMERICAN TOWN...
AND THE EAR OF A FRIEND.
SUDDENLY, A MAGIC WORD IS SPOKEN, AND A STRANGE (YET SOMEWHAT ATTRACTIVE) FIGURE ROCKETS INTO THE SKY!
THE SKY-BORNE SUPER BEING SHOOTS INTO THE STRATOSPHERE, LEAVING EARTHBOUND SPECTATORS STUNNED...
LOOK! UP IN THE SKY...
I DON'T WANNA!
WHY DO YOU HAVE TO BE SO DIFFICULT?!
MEANWHILE... MIRACLEREGGIE HAS LULLED HIS ATTACKERS INTO A FALSE SENSE OF SECURITY BY ALLOWING HIMSELF TO BE BEATEN BRUTALLY ABOUT THE FACE. THE SPACE NINJAS SEEM CERTAIN OF THEIR VICTORY, WHEN SUDDENLY...
BEWARE, VILLAINS, MIRACLETANNER IS HERE!
!
!
!
!
AND YOU'RE MESSING WITH MY MAN!

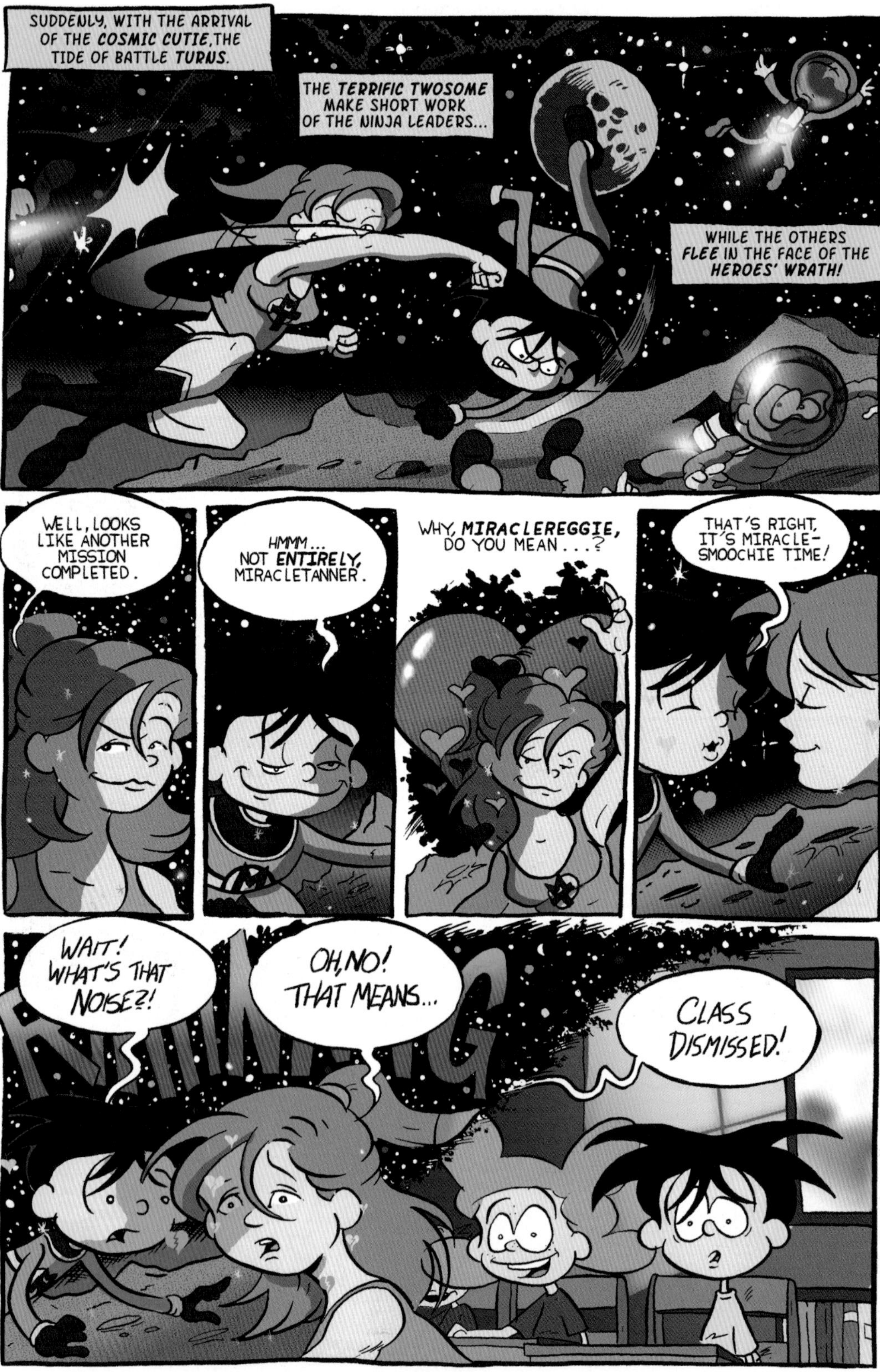
SUDDENLY, WITH THE ARRIVAL OF THE COSMIC CUTIE, THE TIDE OF BATTLE TURNS.
THE TERRIFIC TWOSOME MAKE SHORT WORK OF THE NINJA LEADERS...
WHILE THE OTHERS FLEE IN THE FACE OF THE HEROES' WRATH!
WELL, LOOKS LIKE ANOTHER MISSION COMPLETED.
HMMM... NOT ENTIRELY, MIRACLETANNER.
WHY, MIRACLEREGGIE, DO YOU MEAN . . . ?
THAT'S RIGHT, IT'S MIRACLE-SMOOCHIE TIME!
WAIT! WHAT'S THAT NOISE?!
OH, NO! THAT MEANS...
CLASS DISMISSED!

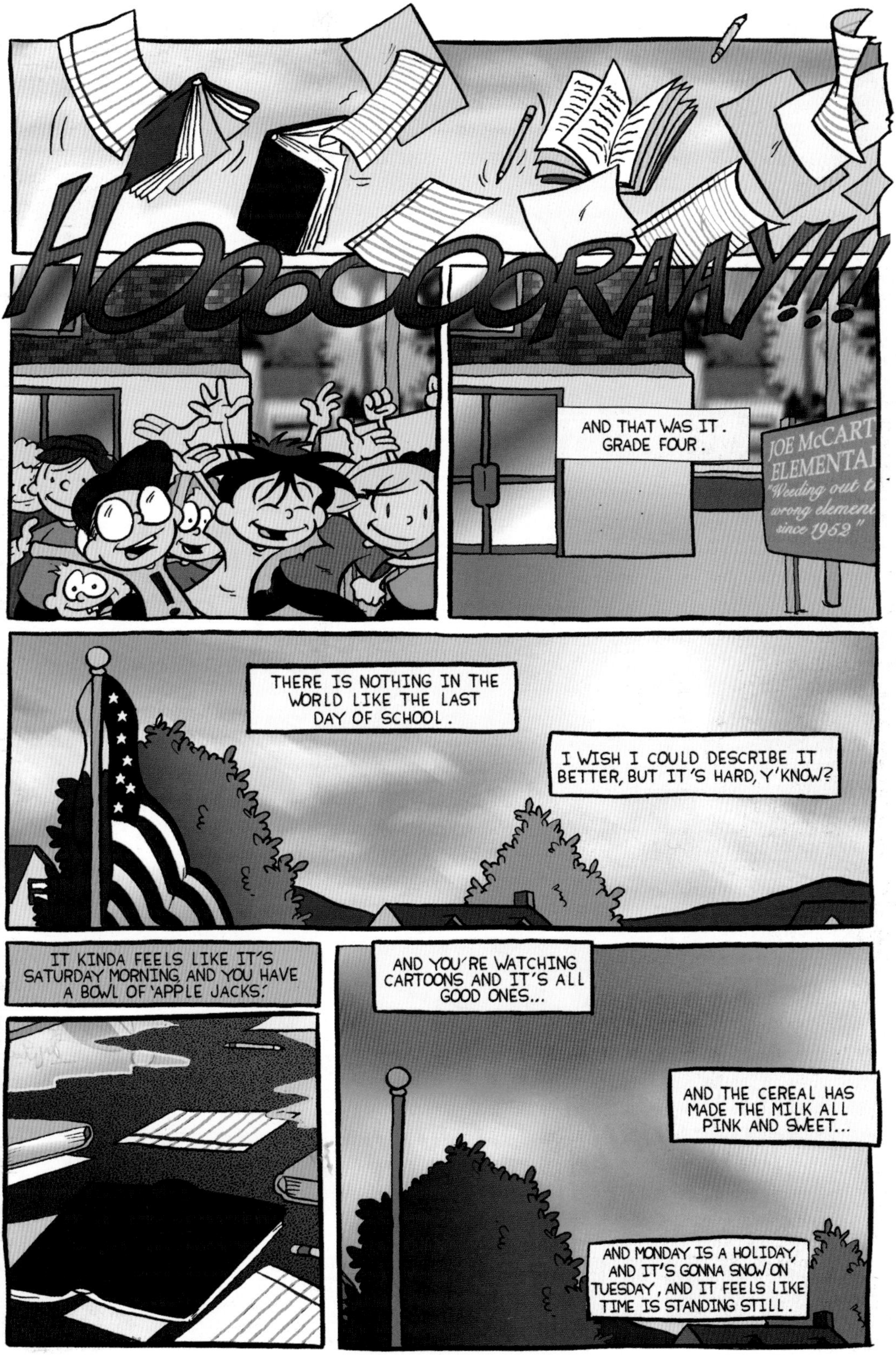
HOOOOOORAAAY!!!
AND THAT WAS IT. GRADE FOUR.
JOE McCART
ELEMENTA
"Weeding out t
wrong element
since 1952"
THERE IS NOTHING IN THE WORLD LIKE THE LAST DAY OF SCHOOL.
I WISH I COULD DESCRIBE IT BETTER, BUT IT'S HARD, Y'KNOW?
IT KINDA FEELS LIKE IT'S SATURDAY MORNING, AND YOU HAVE A BOWL OF 'APPLE JACKS.'
AND YOU'RE WATCHING CARTOONS AND IT'S ALL GOOD ONES...
AND THE CEREAL HAS MADE THE MILK ALL PINK AND SWEET...
AND MONDAY IS A HOLIDAY, AND IT'S GONNA SNOW ON TUESDAY, AND IT FEELS LIKE TIME IS STANDING STILL.

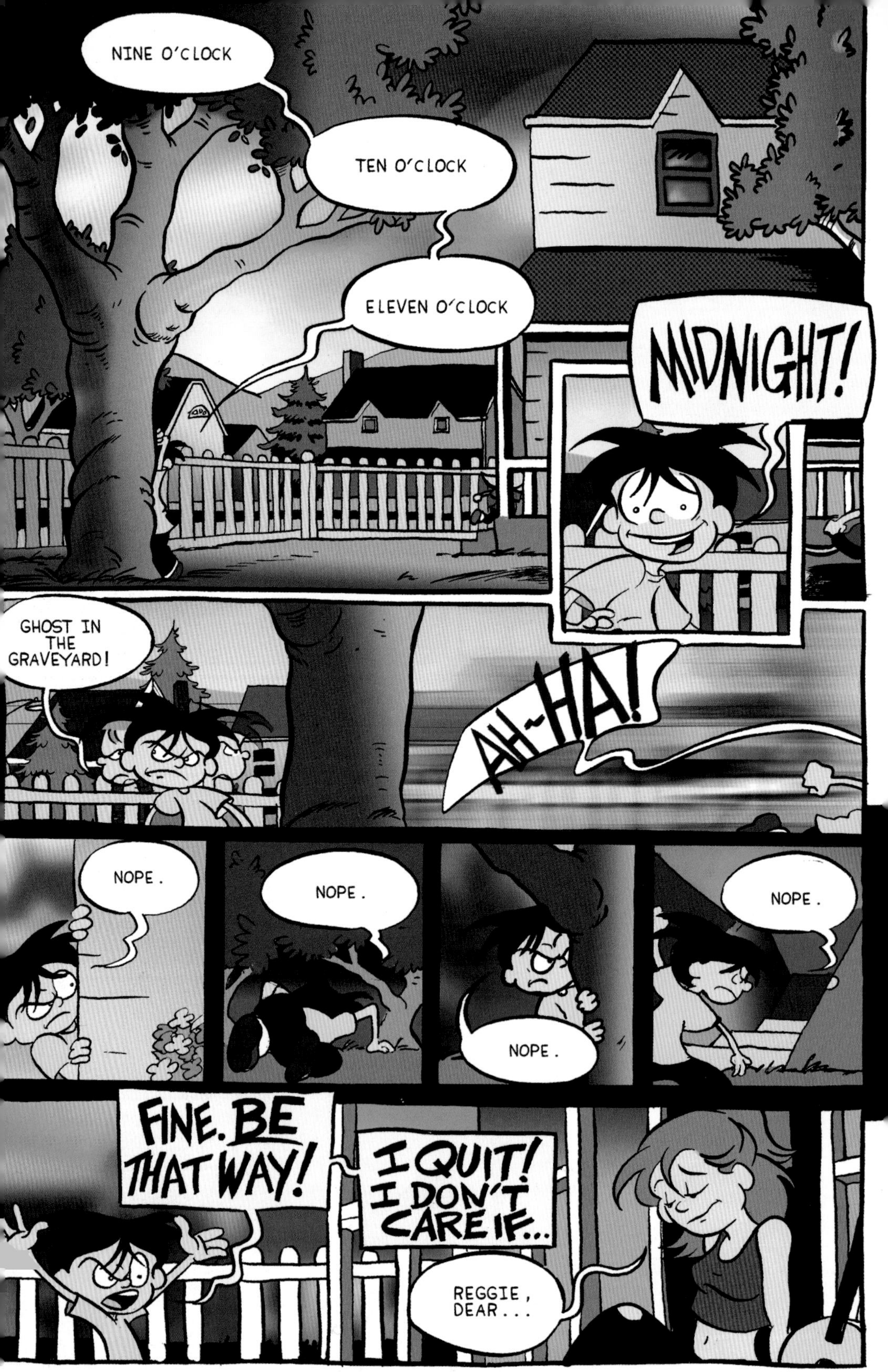
NINE O'CLOCK
TEN O'CLOCK
ELEVEN O'CLOCK
MIDNIGHT!
GHOST IN THE GRAVEYARD!
AH-HA!
NOPE.
NOPE.
NOPE.
NOPE.
FINE. BE THAT WAY!
I QUIT! I DON'T CARE IF...
REGGIE, DEAR...

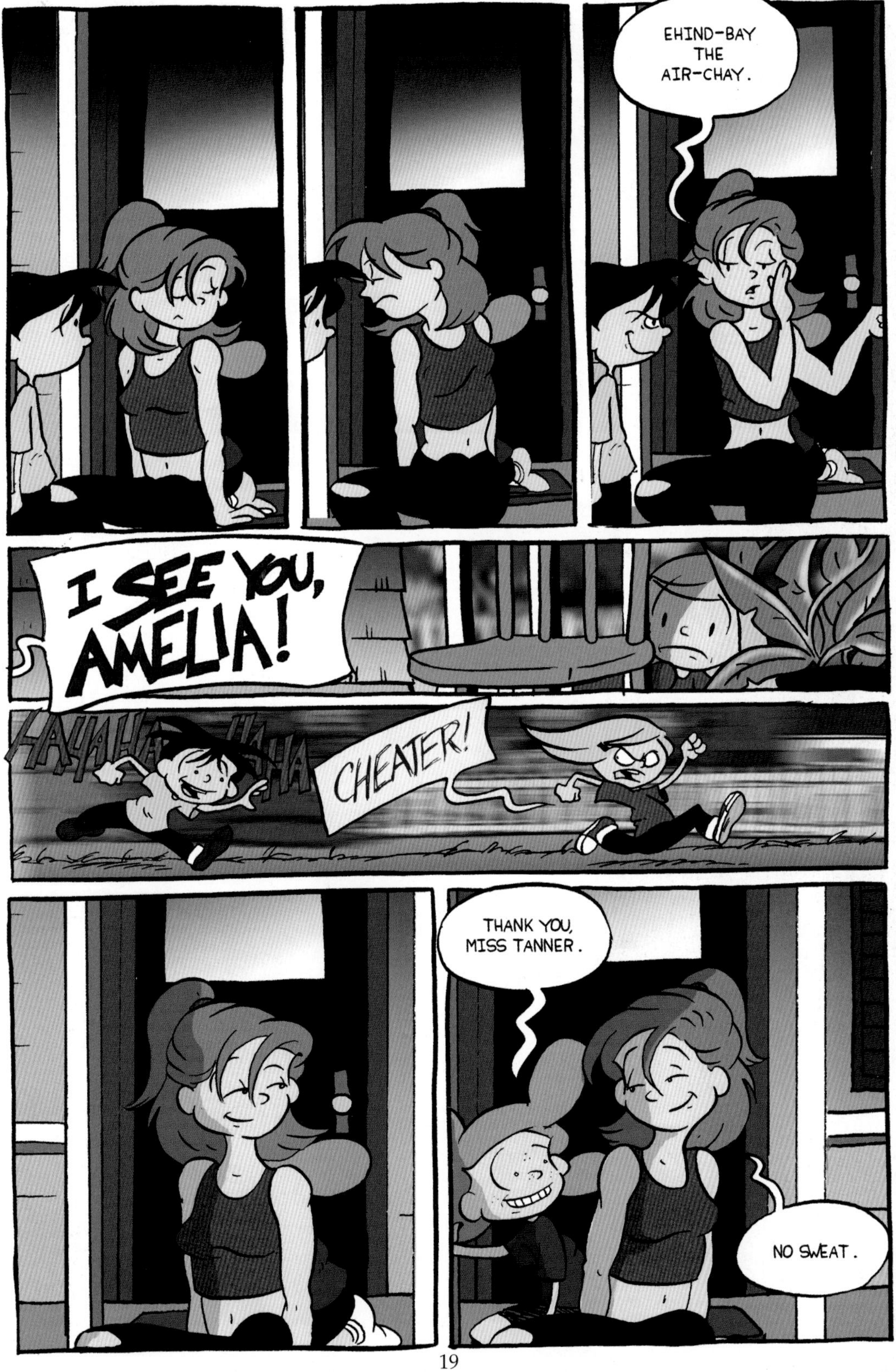
EHIND-BAY THE AIR-CHAY.
I SEE YOU, AMELIA!
HAHAHA HAHA
CHEATER!
THANK YOU, MISS TANNER.
NO SWEAT.

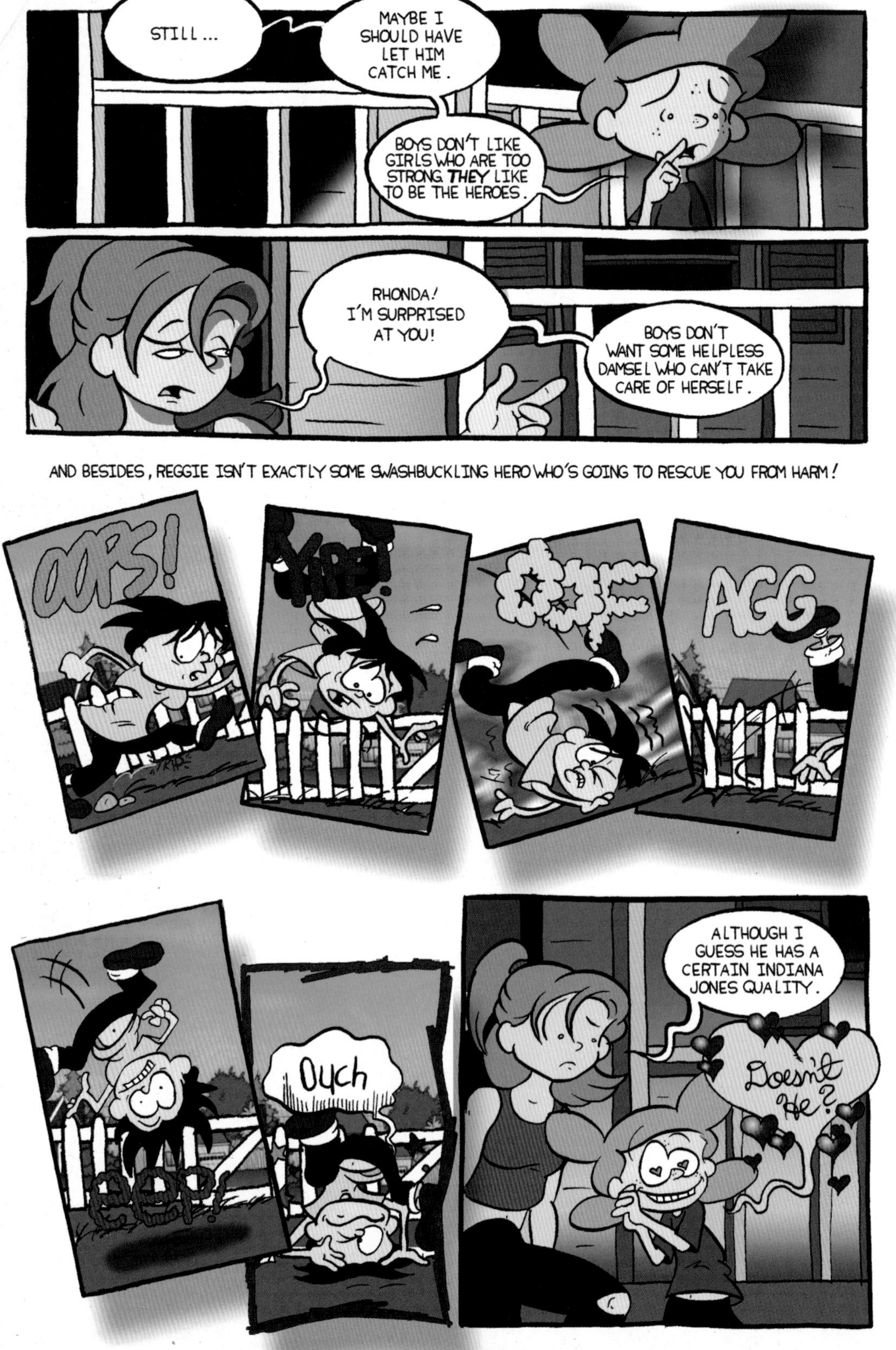
STILL...
MAYBE I SHOULD HAVE LET HIM CATCH ME.
BOYS DON'T LIKE GIRLS WHO ARE TOO STRONG. THEY LIKE TO BE THE HEROES.
RHONDA! I'M SURPRISED AT YOU!
BOYS DON'T WANT SOME HELPLESS DAMSEL WHO CAN'T TAKE CARE OF HERSELF.
AND BESIDES, REGGIE ISN'T EXACTLY SOME SWASHBUCKLING HERO WHO'S GOING TO RESCUE YOU FROM HARM!
OOPS!
YIPE!
OOF
AGG
Ouch
ALTHOUGH I GUESS HE HAS A CERTAIN INDIANA JONES QUALITY.
Doesn't He?

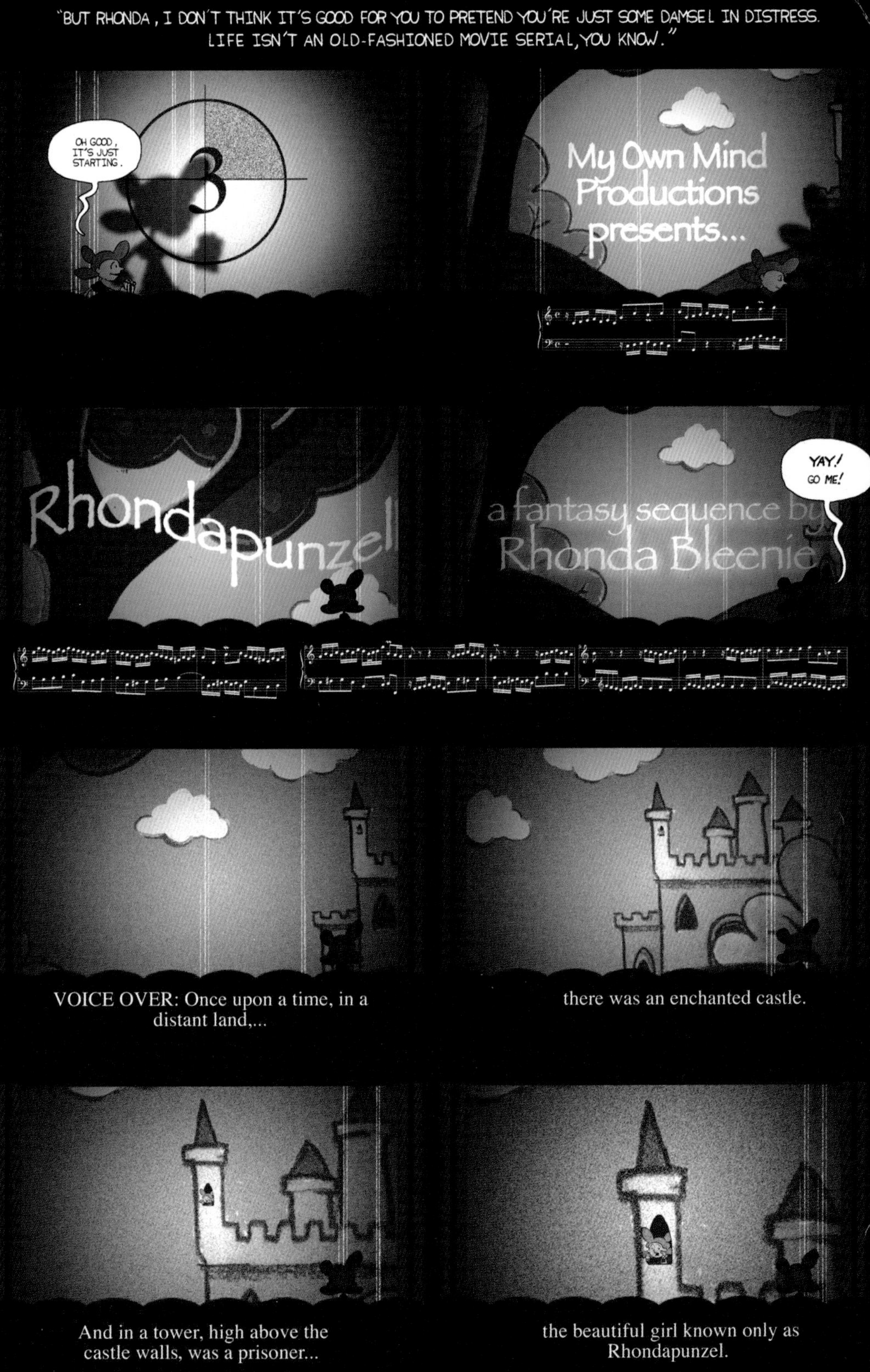
"BUT RHONDA, I DON'T THINK IT'S GOOD FOR YOU TO PRETEND YOU'RE JUST SOME DAMSEL IN DISTRESS. LIFE ISN'T AN OLD-FASHIONED MOVIE SERIAL, YOU KNOW."
OH GOOD, IT'S JUST STARTING.
3
My Own Mind Productions presents...
Rhondapunzel
a fantasy sequence by Rhonda Bleenie
YAY! GO ME!
VOICE OVER: Once upon a time, in a distant land,...
there was an enchanted castle.
And in a tower, high above the castle walls, was a prisoner...
the beautiful girl known only as Rhondapunzel.

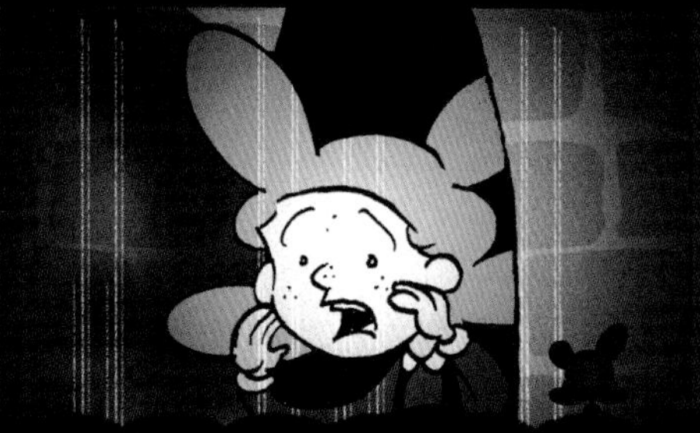

RHONDAPUNZEL: Help! Help! I, Rhondapunzel, am trapped in this tower, and in need of rescuing. (Eligible Princes only need apply.)

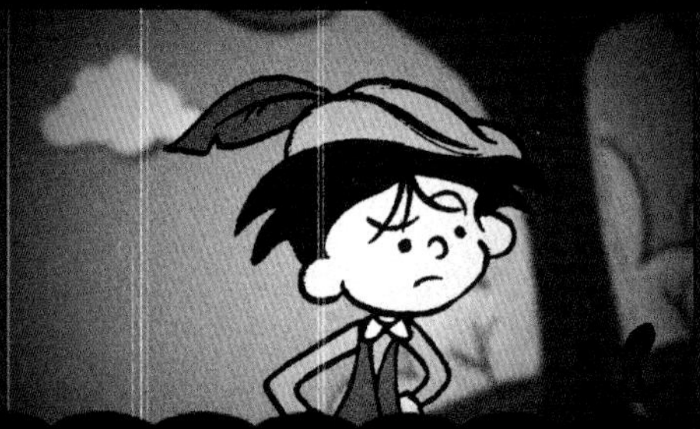

REGINALD: Hark! What doth cometh on yon morn breeze? Zounds! 'Tis the cry of a hot chick in distress!

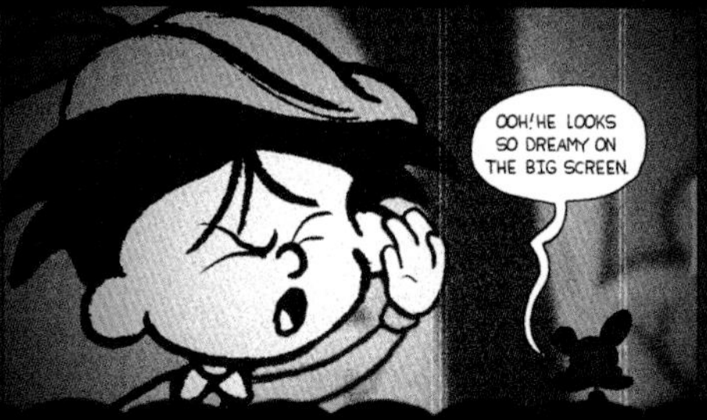
OOH! HE LOOKS SO DREAMY ON THE BIG SCREEN.

REGINALD: Fear not, fair hottie! For Reginald of the Woods is here! Lower your hair and I shall climb up to rescue you anon!

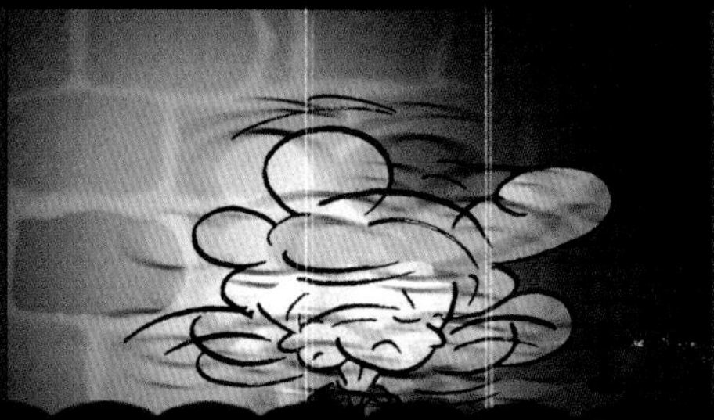

SFX: (Whip Whip Whip)

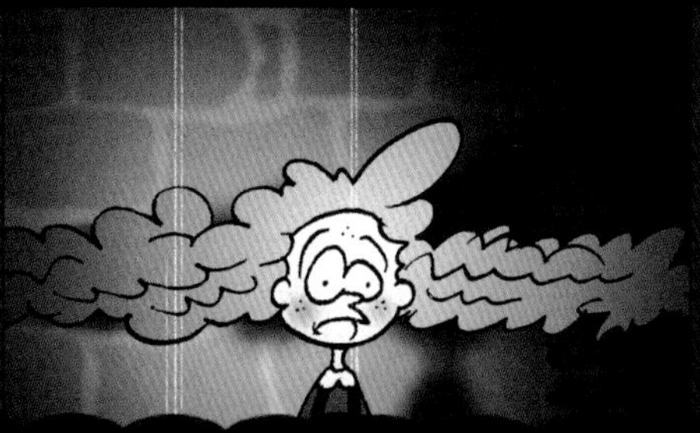

SFX: (Sproing!)
RHONDAPUNZEL: How embarrassing!

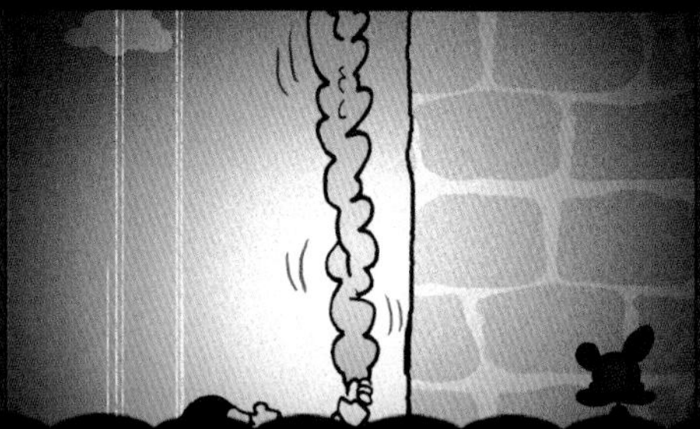

SFX: (Tug Tug)

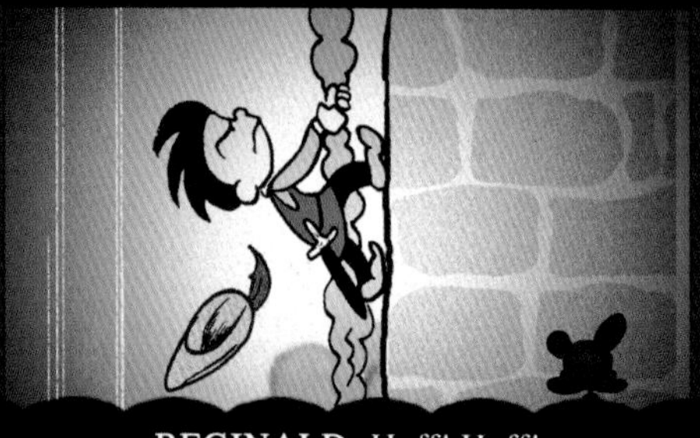

REGINALD: Huff! Huff!

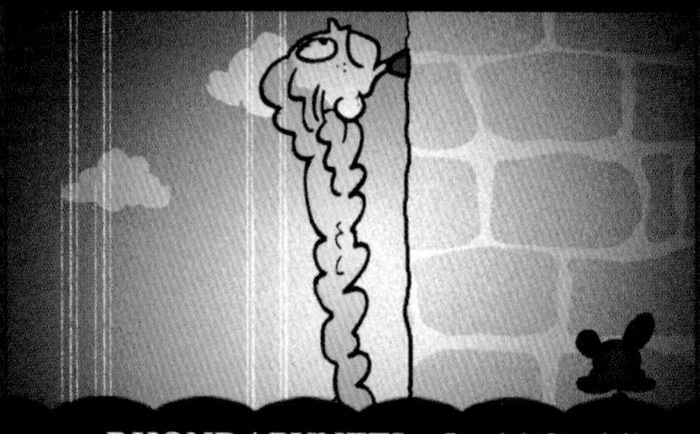

RHONDAPUNZEL: Ouch! Ouch!

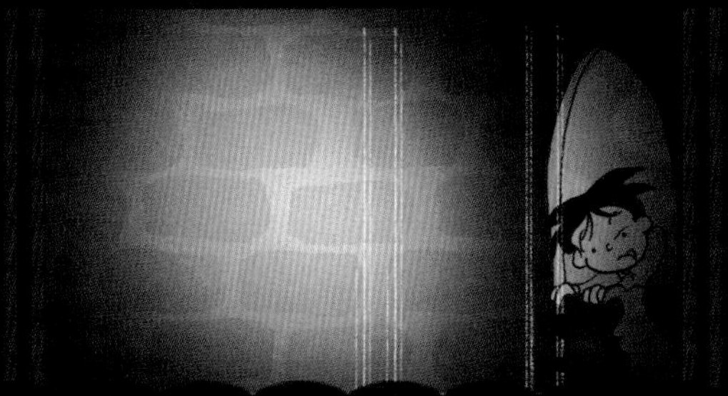

REGINALD: Take heart, fair maiden! For I, Reginald of the Woods, have come to save you.

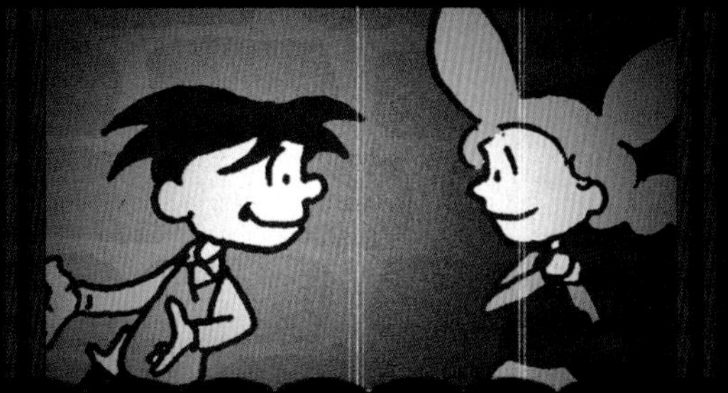

RHONDAPUNZEL: I knew that if I waited long enough, a handsome prince would come to rescue me.

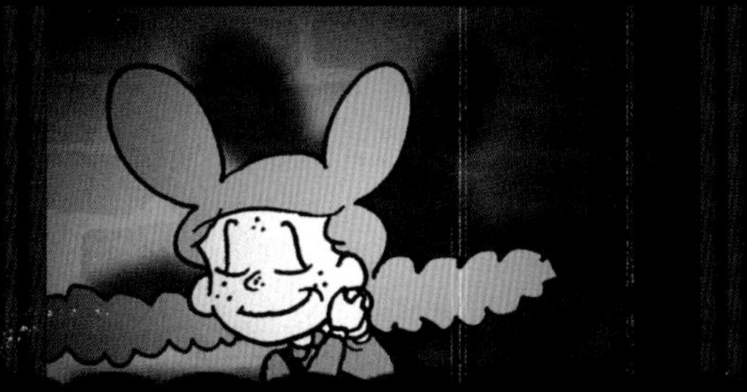

RHONDAPUNZEL: You ARE a prince, aren't you?

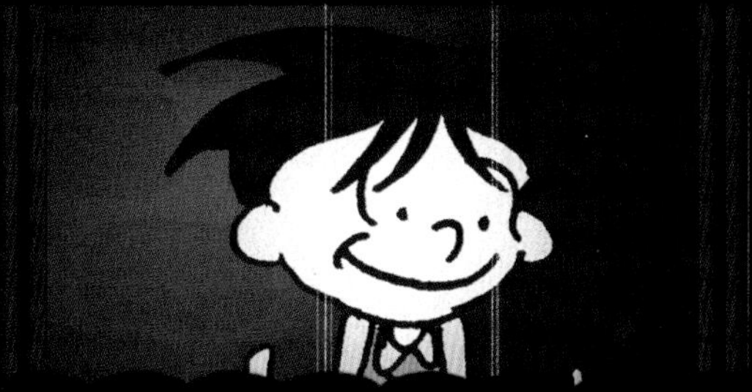

REGINALD: Well, not exactly, but my dad has most of his albums.

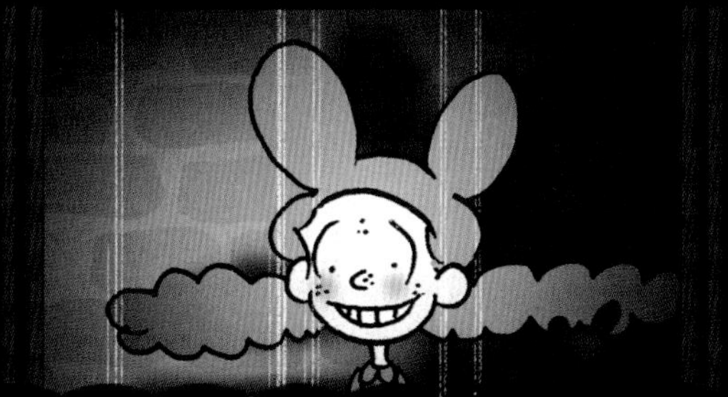

RHONDAPUNZEL: Close enough!

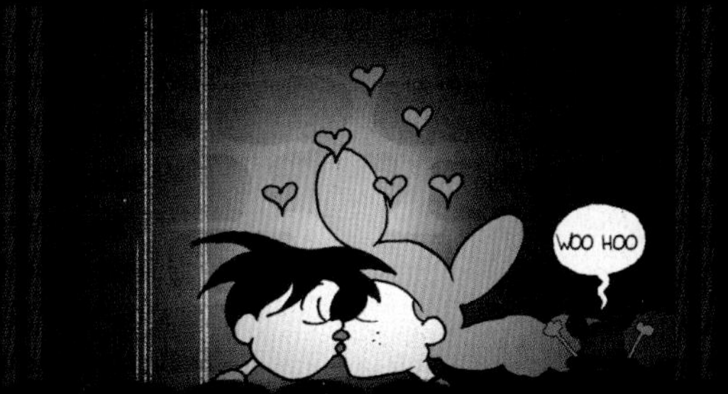
WOO HOO

SFX: Smooooooooooooooch!!

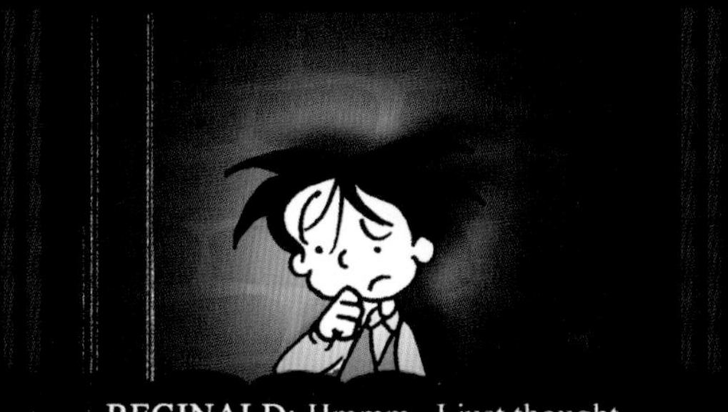

REGINALD: Hmmm...I just thought of something.
RHONDAPUNZEL: Yes, my love?

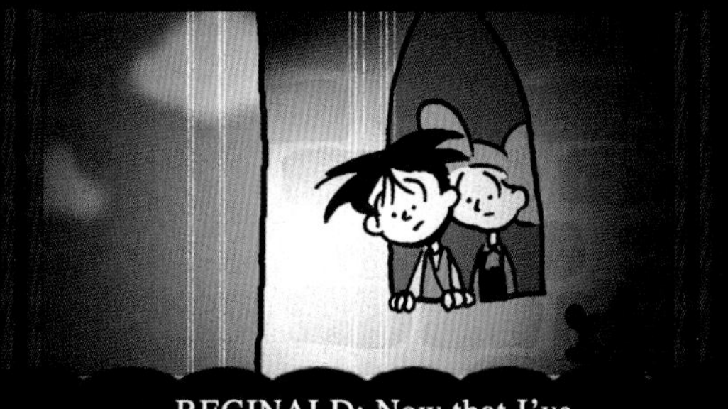

REGINALD: Now that I've rescued you, who is gonna rescue me?

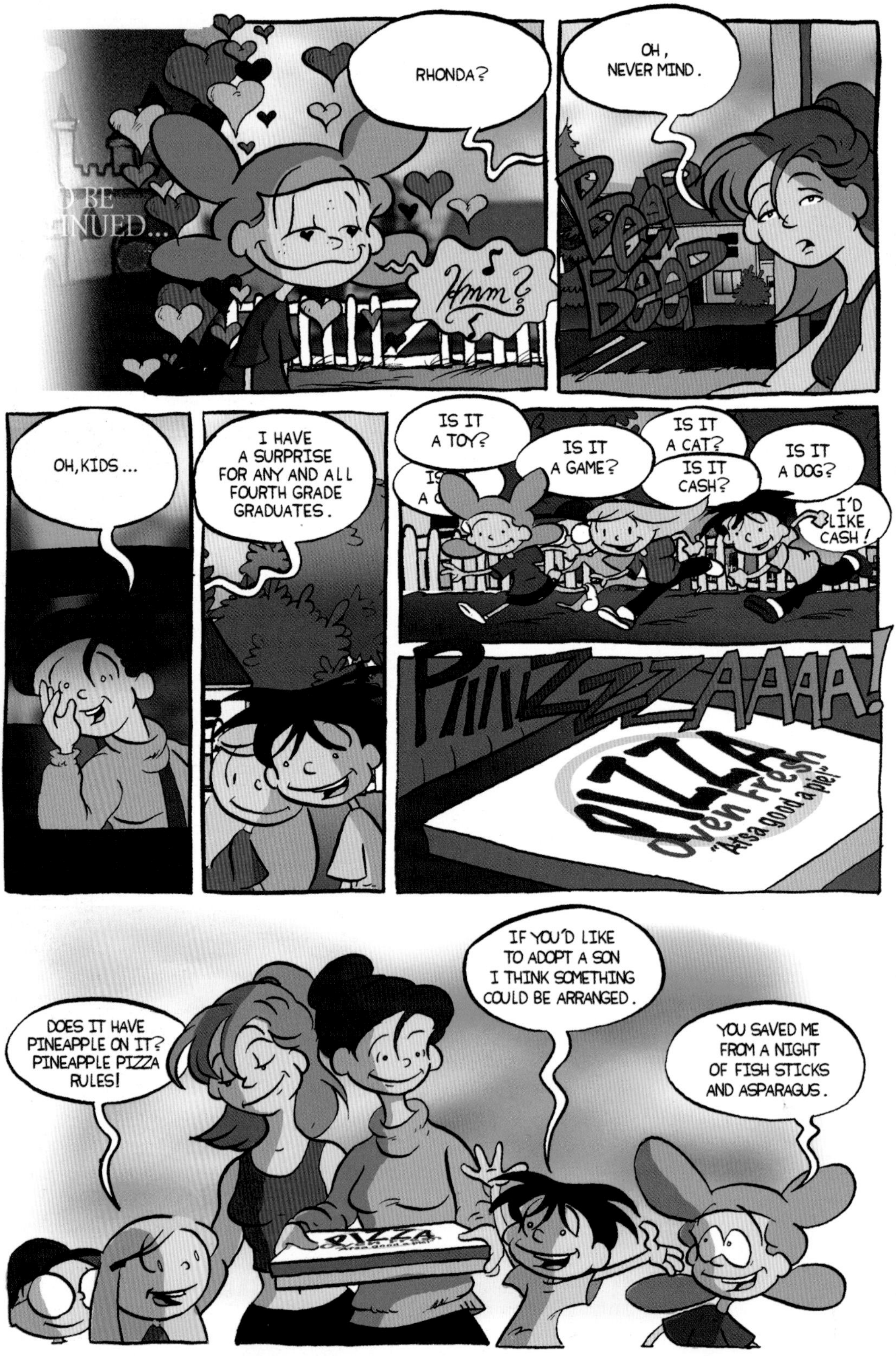
RHONDA?
Hmm?
OH, NEVER MIND.
OH, KIDS...
I HAVE A SURPRISE FOR ANY AND ALL FOURTH GRADE GRADUATES.
IS IT A TOY?
IS IT A GAME?
IS IT A CAT?
IS IT CASH?
IS IT A DOG?
I'D LIKE CASH!
PIIIZZZAAAA!
PIZZA
Oven Fresh
"Atsa good a pie!"
DOES IT HAVE PINEAPPLE ON IT? PINEAPPLE PIZZA RULES!
IF YOU'D LIKE TO ADOPT A SON I THINK SOMETHING COULD BE ARRANGED.
YOU SAVED ME FROM A NIGHT OF FISH STICKS AND ASPARAGUS.

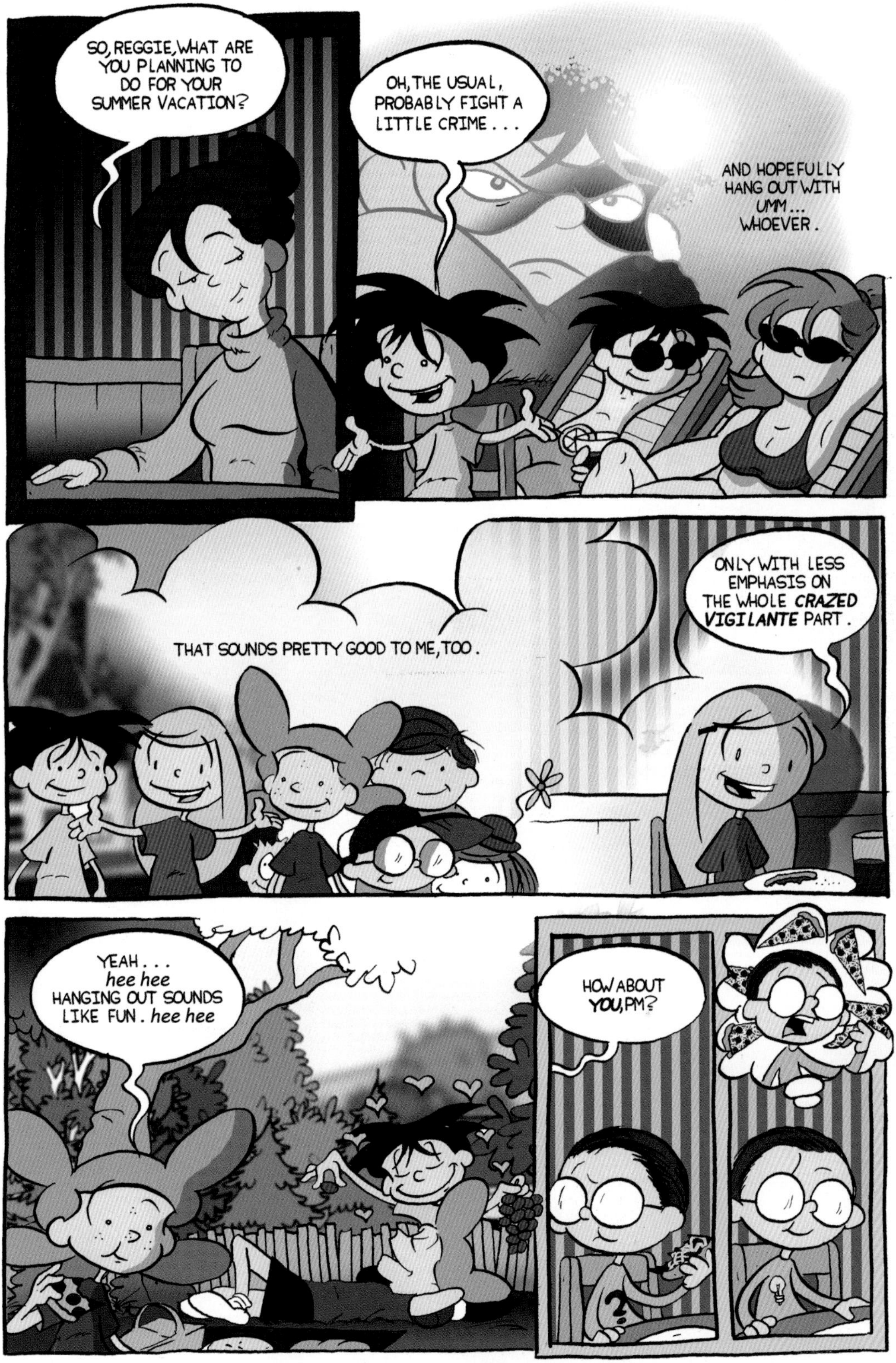
SO, REGGIE, WHAT ARE YOU PLANNING TO DO FOR YOUR SUMMER VACATION?
OH, THE USUAL, PROBABLY FIGHT A LITTLE CRIME . . .
AND HOPEFULLY HANG OUT WITH UMM... WHOEVER.
THAT SOUNDS PRETTY GOOD TO ME, TOO.
ONLY WITH LESS EMPHASIS ON THE WHOLE CRAZED VIGILANTE PART.
YEAH . . . hee hee HANGING OUT SOUNDS LIKE FUN. hee hee
HOW ABOUT YOU, PM?

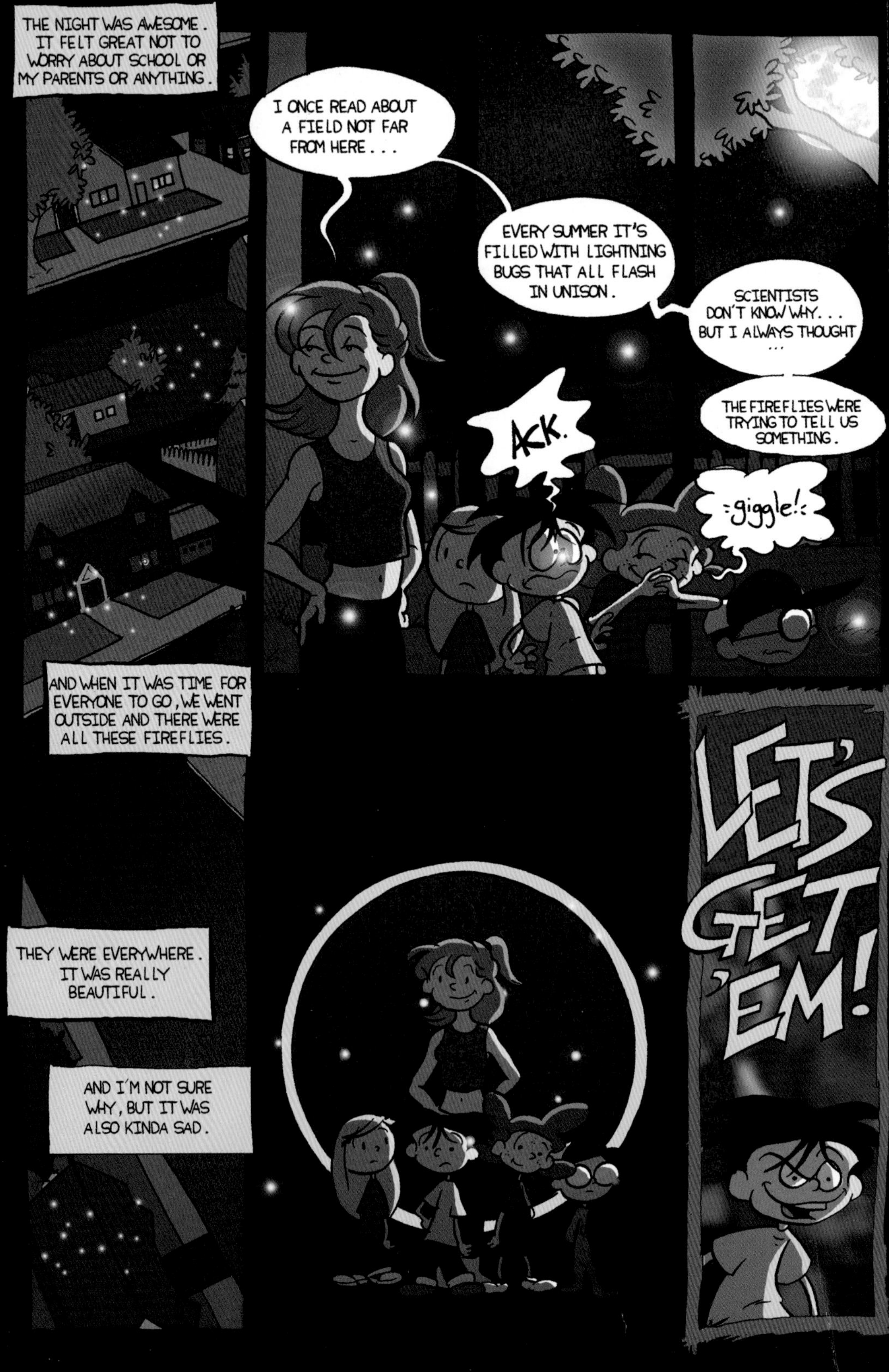

THE NIGHT WAS AWESOME. IT FELT GREAT NOT TO WORRY ABOUT SCHOOL OR MY PARENTS OR ANYTHING.
I ONCE READ ABOUT A FIELD NOT FAR FROM HERE...
EVERY SUMMER IT'S FILLED WITH LIGHTNING BUGS THAT ALL FLASH IN UNISON.
SCIENTISTS DON'T KNOW WHY... BUT I ALWAYS THOUGHT ...
THE FIREFLIES WERE TRYING TO TELL US SOMETHING.
ACK.
:giggle!:
AND WHEN IT WAS TIME FOR EVERYONE TO GO, WE WENT OUTSIDE AND THERE WERE ALL THESE FIREFLIES.
THEY WERE EVERYWHERE. IT WAS REALLY BEAUTIFUL.
AND I'M NOT SURE WHY, BUT IT WAS ALSO KINDA SAD.
LET'S GET 'EM!

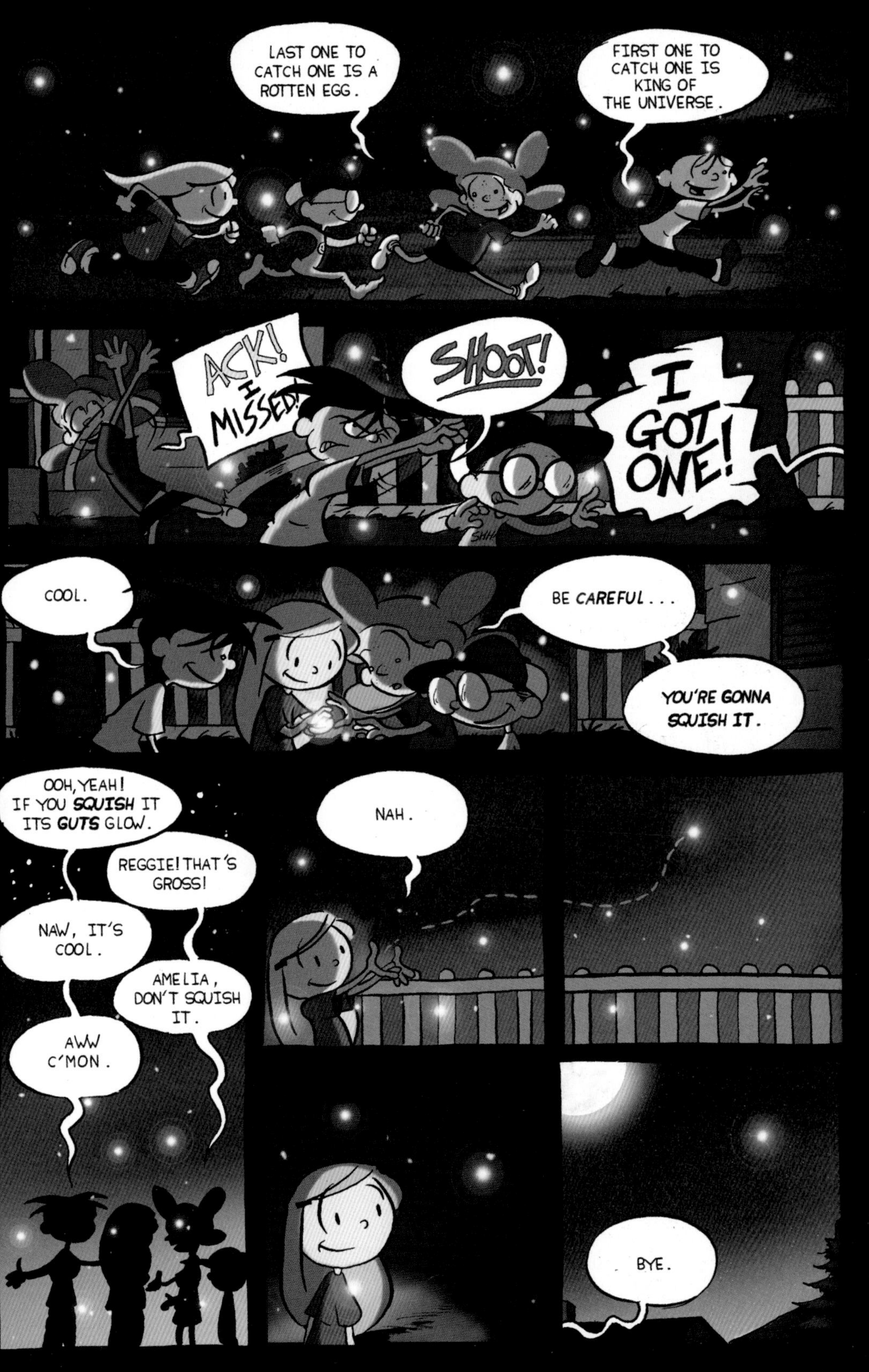

LAST ONE TO CATCH ONE IS A ROTTEN EGG.
FIRST ONE TO CATCH ONE IS KING OF THE UNIVERSE.
ACK! I MISSED!
SHOOT!
I GOT ONE!
SHHH
COOL.
BE CAREFUL...
YOU'RE GONNA SQUISH IT.
OOH, YEAH! IF YOU SQUISH IT ITS GUTS GLOW.
REGGIE! THAT'S GROSS!
NAW, IT'S COOL.
AMELIA, DON'T SQUISH IT.
AWW C'MON.
NAH.
BYE.

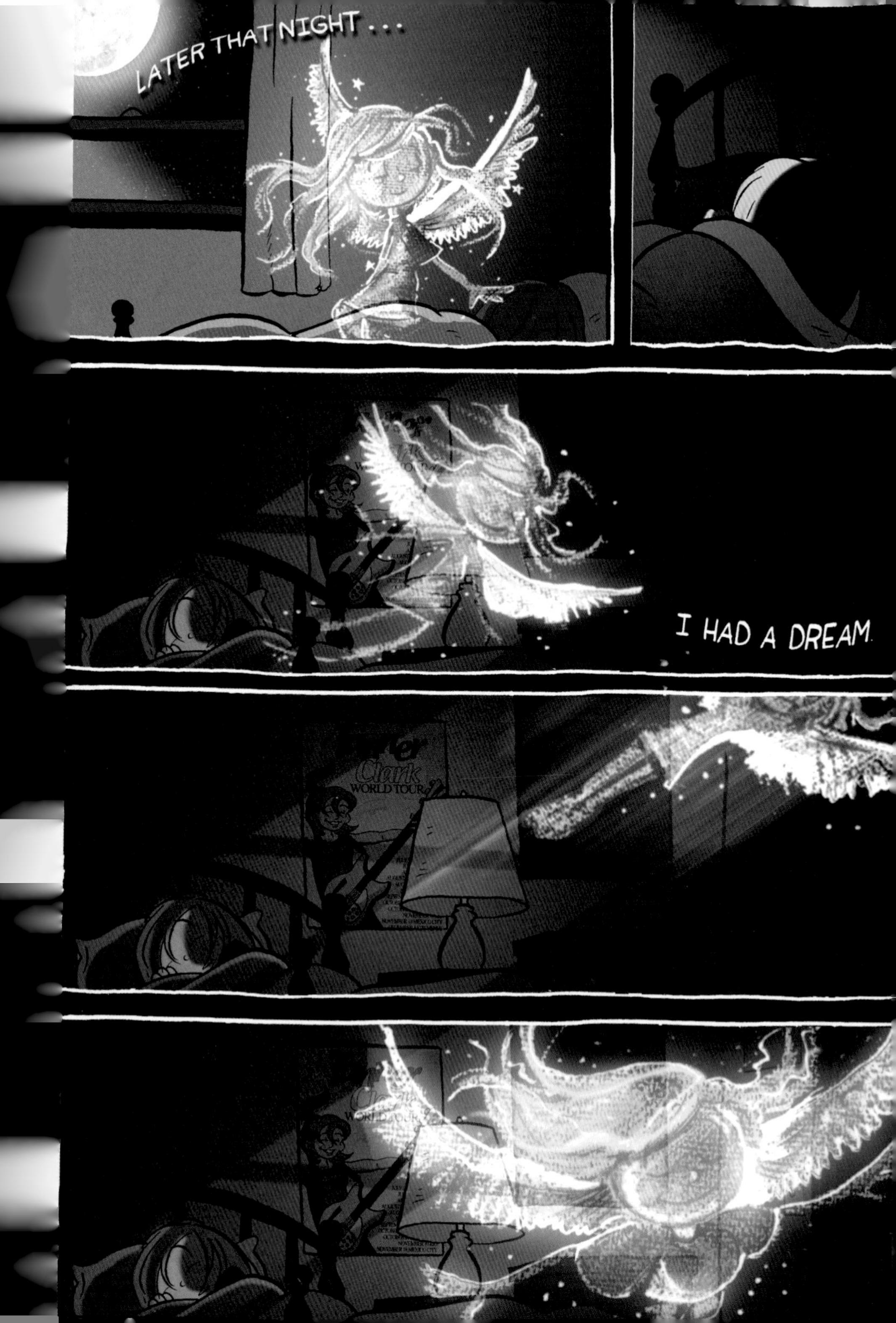
LATER THAT NIGHT . . .
I HAD A DREAM.
Clark
WORLD TOUR

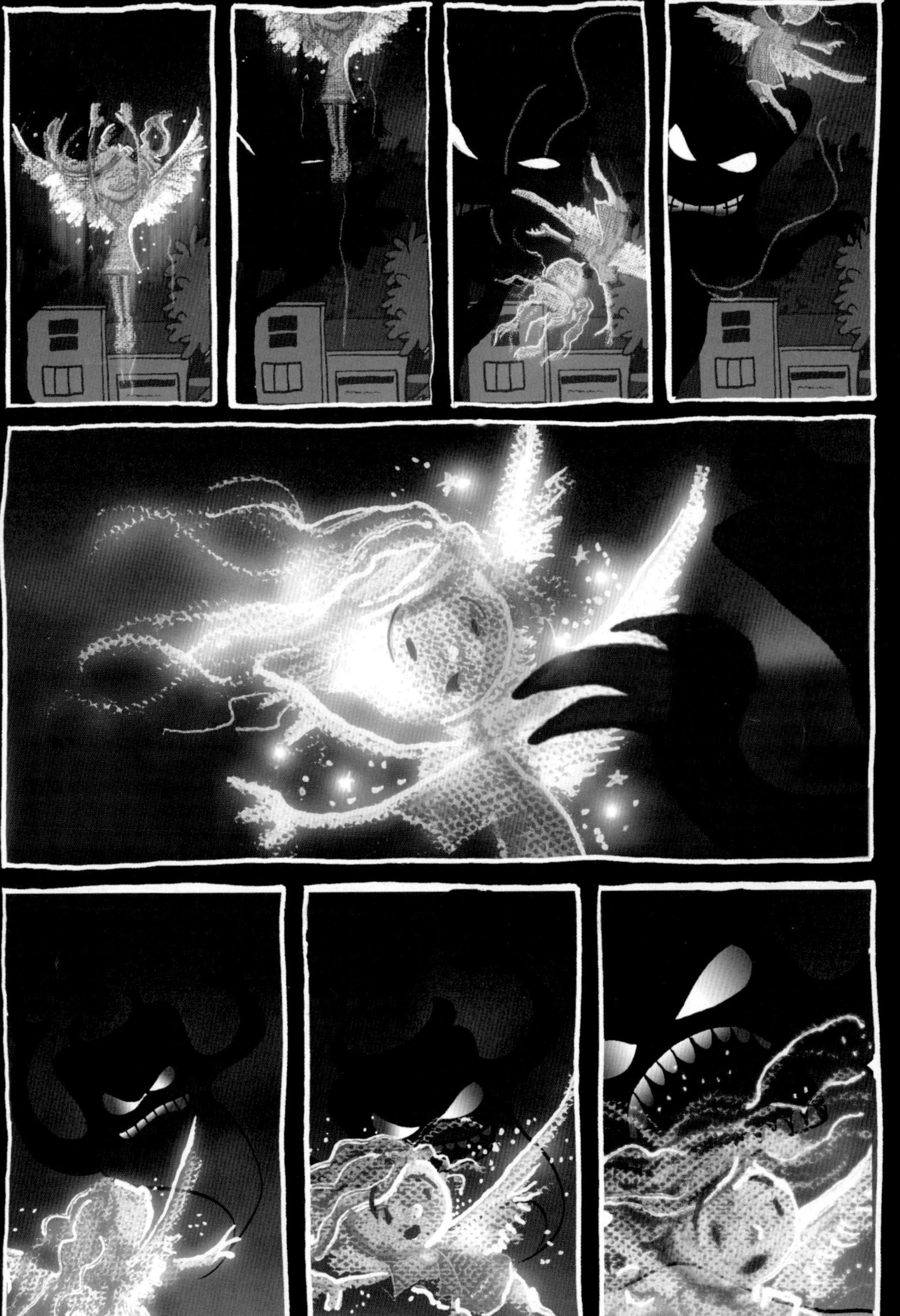

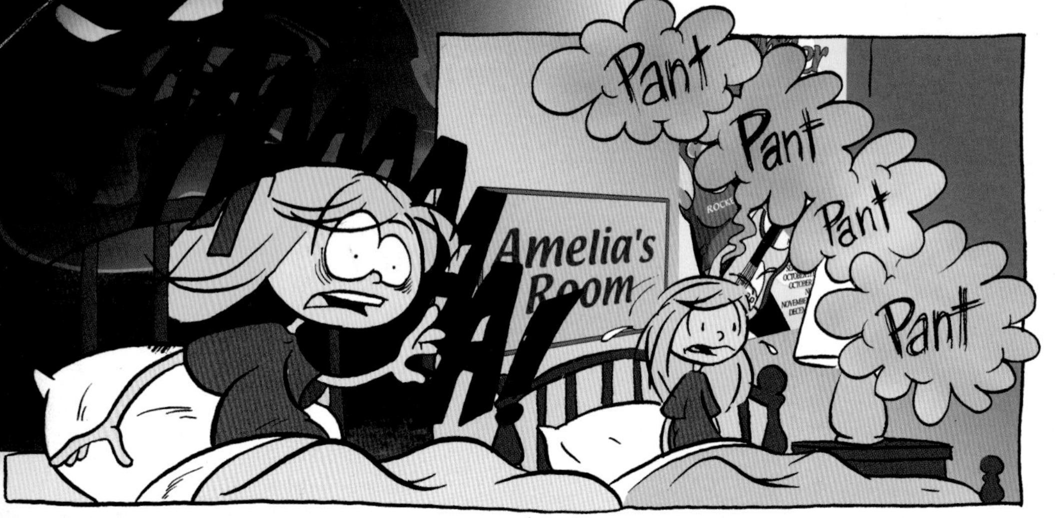
Amelia's Room
Pant
Pant
Pant
Pant

IT TOOK A WHILE FOR ME TO REALIZE THAT IT WAS JUST
A DREAM, AND THAT IT WAS MORNING NOW, AND
THAT I WAS SAFE AND THAT EVERYTHING WAS OKAY.

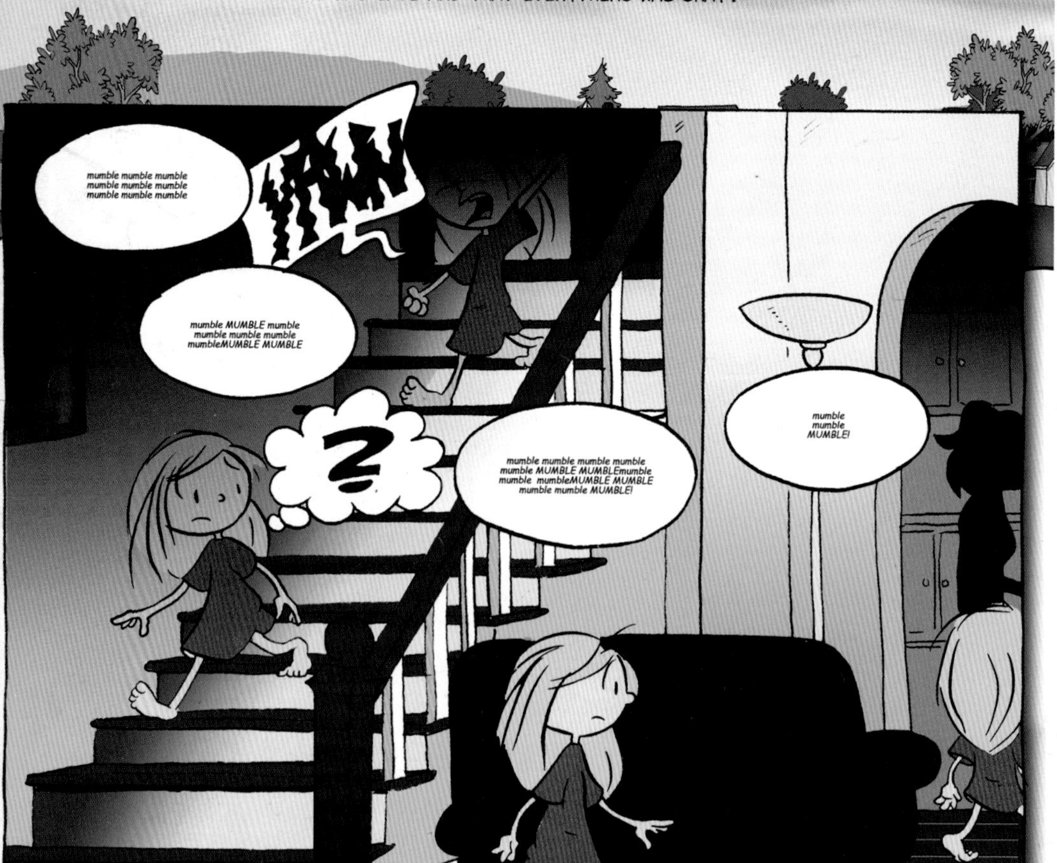
mumble mumble mumble
mumble mumble mumble
mumble mumble mumble
YAWN
mumble MUMBLE mumble
mumble mumble mumble
mumbleMUMBLE MUMBLE
?
mumble mumble mumble mumble
mumble MUMBLE MUMBLEmumble
mumble mumbleMUMBLE MUMBLE
mumble mumble MUMBLE!
mumble
mumble
MUMBLE!

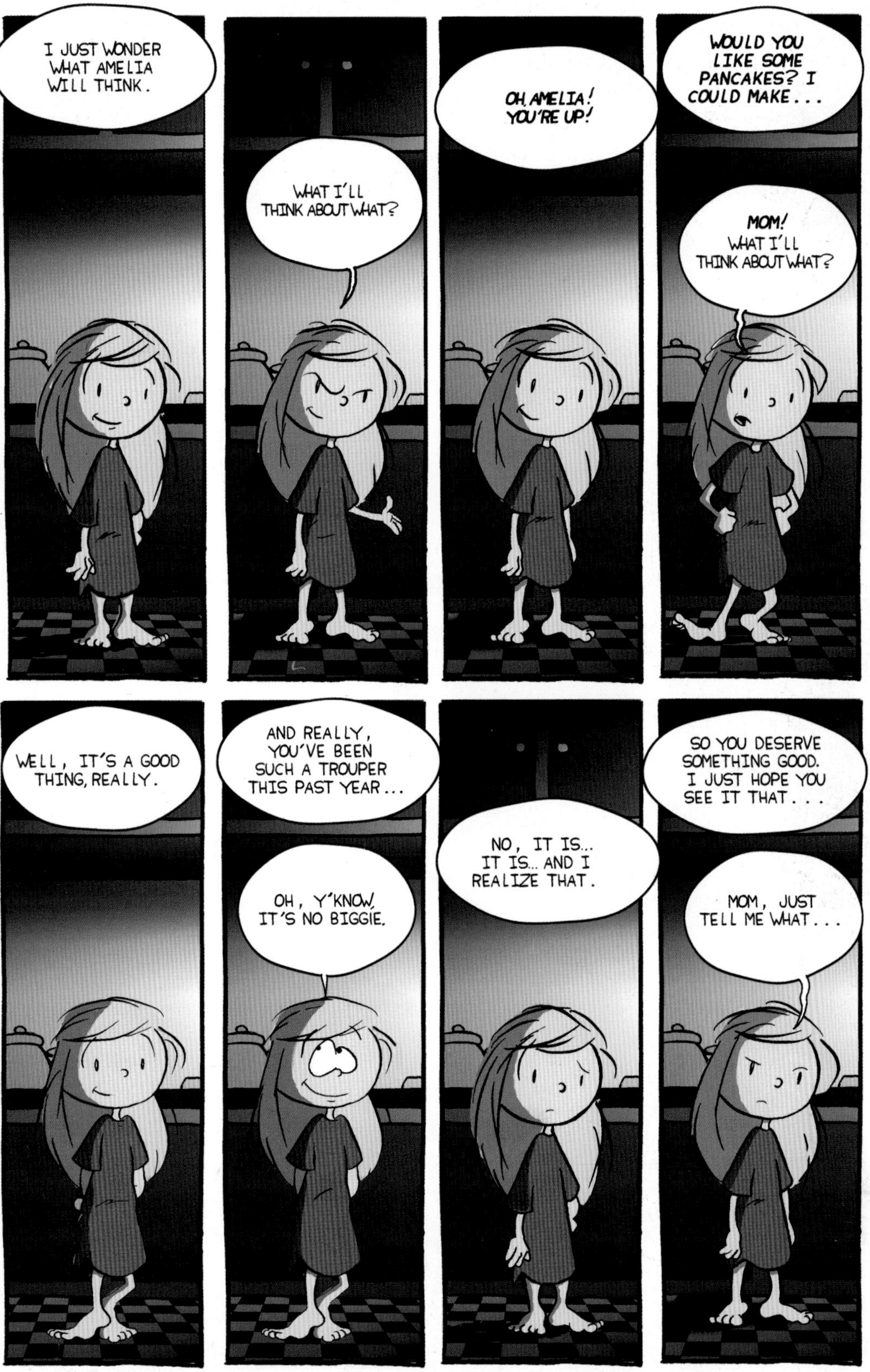
I JUST WONDER WHAT AMELIA WILL THINK.
WHAT I'LL THINK ABOUT WHAT?
OH, AMELIA! YOU'RE UP!
WOULD YOU LIKE SOME PANCAKES? I COULD MAKE...
MOM! WHAT I'LL THINK ABOUT WHAT?
WELL, IT'S A GOOD THING, REALLY.
AND REALLY, YOU'VE BEEN SUCH A TROUPER THIS PAST YEAR...
OH, Y'KNOW, IT'S NO BIGGIE.
NO, IT IS... IT IS... AND I REALIZE THAT.
SO YOU DESERVE SOMETHING GOOD. I JUST HOPE YOU SEE IT THAT...
MOM, JUST TELL ME WHAT...

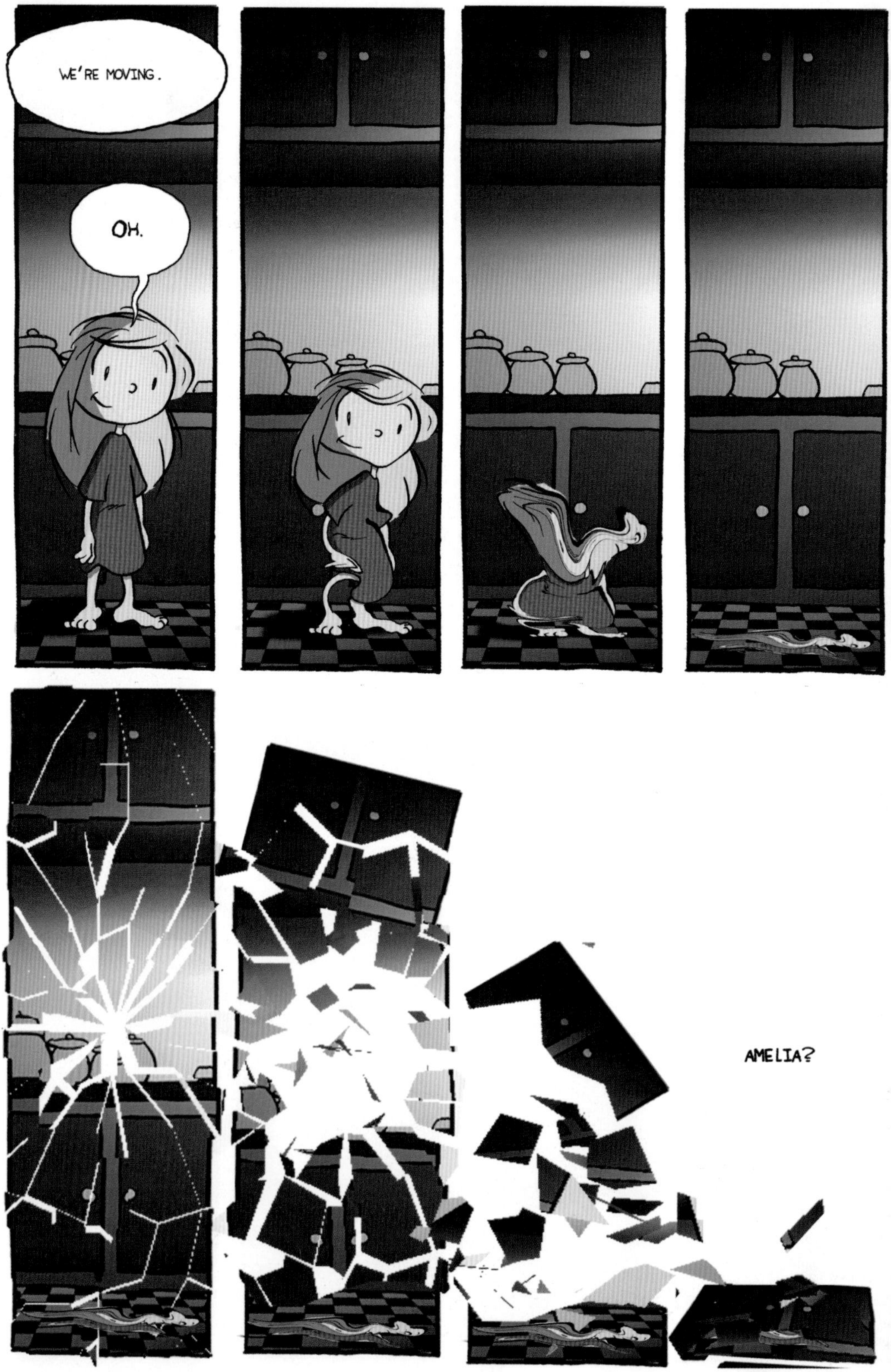
WE'RE MOVING.
OH.
AMELIA?

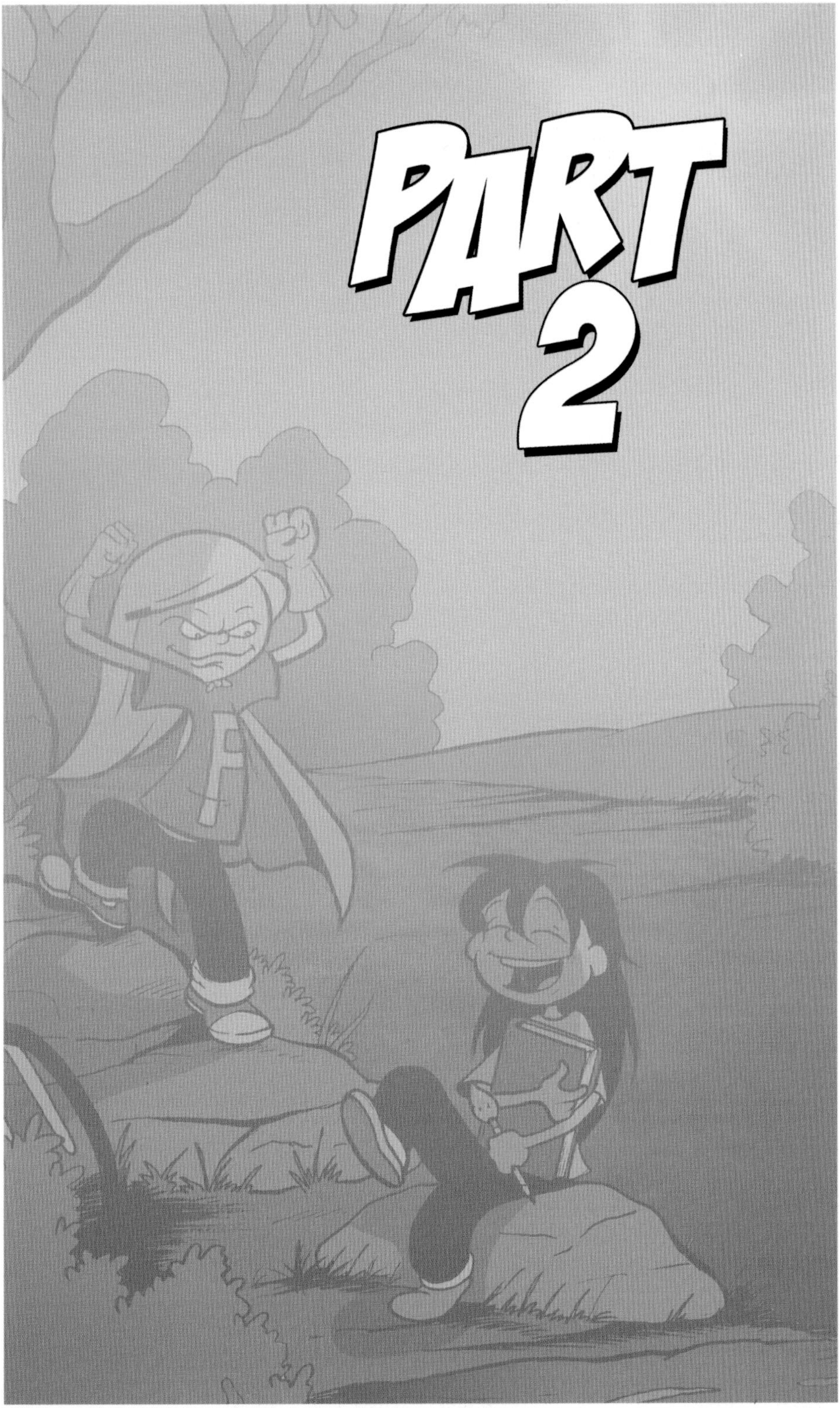
PART 2

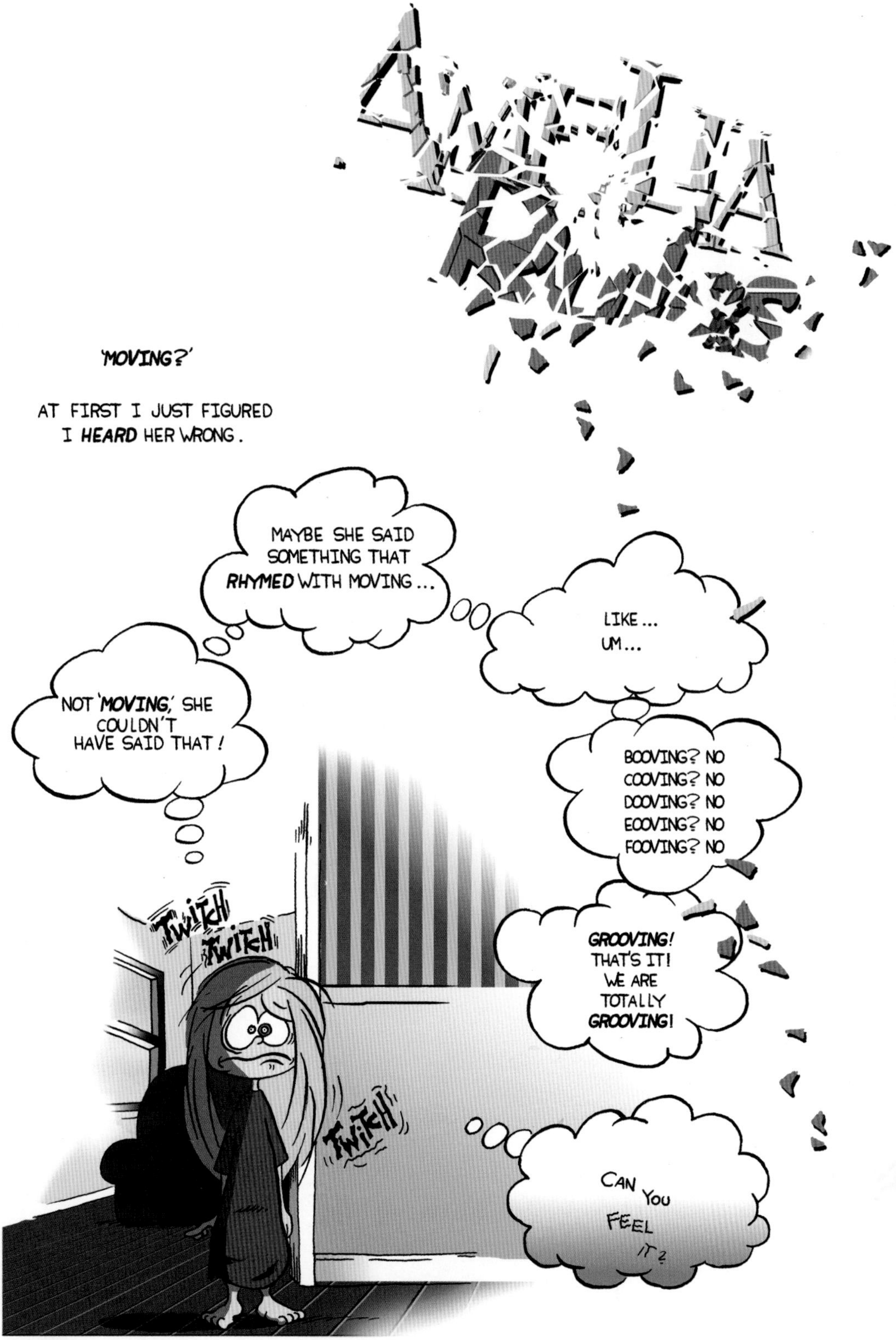
'MOVING?'
AT FIRST I JUST FIGURED I HEARD HER WRONG.
MAYBE SHE SAID SOMETHING THAT RHYMED WITH MOVING...
LIKE... UM...
BOOVING? NO
COOVING? NO
DOOVING? NO
EOOVING? NO
FOOVING? NO
GROOVING! THAT'S IT! WE ARE TOTALLY GROOVING!
CAN YOU FEEL IT?
NOT 'MOVING,' SHE COULDN'T HAVE SAID THAT!
TWITCH
TWITCH
TWITCH

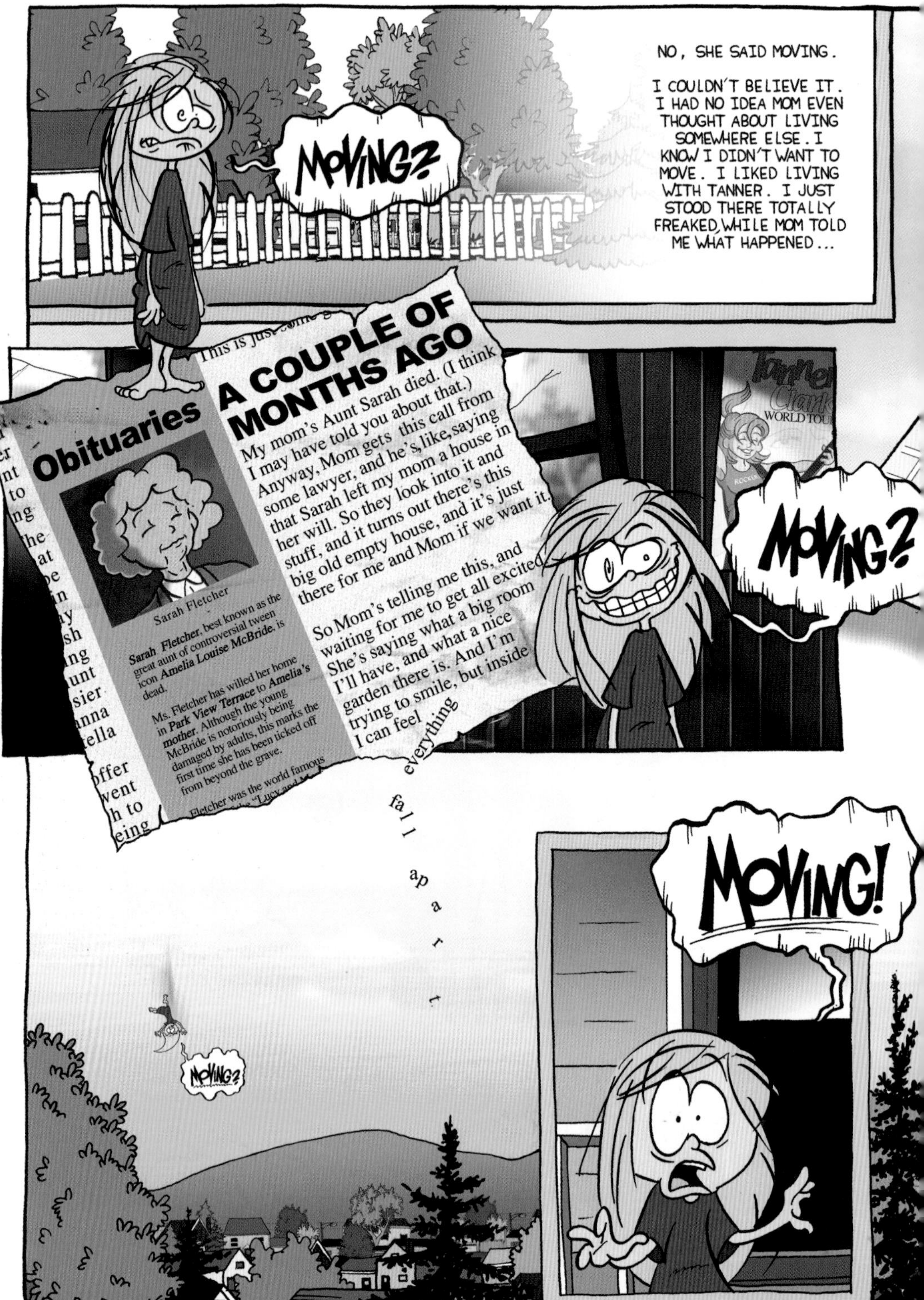

NO, SHE SAID MOVING.
I COULDN'T BELIEVE IT. I HAD NO IDEA MOM EVEN THOUGHT ABOUT LIVING SOMEWHERE ELSE. I KNOW I DIDN'T WANT TO MOVE. I LIKED LIVING WITH TANNER. I JUST STOOD THERE TOTALLY FREAKED, WHILE MOM TOLD ME WHAT HAPPENED...
MOVING?
Obituaries
Sarah Fletcher
Sarah Fletcher, best known as the great aunt of controversial tween icon Amelia Louise McBride, is dead.
Ms. Fletcher has willed her home in Park View Terrace to Amelia's mother. Although the young McBride is notoriously being damaged by adults, this marks the first time she has been ticked off from beyond the grave.
Fletcher was the world famous
A COUPLE OF MONTHS AGO
My mom's Aunt Sarah died. (I think I may have told you about that.) Anyway, Mom gets this call from some lawyer, and he's, like, saying that Sarah left my mom a house in her will. So they look into it and stuff, and it turns out there's this big old empty house, and it's just there for me and Mom if we want it.
So Mom's telling me this, and waiting for me to get all excited. She's saying what a big room I'll have, and what a nice garden there is. And I'm trying to smile, but inside I can feel everything fall apart.
Tanner Clark WORLD TOUR
MOVING?
MOVING!
MOVING?

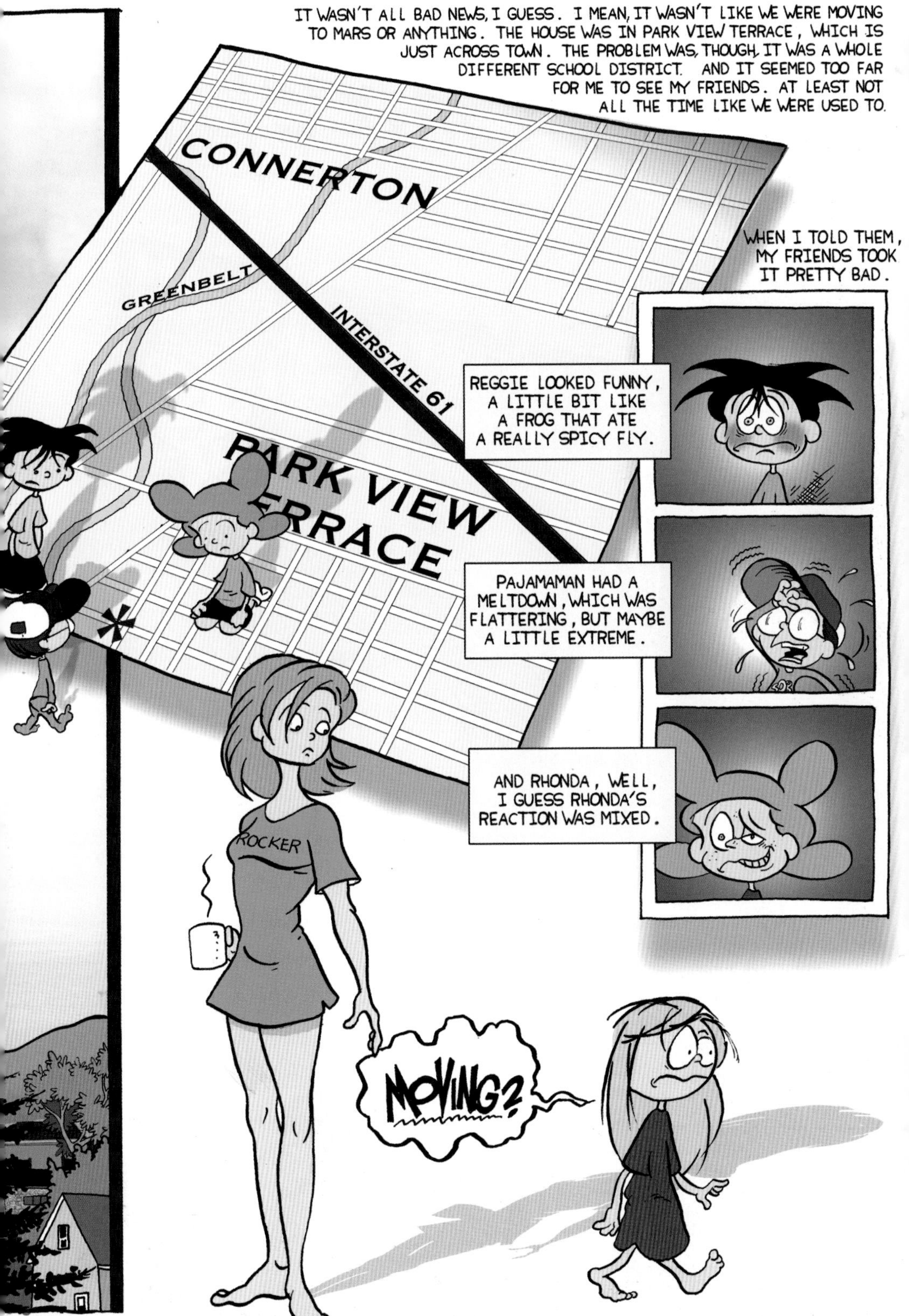
IT WASN'T ALL BAD NEWS, I GUESS. I MEAN, IT WASN'T LIKE WE WERE MOVING TO MARS OR ANYTHING. THE HOUSE WAS IN PARK VIEW TERRACE, WHICH IS JUST ACROSS TOWN. THE PROBLEM WAS, THOUGH, IT WAS A WHOLE DIFFERENT SCHOOL DISTRICT. AND IT SEEMED TOO FAR FOR ME TO SEE MY FRIENDS. AT LEAST NOT ALL THE TIME LIKE WE WERE USED TO.
CONNERTON
GREENBELT
INTERSTATE 61
PARK VIEW TERRACE
WHEN I TOLD THEM, MY FRIENDS TOOK IT PRETTY BAD.
REGGIE LOOKED FUNNY, A LITTLE BIT LIKE A FROG THAT ATE A REALLY SPICY FLY.
PAJAMAMAN HAD A MELTDOWN, WHICH WAS FLATTERING, BUT MAYBE A LITTLE EXTREME.
AND RHONDA, WELL, I GUESS RHONDA'S REACTION WAS MIXED.
ROCKER
MOVING?

chapter Two: Into Graceland

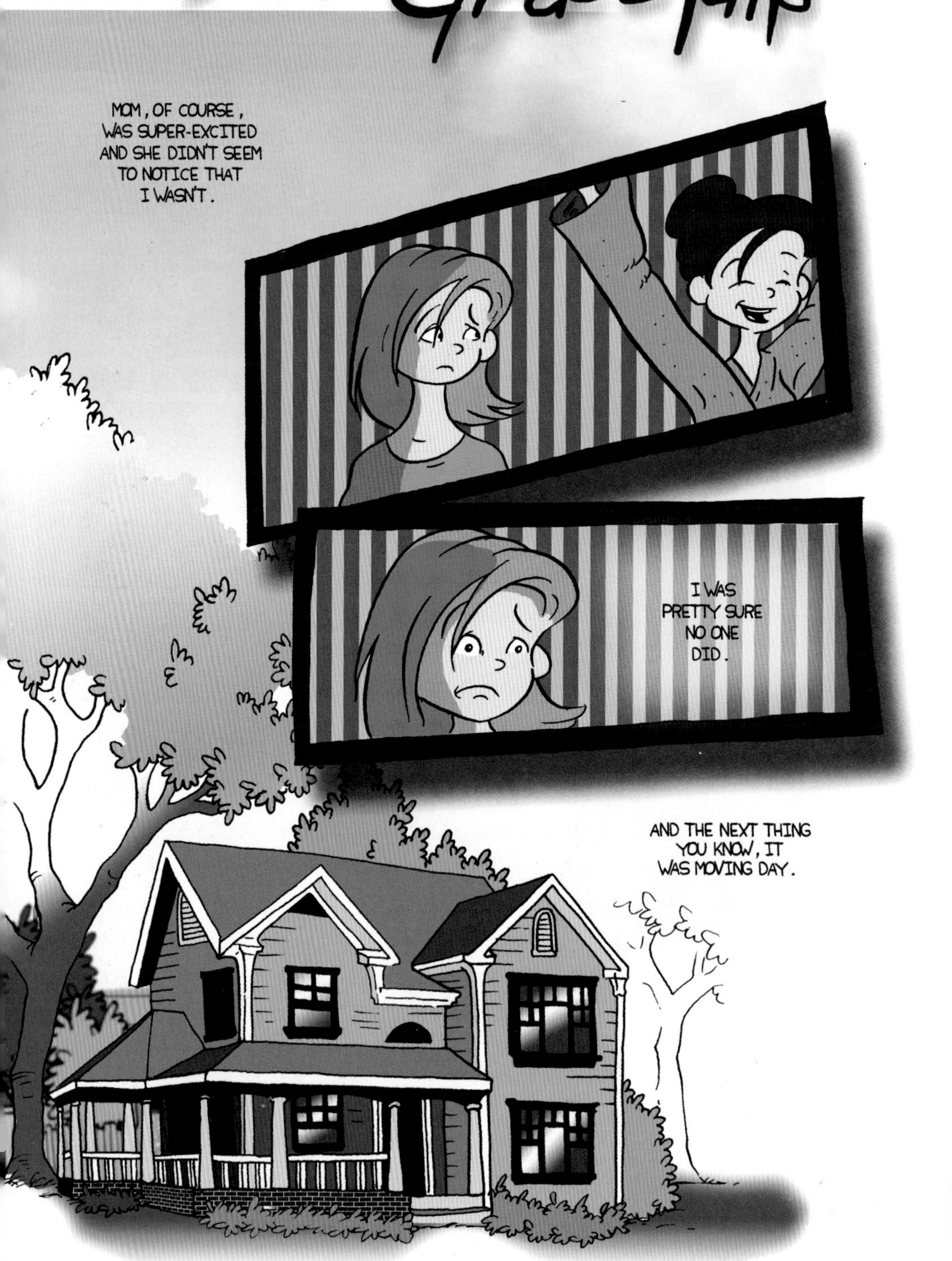
MOM, OF COURSE, WAS SUPER-EXCITED AND SHE DIDN'T SEEM TO NOTICE THAT I WASN'T.
I WAS PRETTY SURE NO ONE DID.
AND THE NEXT THING YOU KNOW, IT WAS MOVING DAY.

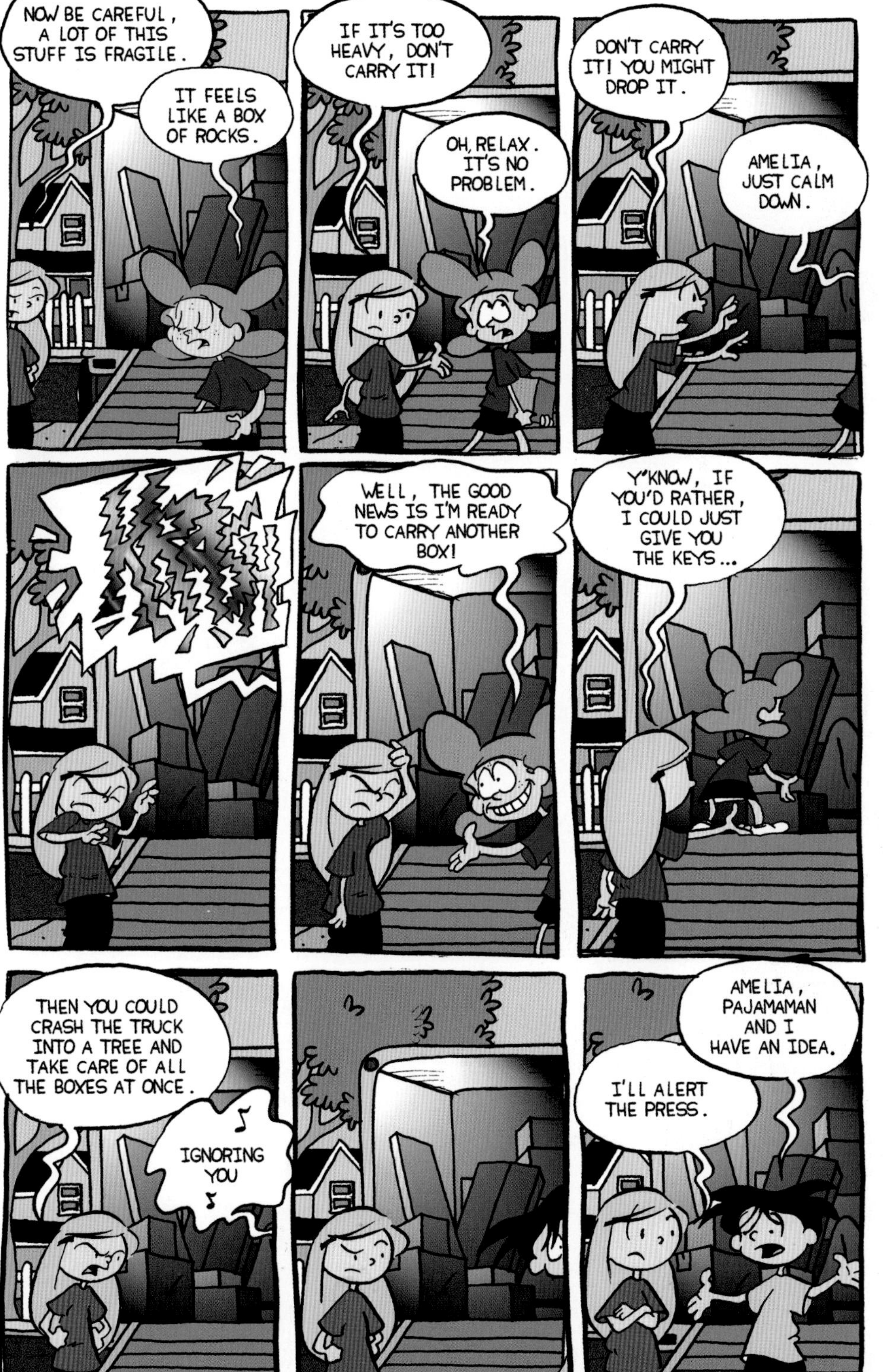
NOW BE CAREFUL, A LOT OF THIS STUFF IS FRAGILE.
IT FEELS LIKE A BOX OF ROCKS.
IF IT'S TOO HEAVY, DON'T CARRY IT!
OH, RELAX. IT'S NO PROBLEM.
DON'T CARRY IT! YOU MIGHT DROP IT.
AMELIA, JUST CALM DOWN.
WELL, THE GOOD NEWS IS I'M READY TO CARRY ANOTHER BOX!
Y'KNOW, IF YOU'D RATHER, I COULD JUST GIVE YOU THE KEYS...
THEN YOU COULD CRASH THE TRUCK INTO A TREE AND TAKE CARE OF ALL THE BOXES AT ONCE.
IGNORING YOU
AMELIA, PAJAMAMAN AND I HAVE AN IDEA.
I'LL ALERT THE PRESS.

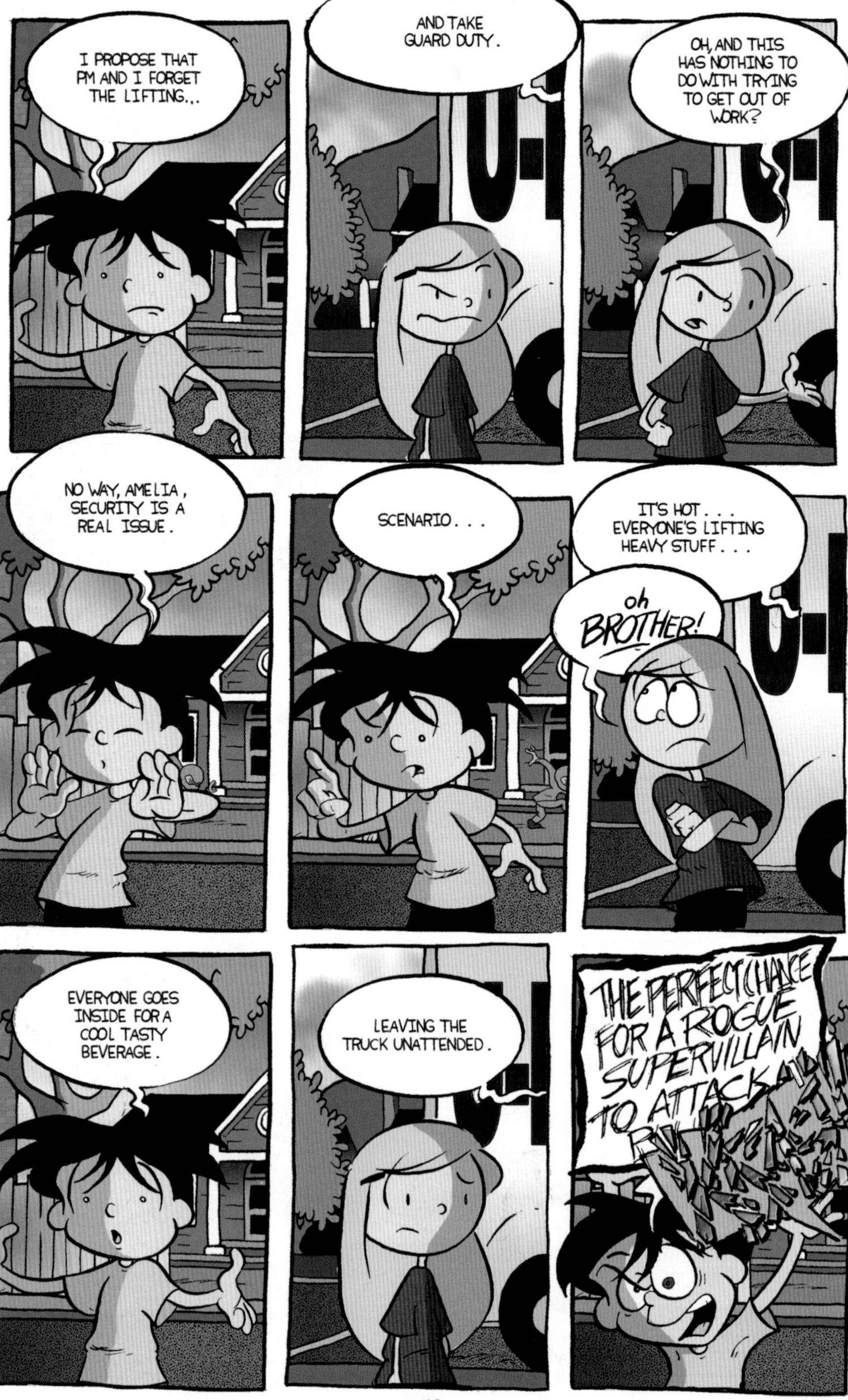
I PROPOSE THAT PM AND I FORGET THE LIFTING...
AND TAKE GUARD DUTY.
OH, AND THIS HAS NOTHING TO DO WITH TRYING TO GET OUT OF WORK?
NO WAY, AMELIA, SECURITY IS A REAL ISSUE.
SCENARIO . . .
IT'S HOT . . . EVERYONE'S LIFTING HEAVY STUFF . . .
oh BROTHER!
EVERYONE GOES INSIDE FOR A COOL TASTY BEVERAGE.
LEAVING THE TRUCK UNATTENDED.
THE PERFECT CHANCE FOR A ROGUE SUPERVILLAIN TO ATTACK!

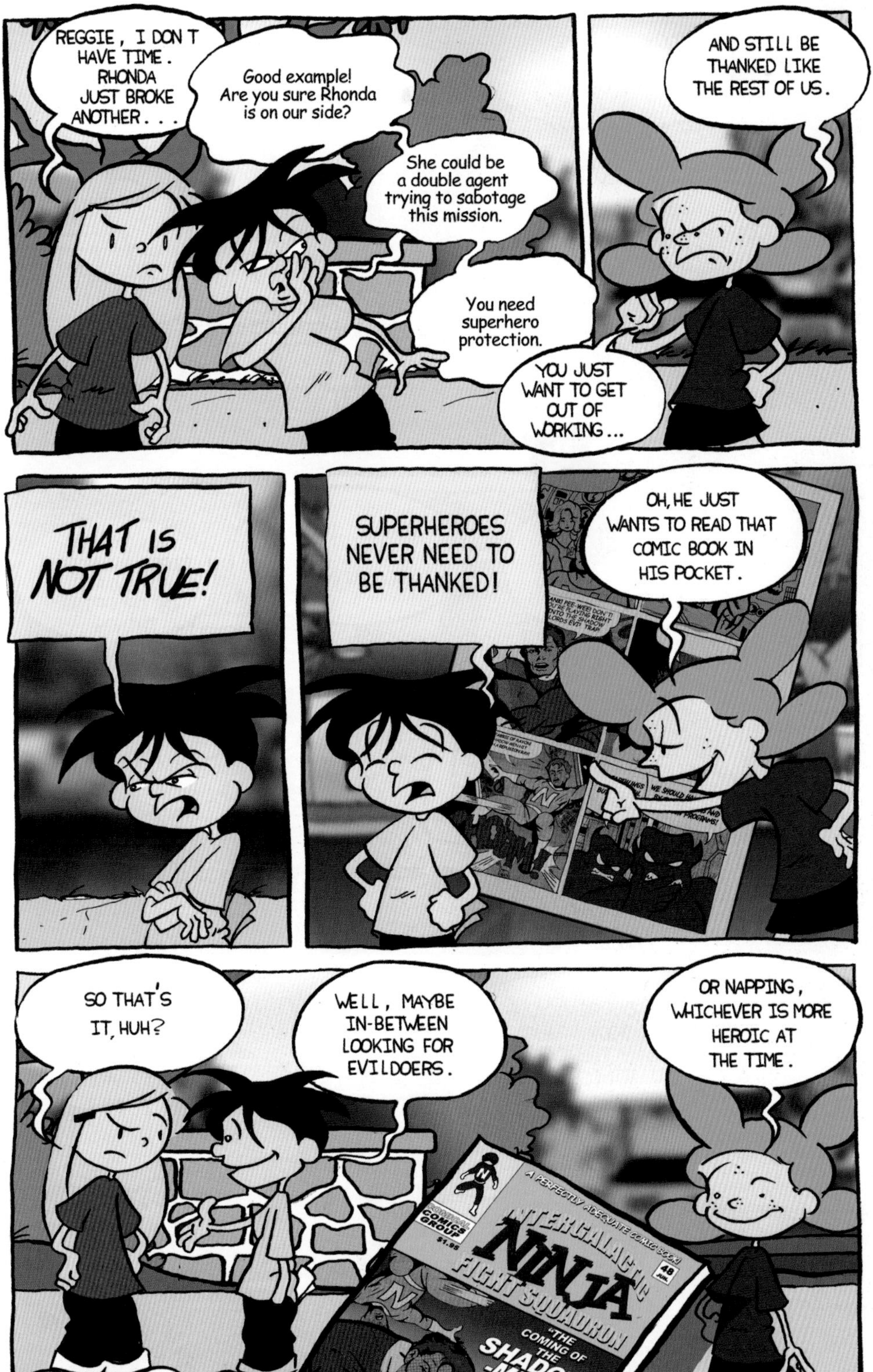
REGGIE, I DON T HAVE TIME. RHONDA JUST BROKE ANOTHER . . .
Good example! Are you sure Rhonda is on our side?
She could be a double agent trying to sabotage this mission.
You need superhero protection.
YOU JUST WANT TO GET OUT OF WORKING ...
AND STILL BE THANKED LIKE THE REST OF US.
THAT IS NOT TRUE!
SUPERHEROES NEVER NEED TO BE THANKED!
OH, HE JUST WANTS TO READ THAT COMIC BOOK IN HIS POCKET.
SO THAT'S IT, HUH?
WELL, MAYBE IN-BETWEEN LOOKING FOR EVILDOERS.
OR NAPPING, WHICHEVER IS MORE HEROIC AT THE TIME.
A PERFECTLY ADEQUATE COMIC BOOK!
COMICS GROUP
$1.95
48
INTERGALACTIC NINJA FIGHT SQUADRON
"THE COMING OF THE SHADOW-MEN"

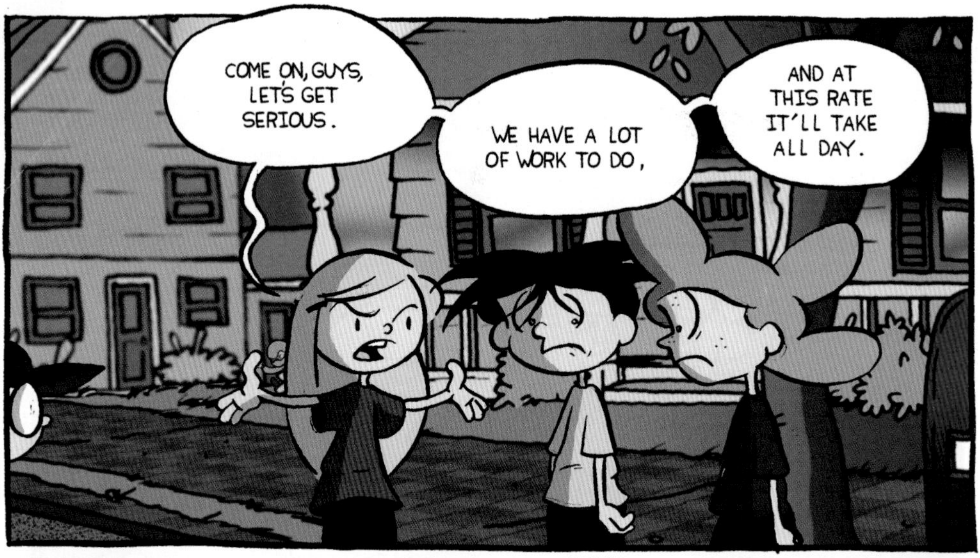
COME ON, GUYS, LET'S GET SERIOUS.
WE HAVE A LOT OF WORK TO DO,
AND AT THIS RATE IT'LL TAKE ALL DAY.

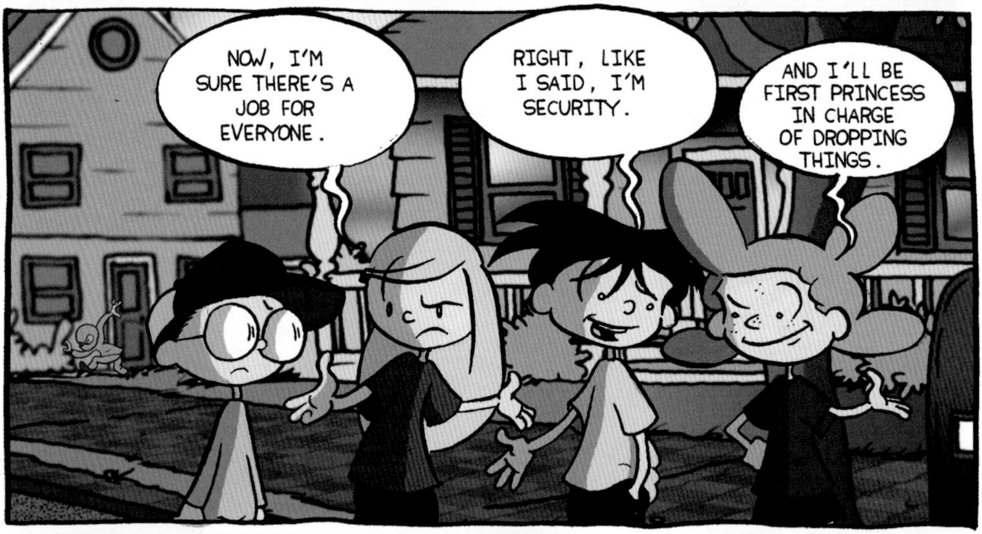
NOW, I'M SURE THERE'S A JOB FOR EVERYONE.
RIGHT, LIKE I SAID, I'M SECURITY.
AND I'LL BE FIRST PRINCESS IN CHARGE OF DROPPING THINGS.

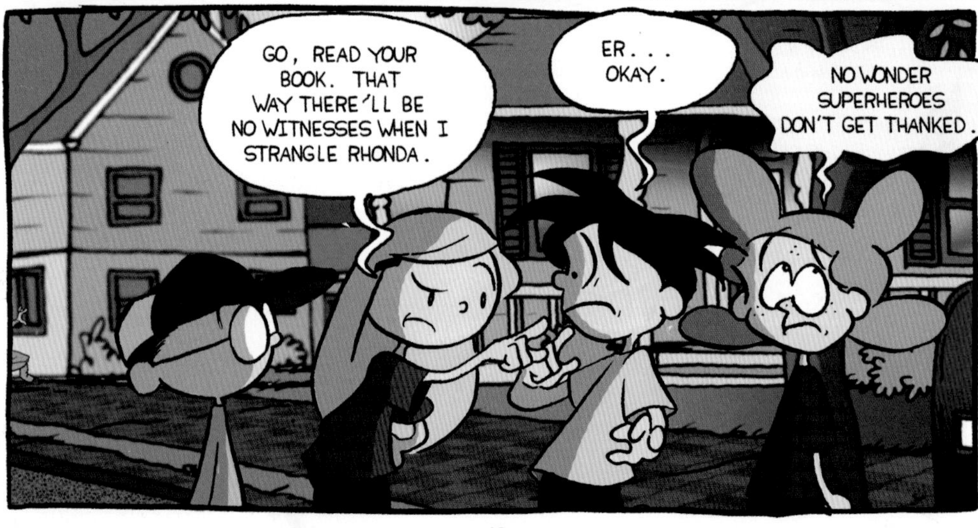
GO, READ YOUR BOOK. THAT WAY THERE'LL BE NO WITNESSES WHEN I STRANGLE RHONDA.
ER... OKAY.
NO WONDER SUPERHEROES DON'T GET THANKED.

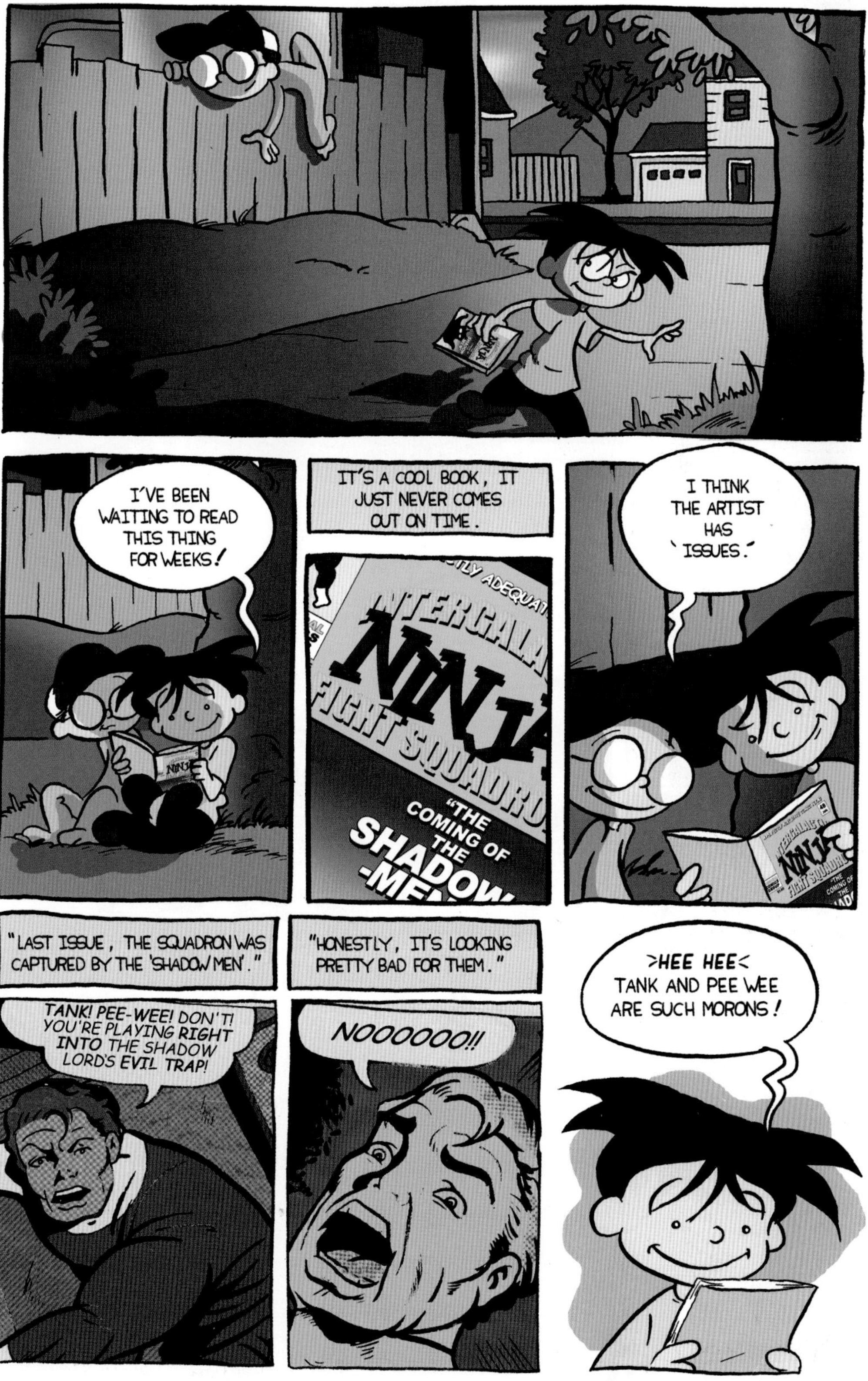
I'VE BEEN WAITING TO READ THIS THING FOR WEEKS!
IT'S A COOL BOOK, IT JUST NEVER COMES OUT ON TIME.
INTERGALA
NINJA
FIGHT SQUADRO
"THE COMING OF THE SHADOW-MEN
I THINK THE ARTIST HAS 'ISSUES.'
"LAST ISSUE, THE SQUADRON WAS CAPTURED BY THE 'SHADOW MEN'."
TANK! PEE-WEE! DON'T! YOU'RE PLAYING RIGHT INTO THE SHADOW LORD'S EVIL TRAP!
"HONESTLY, IT'S LOOKING PRETTY BAD FOR THEM."
NOOOOOO!!
>HEE HEE< TANK AND PEE WEE ARE SUCH MORONS!

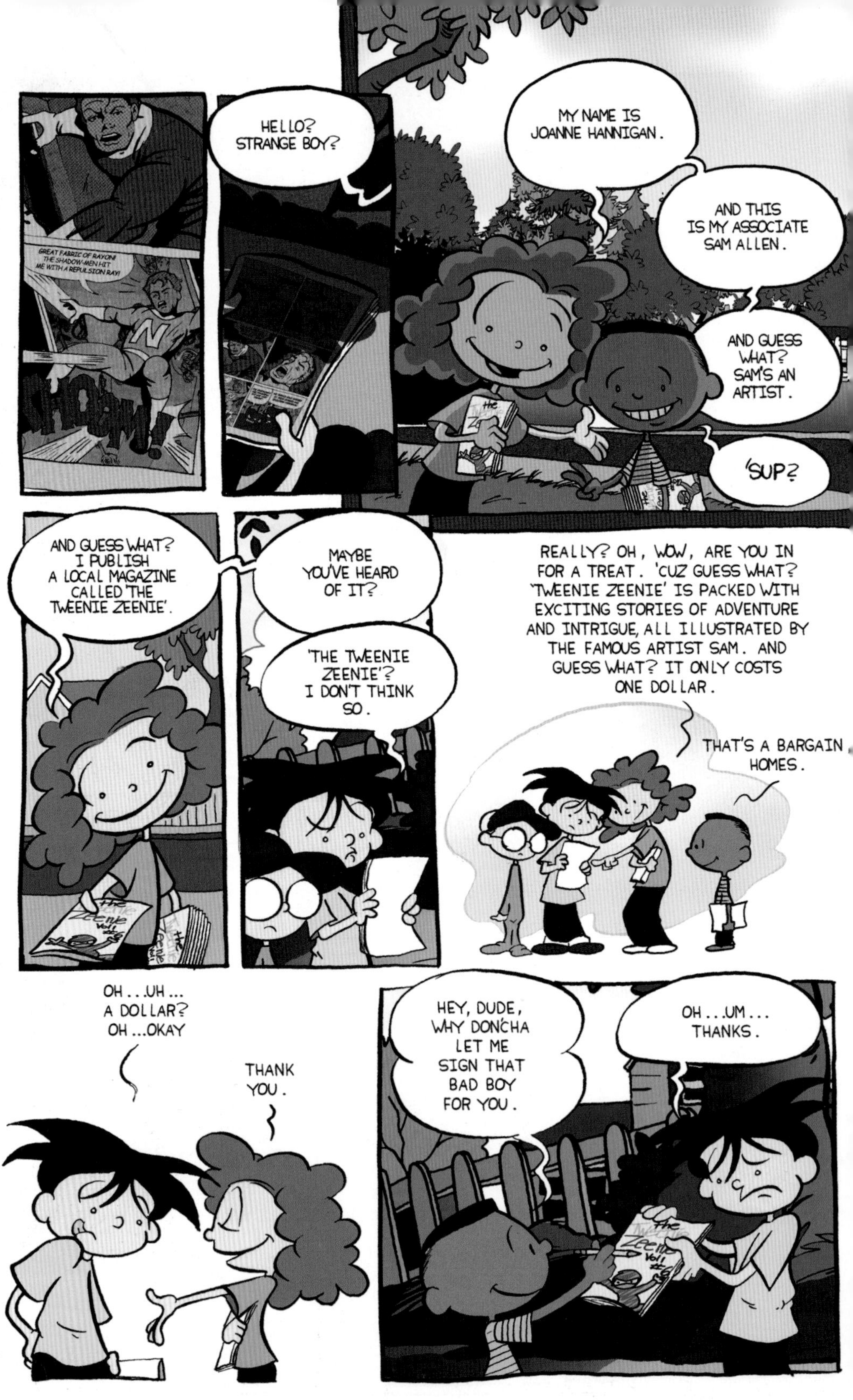
GREAT FABRIC OF RAYON! THE SHADOW-MEN HIT ME WITH A REPULSION RAY!
HELLO? STRANGE BOY?
MY NAME IS JOANNE HANNIGAN.
AND THIS IS MY ASSOCIATE SAM ALLEN.
AND GUESS WHAT? SAM'S AN ARTIST.
'SUP?
AND GUESS WHAT? I PUBLISH A LOCAL MAGAZINE CALLED 'THE TWEENIE ZEENIE'.
MAYBE YOU'VE HEARD OF IT?
'THE TWEENIE ZEENIE'? I DON'T THINK SO.
REALLY? OH, WOW, ARE YOU IN FOR A TREAT. 'CUZ GUESS WHAT? 'TWEENIE ZEENIE' IS PACKED WITH EXCITING STORIES OF ADVENTURE AND INTRIGUE, ALL ILLUSTRATED BY THE FAMOUS ARTIST SAM. AND GUESS WHAT? IT ONLY COSTS ONE DOLLAR.
THAT'S A BARGAIN HOMES.
OH...UH... A DOLLAR? OH...OKAY
THANK YOU.
HEY, DUDE, WHY DON'CHA LET ME SIGN THAT BAD BOY FOR YOU.
OH...UM... THANKS.

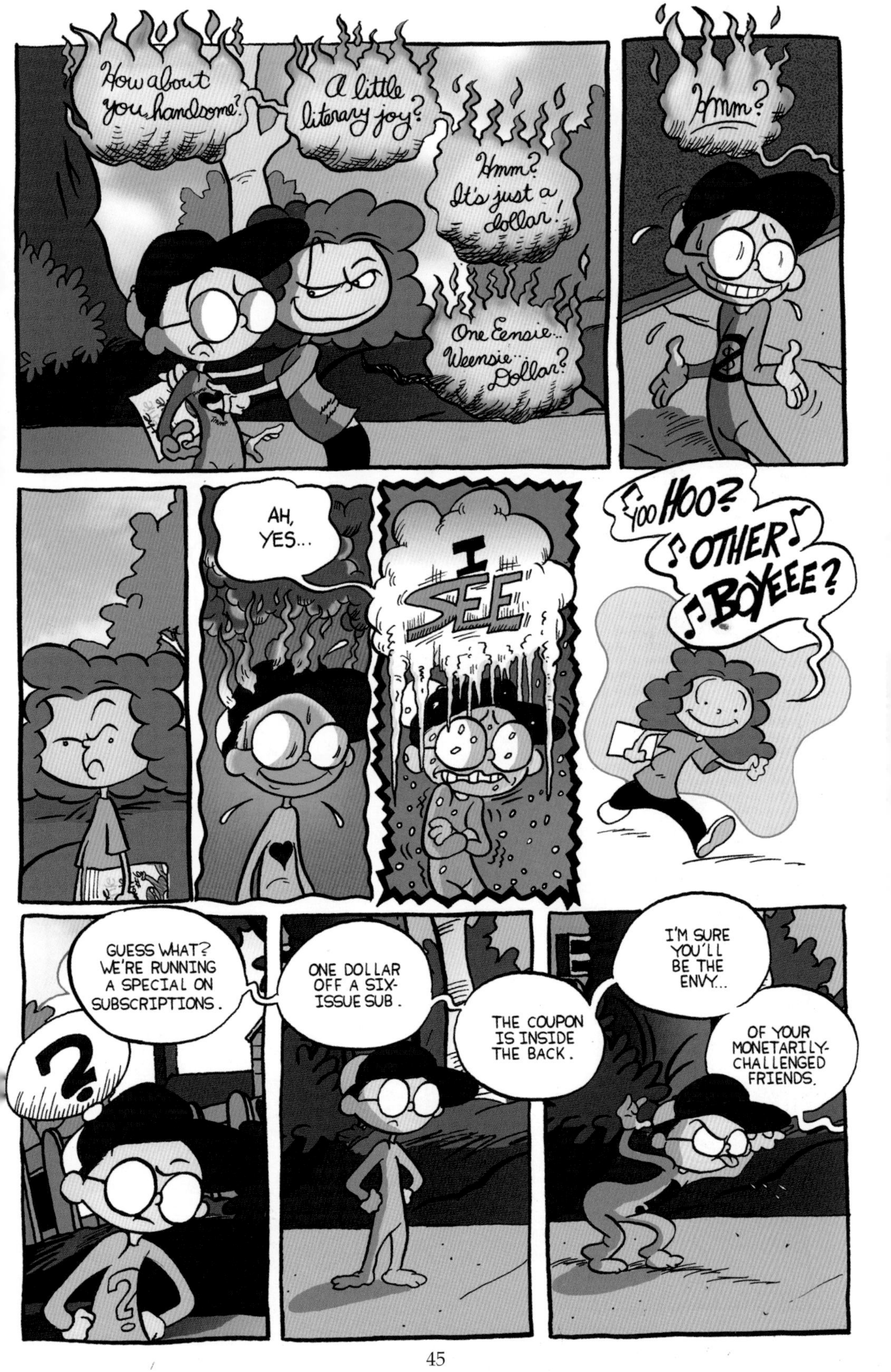
How about you, handsome?
A little literary joy?
Hmm? It's just a dollar!
One Eensie... Weensie... Dollar?
Hmm?
AH, YES...
I SEE
YOO HOO? OTHER BOYEEE?
GUESS WHAT? WE'RE RUNNING A SPECIAL ON SUBSCRIPTIONS.
?
ONE DOLLAR OFF A SIX-ISSUE SUB.
THE COUPON IS INSIDE THE BACK.
I'M SURE YOU'LL BE THE ENVY...
OF YOUR MONETARILY-CHALLENGED FRIENDS.

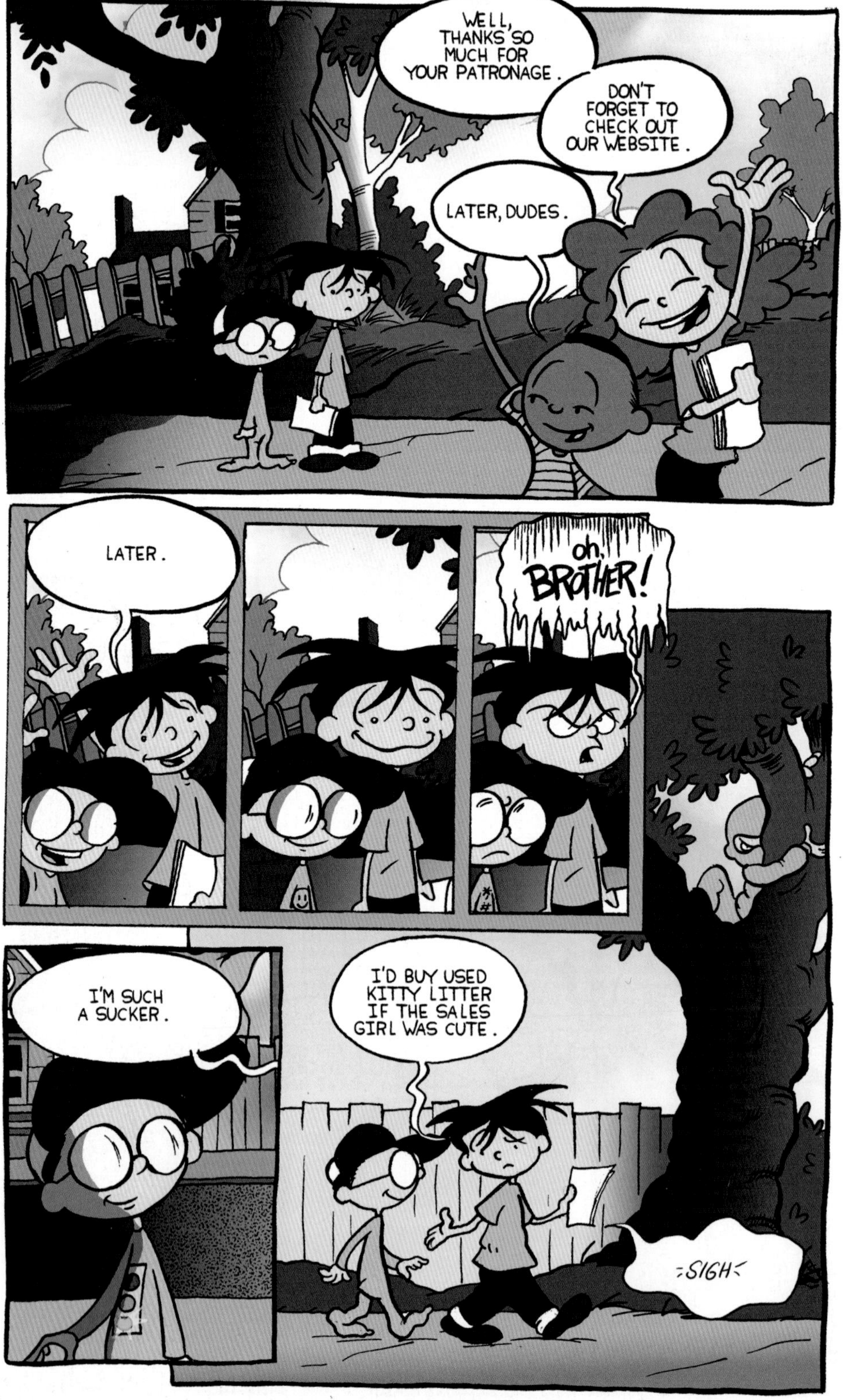
WELL, THANKS SO MUCH FOR YOUR PATRONAGE.
DON'T FORGET TO CHECK OUT OUR WEBSITE.
LATER, DUDES.
LATER.
oh, BROTHER!
I'M SUCH A SUCKER.
I'D BUY USED KITTY LITTER IF THE SALES GIRL WAS CUTE.
SIGH

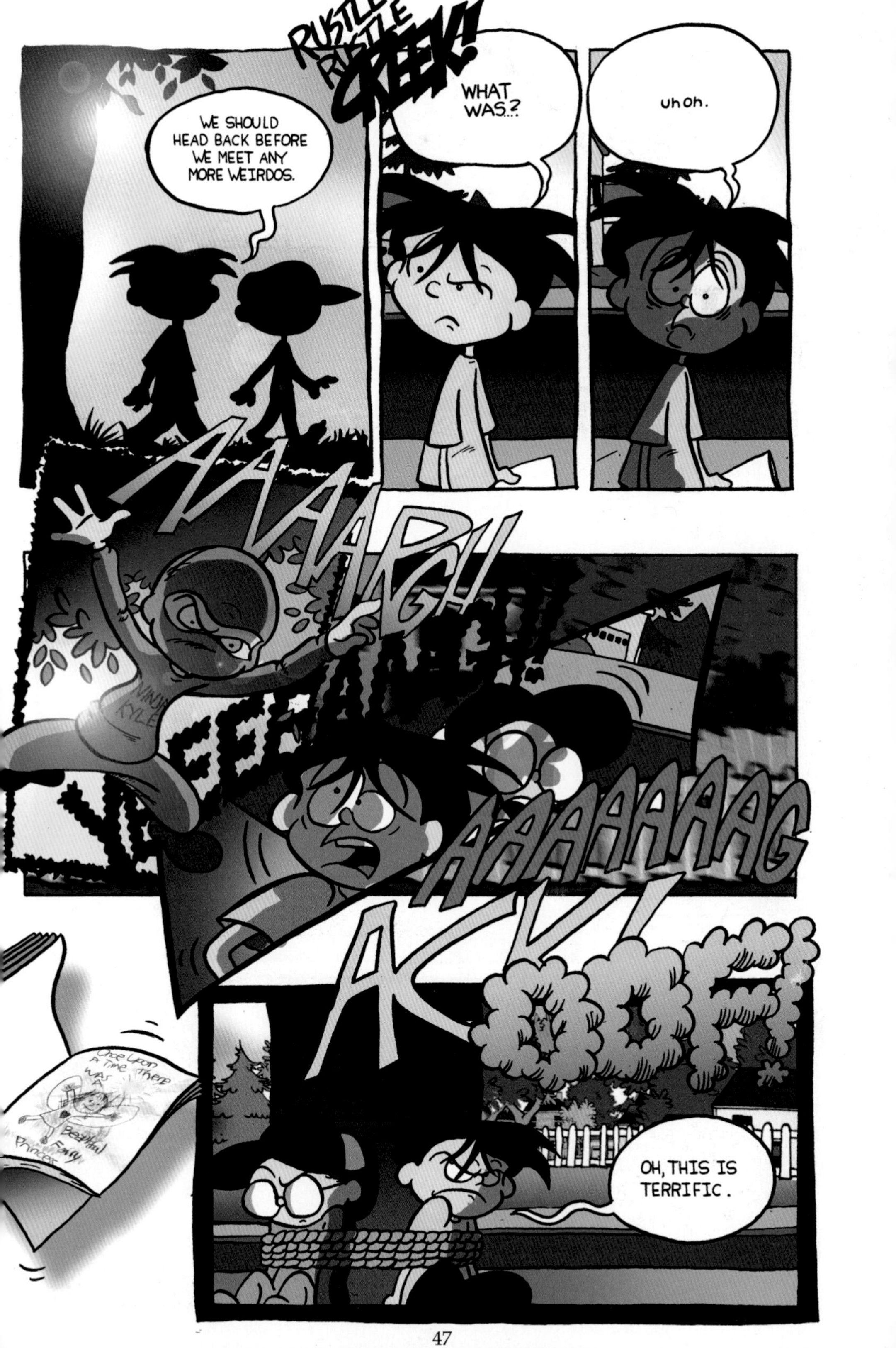
RUSTLE
RUSTLE
CREEK!
WE SHOULD HEAD BACK BEFORE WE MEET ANY MORE WEIRDOS.
WHAT WAS...?
uh oh.
AAAAAGH!
NINJA KYLE
AAAAAAAAG
ACK!
OOOF!
Once Upon A Time There WAS A Beautiful Fairy Princess
OH, THIS IS TERRIFIC.

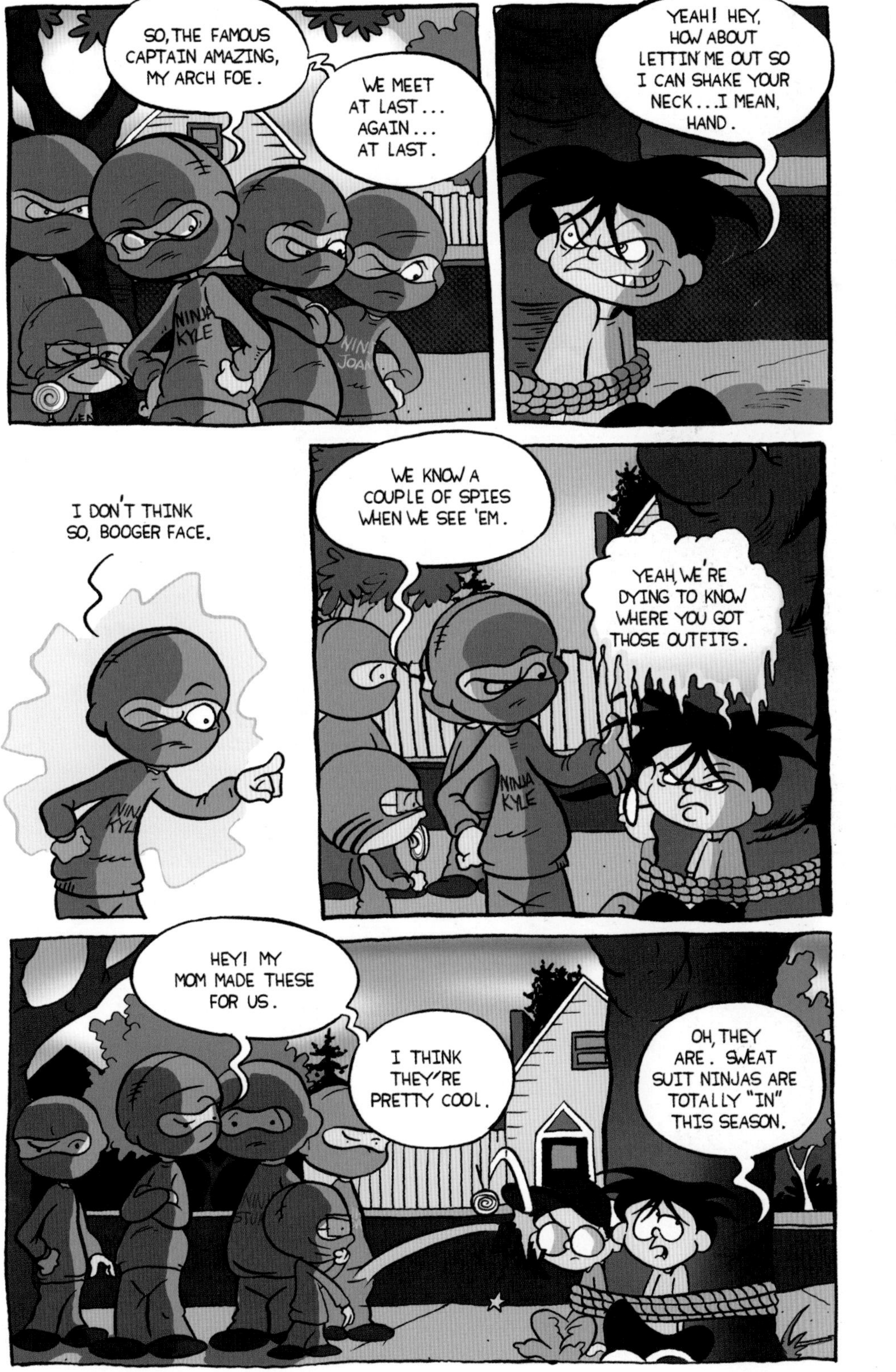
SO, THE FAMOUS CAPTAIN AMAZING, MY ARCH FOE.
WE MEET AT LAST... AGAIN... AT LAST.
YEAH! HEY, HOW ABOUT LETTIN' ME OUT SO I CAN SHAKE YOUR NECK...I MEAN, HAND.
I DON'T THINK SO, BOOGER FACE.
WE KNOW A COUPLE OF SPIES WHEN WE SEE 'EM.
YEAH, WE'RE DYING TO KNOW WHERE YOU GOT THOSE OUTFITS.
HEY! MY MOM MADE THESE FOR US.
I THINK THEY'RE PRETTY COOL.
OH, THEY ARE. SWEAT SUIT NINJAS ARE TOTALLY "IN" THIS SEASON.

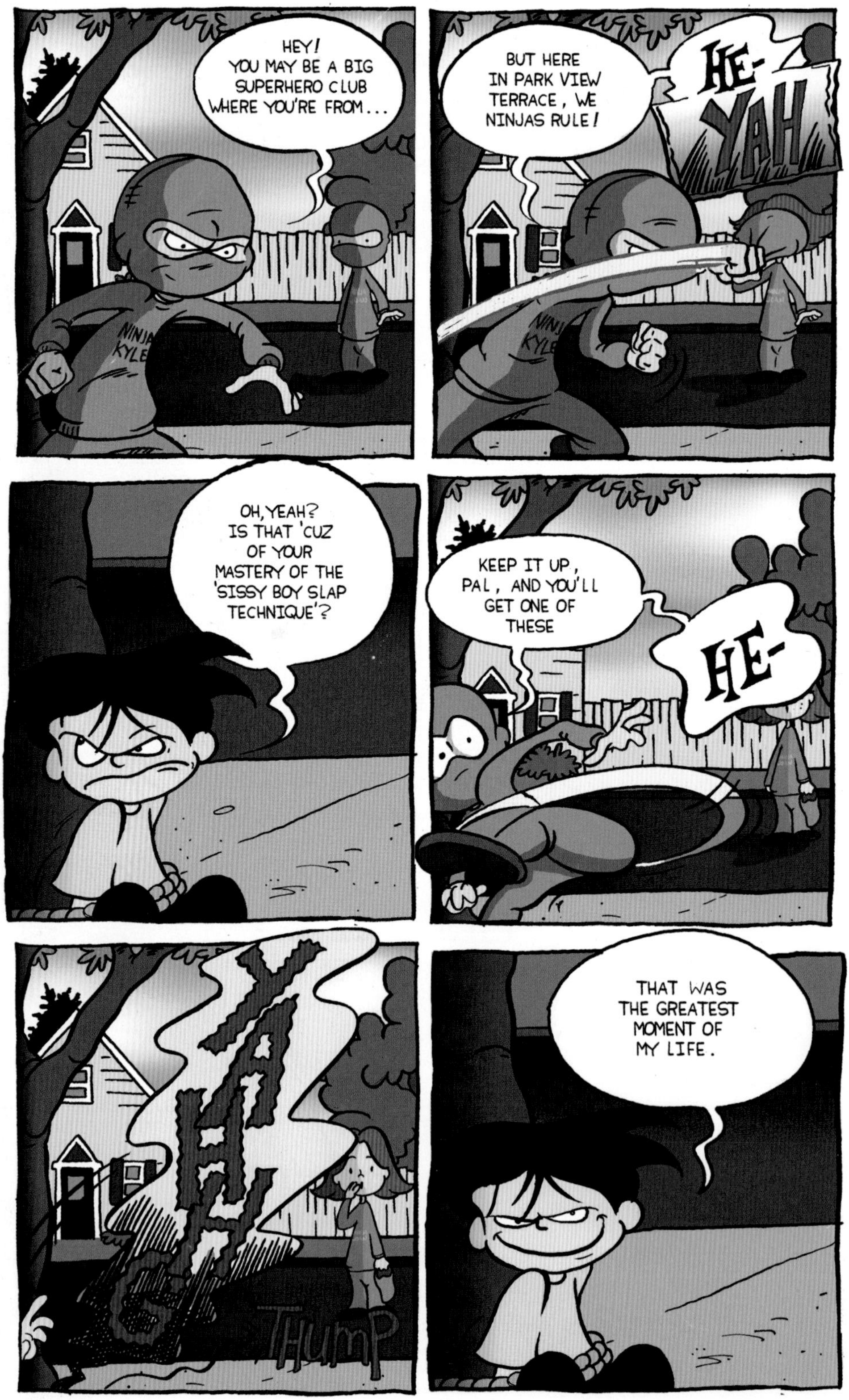
HEY! YOU MAY BE A BIG SUPERHERO CLUB WHERE YOU'RE FROM...
NINJA KYLE
BUT HERE IN PARK VIEW TERRACE, WE NINJAS RULE!
HE-YAH
OH, YEAH? IS THAT 'CUZ OF YOUR MASTERY OF THE 'SISSY BOY SLAP TECHNIQUE'?
KEEP IT UP, PAL, AND YOU'LL GET ONE OF THESE
HE-
YAH
THUMP
THAT WAS THE GREATEST MOMENT OF MY LIFE.

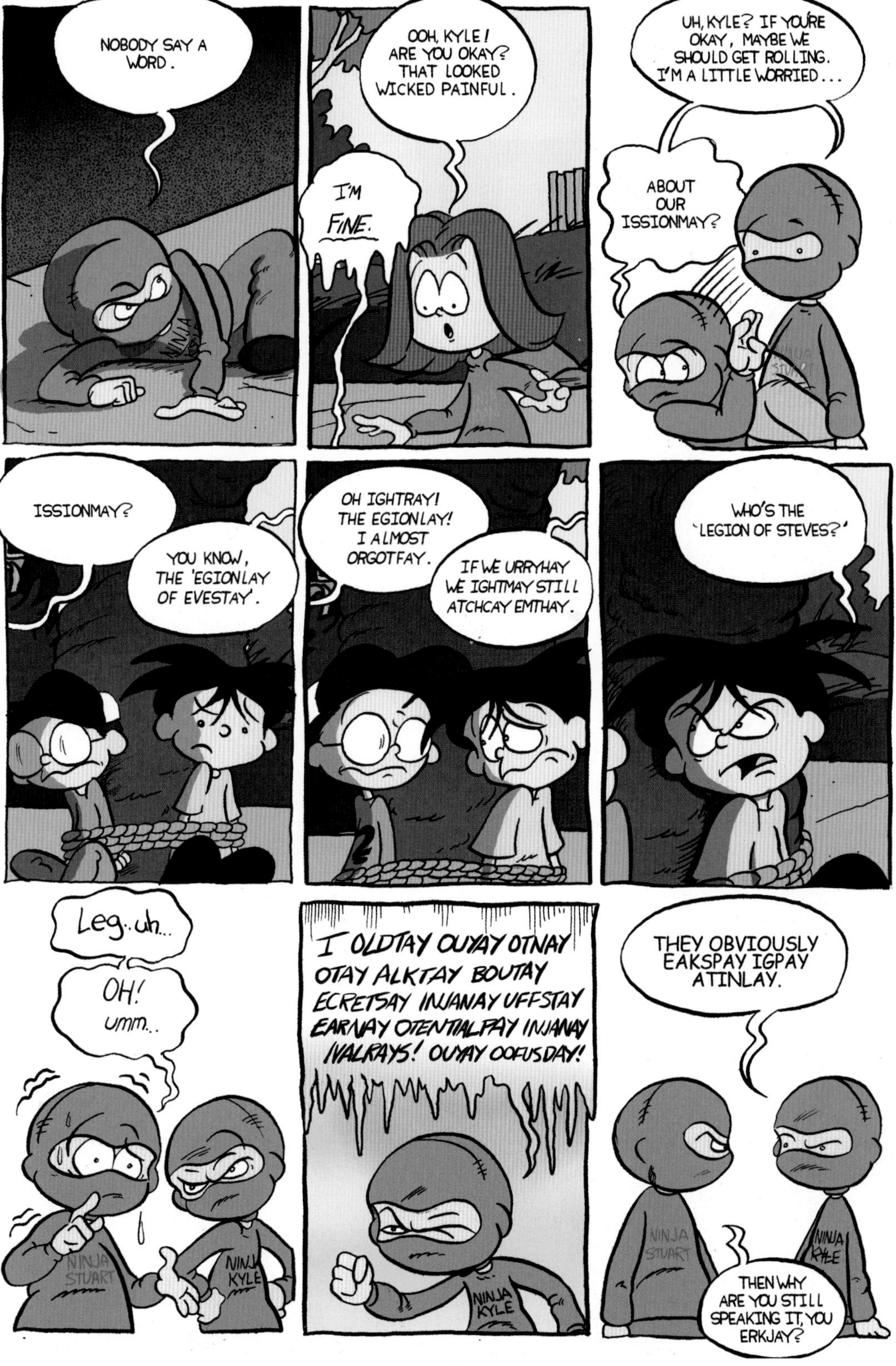
NOBODY SAY A WORD.
OOH, KYLE! ARE YOU OKAY? THAT LOOKED WICKED PAINFUL.
I'M FINE.
UH, KYLE? IF YOU'RE OKAY, MAYBE WE SHOULD GET ROLLING. I'M A LITTLE WORRIED...
ABOUT OUR ISSIONMAY?
ISSIONMAY?
YOU KNOW, THE 'EGIONLAY OF EVESTAY'.
OH IGHTRAY! THE EGIONLAY! I ALMOST ORGOTFAY.
IF WE URRYHAY WE IGHTMAY STILL ATCHCAY EMTHAY.
WHO'S THE 'LEGION OF STEVES?'
Leg..uh...
OH! umm...
I OLDTAY OUYAY OTNAY OTAY ALKTAY BOUTAY ECRETSAY INJANAY UFFSTAY EARNAY OTENTIALPAY INJANAY IVALRAYS! OUYAY OOFUSDAY!
THEY OBVIOUSLY EAKSPAY IGPAY ATINLAY.
THEN WHY ARE YOU STILL SPEAKING IT, YOU ERKJAY?

BEFORE YOU KNEW IT, MOST OF THE STUFF WAS MOVED IN AND IT WAS TIME TO SAY GOOD-BYE.

IF YOU WANT TO KNOW JUST HOW MUCH EVERYTHING CHANGED, JUST IMAGINE . . .

OH, HECK, WHY DON'T I JUST TELL YOU THE REST OF THE STORY NOW. . . .

I DON'T SEE MUCH OF MY FRIENDS AFTER I MOVE, WITH THE DIFFERENT SCHOOLS AND ALL. SO IN A FEW MONTHS I JOIN THE NINJAS. I DON'T LAST LONG, THOUGH, 'CUZ KYLE KICKS ME OUT FOR NOT WEARING THE MASK. TWO YEARS LATER, ALL IS FORGIVEN AND HE BECOMES MY FIRST BOYFRIEND. EVENTUALLY HE DUMPS ME. (JERK!)

BUT I REBOUND BY BECOMING HEAD CHEERLEADER AT PARK VIEW HIGH.

NINJA AMELIA

52

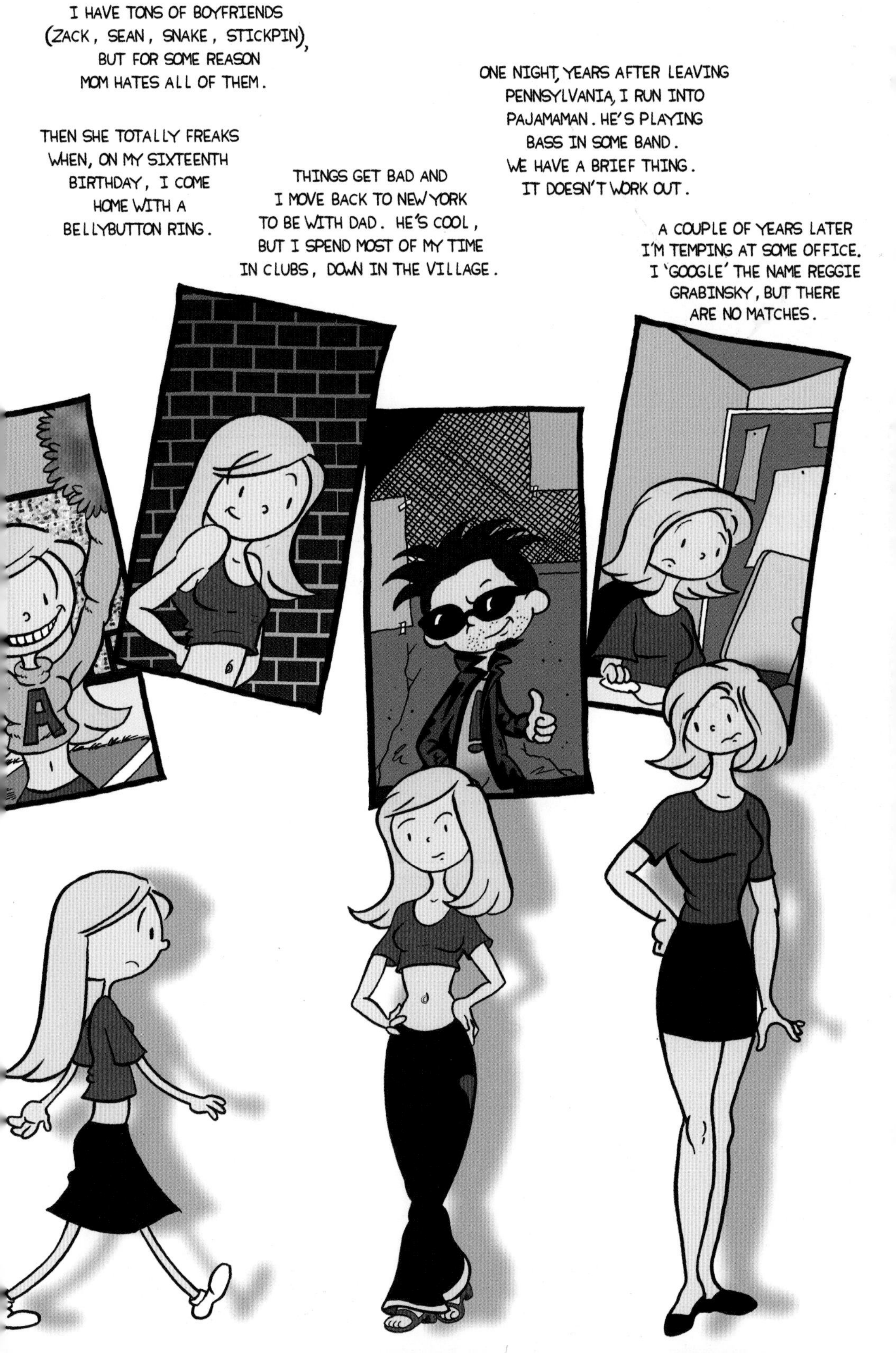
I HAVE TONS OF BOYFRIENDS (ZACK, SEAN, SNAKE, STICKPIN), BUT FOR SOME REASON MOM HATES ALL OF THEM.
THEN SHE TOTALLY FREAKS WHEN, ON MY SIXTEENTH BIRTHDAY, I COME HOME WITH A BELLYBUTTON RING.
THINGS GET BAD AND I MOVE BACK TO NEW YORK TO BE WITH DAD. HE'S COOL, BUT I SPEND MOST OF MY TIME IN CLUBS, DOWN IN THE VILLAGE.
ONE NIGHT, YEARS AFTER LEAVING PENNSYLVANIA, I RUN INTO PAJAMAMAN. HE'S PLAYING BASS IN SOME BAND. WE HAVE A BRIEF THING. IT DOESN'T WORK OUT.
A COUPLE OF YEARS LATER I'M TEMPING AT SOME OFFICE. I 'GOOGLE' THE NAME REGGIE GRABINSKY, BUT THERE ARE NO MATCHES.

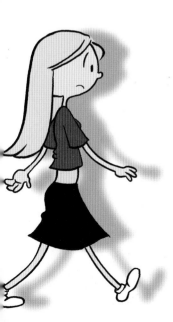

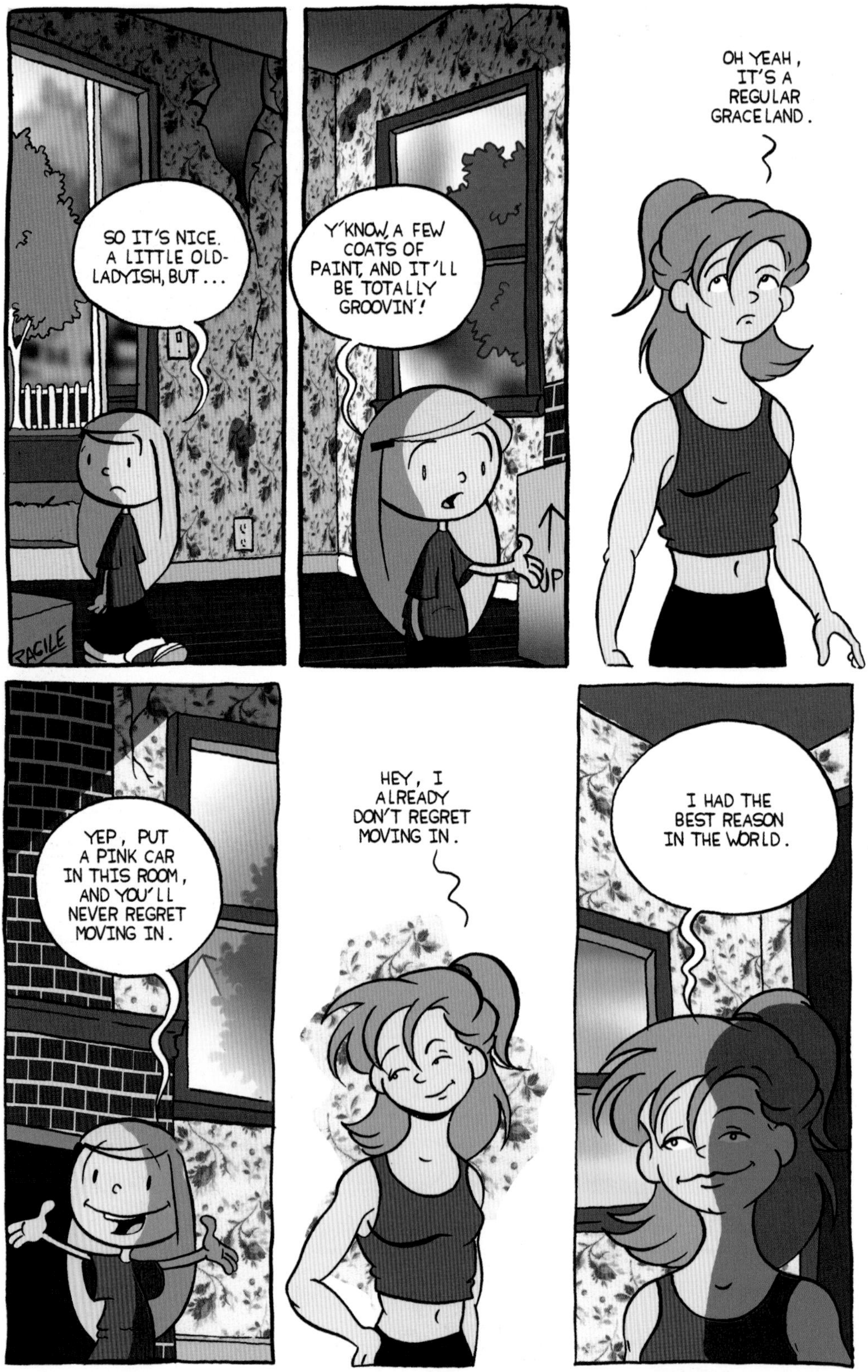
SO IT'S NICE. A LITTLE OLD-LADYISH, BUT . . .
RAGILE
Y'KNOW, A FEW COATS OF PAINT, AND IT'LL BE TOTALLY GROOVIN'!
UP
OH YEAH, IT'S A REGULAR GRACELAND.
YEP, PUT A PINK CAR IN THIS ROOM, AND YOU'LL NEVER REGRET MOVING IN.
HEY, I ALREADY DON'T REGRET MOVING IN.
I HAD THE BEST REASON IN THE WORLD.

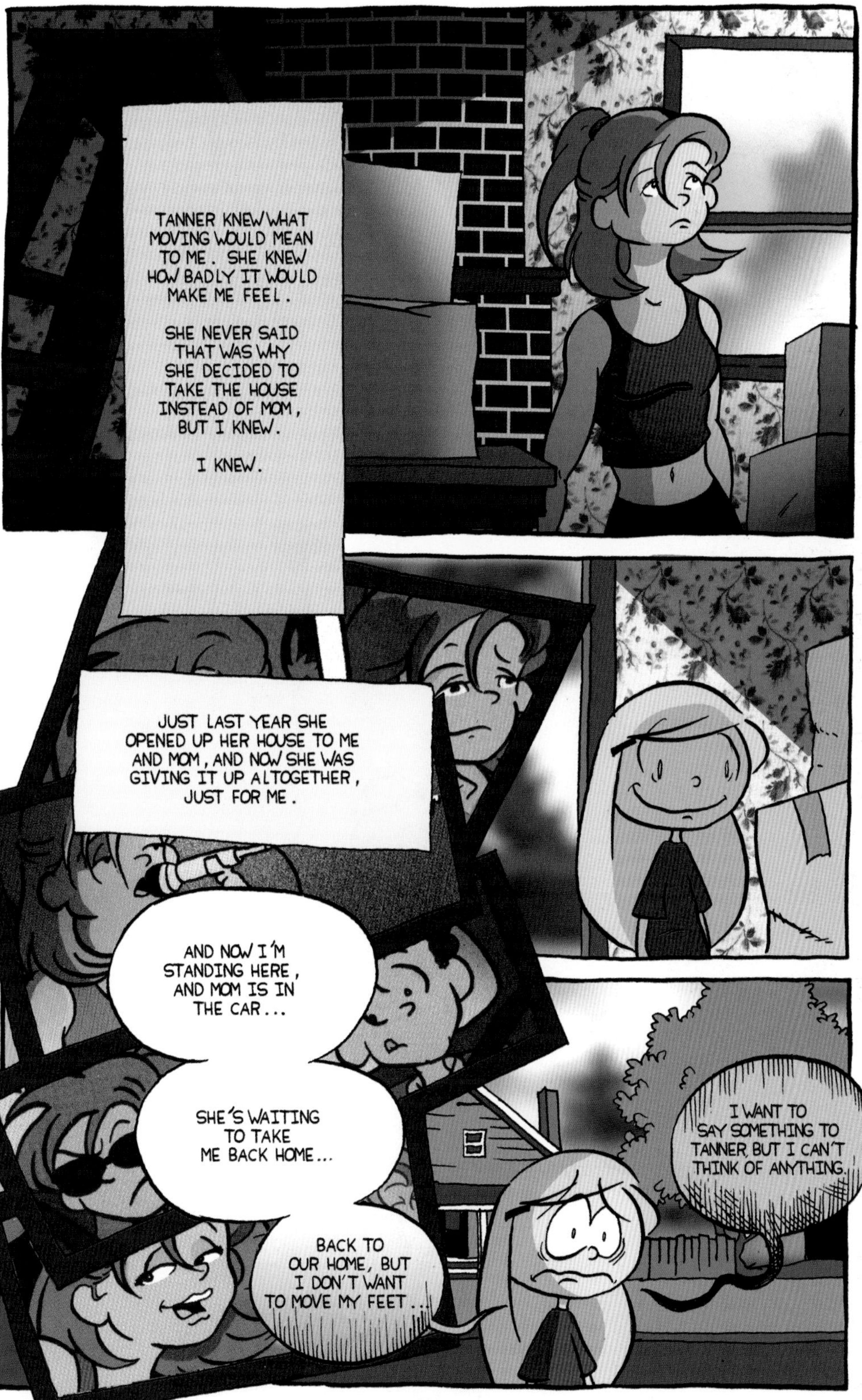
TANNER KNEW WHAT MOVING WOULD MEAN TO ME. SHE KNEW HOW BADLY IT WOULD MAKE ME FEEL.
SHE NEVER SAID THAT WAS WHY SHE DECIDED TO TAKE THE HOUSE INSTEAD OF MOM, BUT I KNEW.
I KNEW.
JUST LAST YEAR SHE OPENED UP HER HOUSE TO ME AND MOM, AND NOW SHE WAS GIVING IT UP ALTOGETHER, JUST FOR ME.
AND NOW I'M STANDING HERE, AND MOM IS IN THE CAR...
SHE'S WAITING TO TAKE ME BACK HOME...
BACK TO OUR HOME, BUT I DON'T WANT TO MOVE MY FEET...
I WANT TO SAY SOMETHING TO TANNER, BUT I CAN'T THINK OF ANYTHING.

SO I RUN BACK IN, AND
I JUMP UP ON HER, AND
I'M HUGGING HER AROUND
HER NECK, AND I START
CRYING, AND SHE STARTS
LAUGHING, AND I
STILL CAN'T THINK
OF ANYTHING TO SAY.

BUT IT DOESN'T MATTER,
'CUZ SUPERHEROES
NEVER NEED TO BE
THANKED ANYWAY.

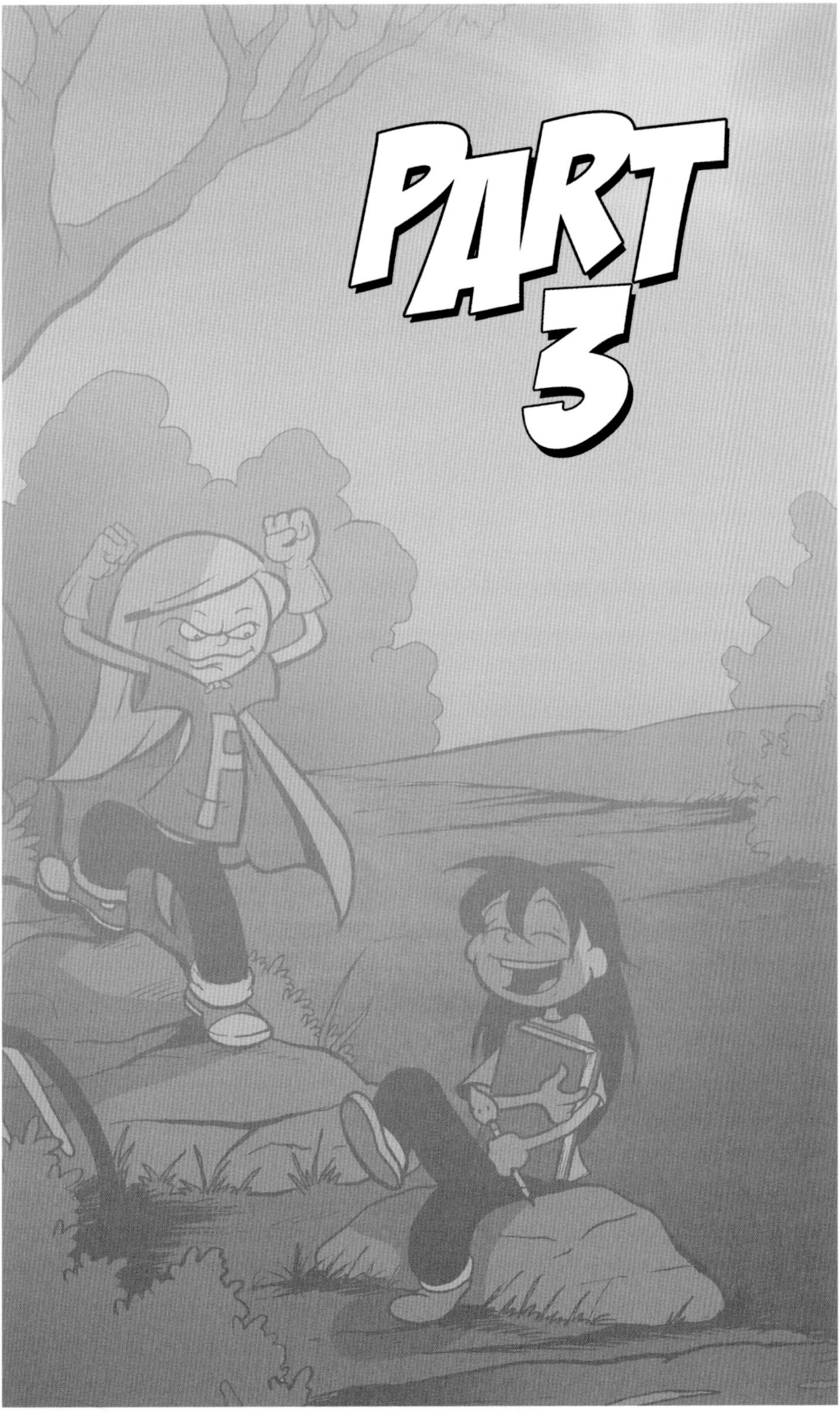
PART
3

SUMMER WAS GETTING WEIRD...

AFTER WE FOUND REGGIE AND PAJAMAMAN TIED TO THAT TREE, IT SEEMED LIKE REGGIE BECAME *OBSESSED* WITH THE NINJAS. PLUS THERE WAS SOME NEW GROUP CALLED THE **LEGION OF STEVES** THAT HE WAS ALWAYS RANTING ABOUT.

TWO WEEKS PASSED SINCE TANNER HAD MOVED OUT, AND EVEN THOUGH SHE WAS JUST ACROSS TOWN, I WAS REALLY **MISSING** HER. AND BECAUSE I'M APPARENTLY A MORON, I DECIDED TO DISCUSS MY FEELINGS WITH **RHONDA**...

KID LIGHTNING, I GIVE YOU THE NEW *AMAZING* MOBILE... THE MOST **POWERFUL** CRIME-FIGHTING VEHICLE SEEN, SINCE I DROVE THE LAST AMAZING MOBILE OFF THAT CLIFF.

WITH IT, WE WILL INVADE THE NINJAS' *HEADQUARTERS*, AND DISCOVER WHAT THEY KNOW ABOUT THIS MYSTERIOUS "*LEGION OF STEVES*".

IT'S REALLY THE *LITTLE* THINGS THAT I MISS THE MOST, Y'KNOW? LIKE SHE USED TO PLAY HER GUITAR UP IN THE ATTIC.

PERHAPS THEY WILL BE OUR ALLIES IN OUR STRUGGLE AGAINST THE NINJAS. FOR LIKE THE OLD SAYING GOES...

Mmm Hmm

Amelia Rules!

Chapter Three:

Old Friends Who Just Met

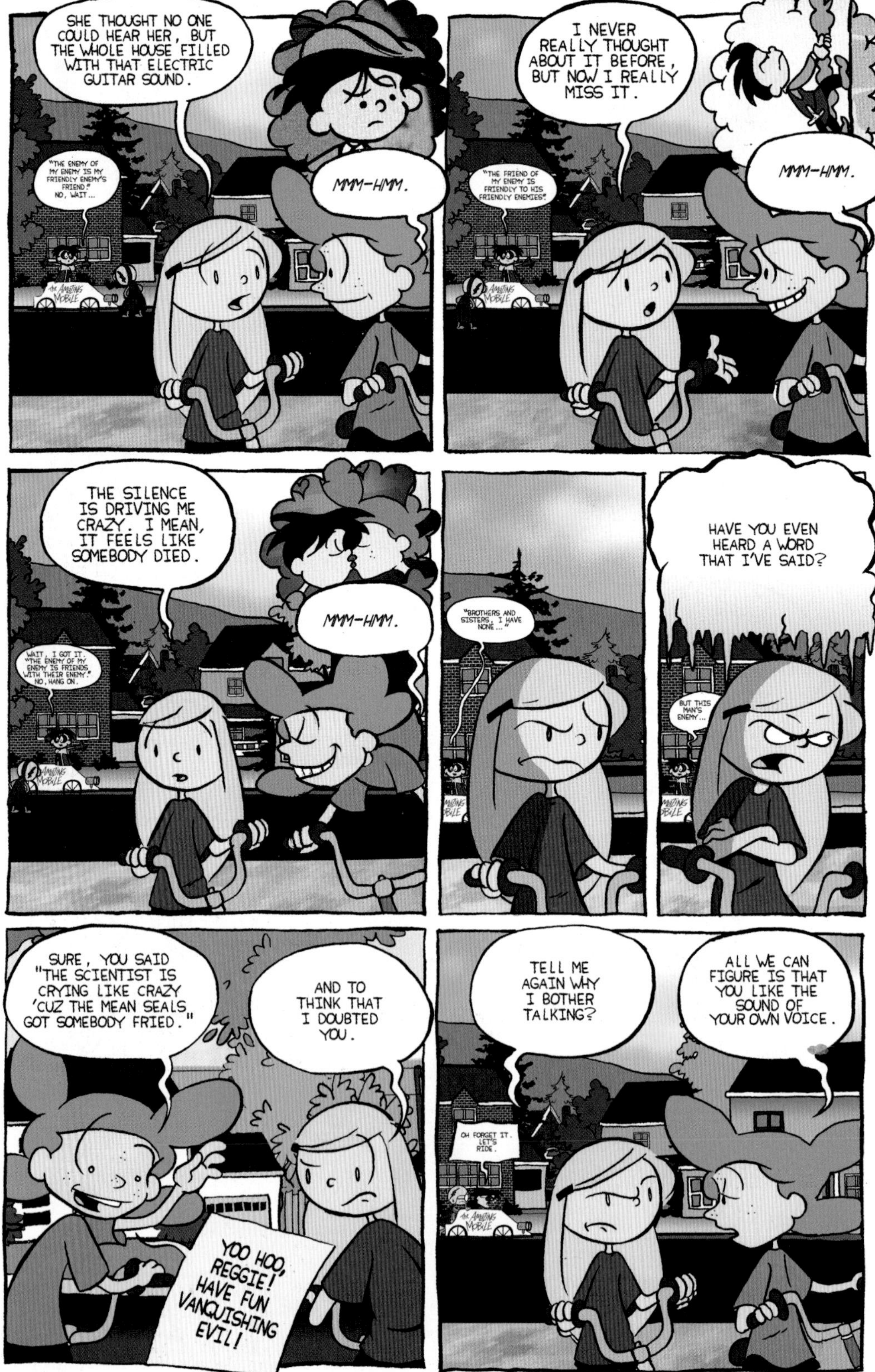
SHE THOUGHT NO ONE COULD HEAR HER, BUT THE WHOLE HOUSE FILLED WITH THAT ELECTRIC GUITAR SOUND.
MMM-HMM.
"THE ENEMY OF MY ENEMY IS MY FRIENDlY ENEMY'S FRIEND." NO, WAIT...
THE AMAZING MOBILE
I NEVER REALLY THOUGHT ABOUT IT BEFORE, BUT NOW I REALLY MISS IT.
MMM-HMM.
"THE FRIEND OF MY ENEMY IS FRIENDlY TO HIS FRIENDlY ENEMIES."
THE SILENCE IS DRIVING ME CRAZY. I MEAN, IT FEELS LIKE SOMEBODY DIED.
MMM-HMM.
WAIT, I GOT IT. "THE ENEMY OF MY ENEMY IS FRIENDS WITH THEIR ENEMY." NO, HANG ON.
"BROTHERS AND SISTERS, I HAVE NONE..."
HAVE YOU EVEN HEARD A WORD THAT I'VE SAID?
BUT THIS MAN'S ENEMY...
SURE, YOU SAID "THE SCIENTIST IS CRYING LIKE CRAZY 'CUZ THE MEAN SEALS GOT SOMEBODY FRIED."
AND TO THINK THAT I DOUBTED YOU.
YOO HOO, REGGIE! HAVE FUN VANQUISHING EVIL!
TELL ME AGAIN WHY I BOTHER TALKING?
ALL WE CAN FIGURE IS THAT YOU LIKE THE SOUND OF YOUR OWN VOICE.
OH FORGET IT. LET'S RIDE.
THE AMAZING MOBILE

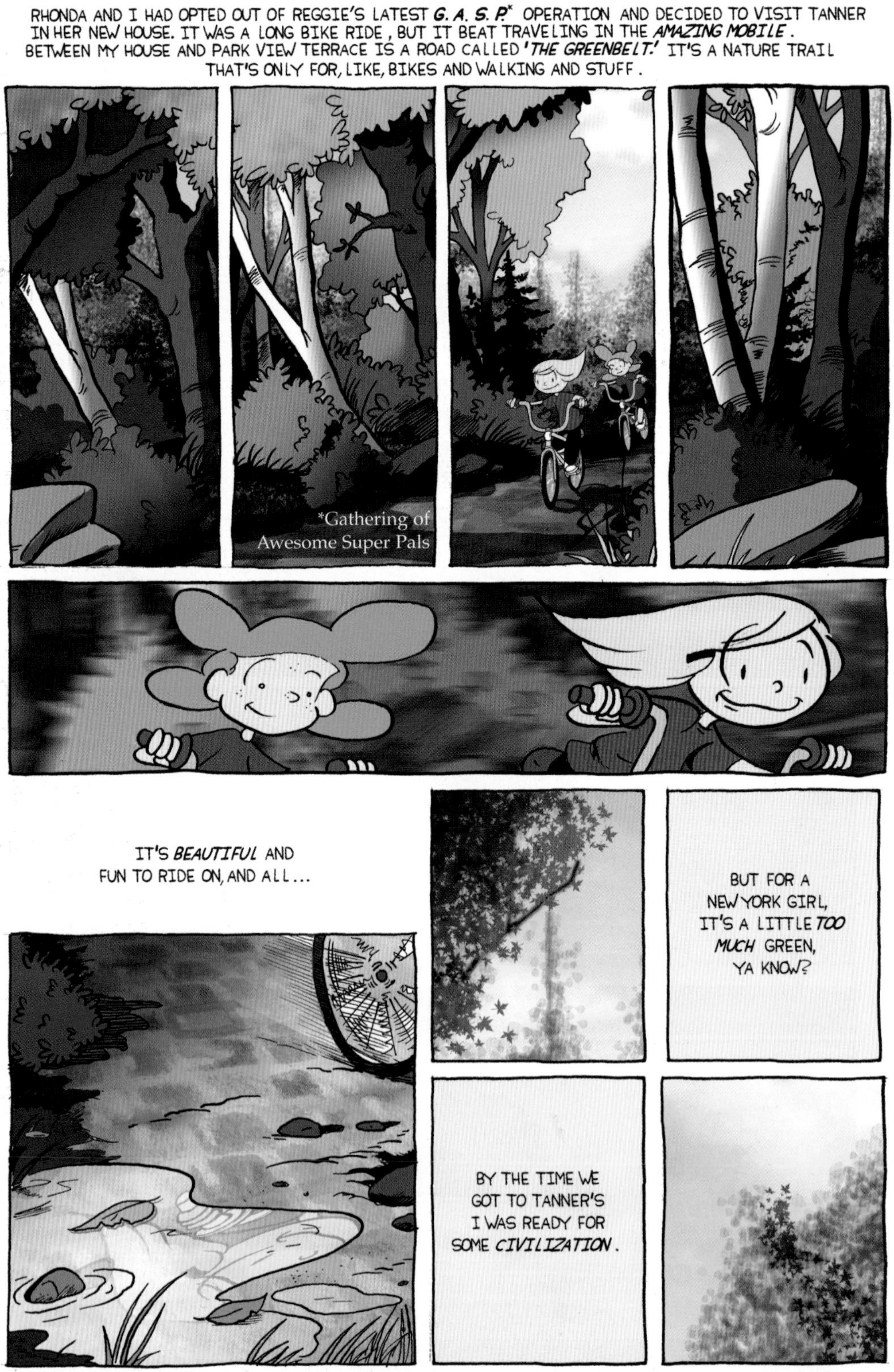
RHONDA AND I HAD OPTED OUT OF REGGIE'S LATEST *G. A. S. P.** OPERATION AND DECIDED TO VISIT TANNER IN HER NEW HOUSE. IT WAS A LONG BIKE RIDE, BUT IT BEAT TRAVELING IN THE *AMAZING MOBILE*.
BETWEEN MY HOUSE AND PARK VIEW TERRACE IS A ROAD CALLED *'THE GREENBELT.'* IT'S A NATURE TRAIL THAT'S ONLY FOR, LIKE, BIKES AND WALKING AND STUFF.
*Gathering of Awesome Super Pals
IT'S *BEAUTIFUL* AND FUN TO RIDE ON, AND ALL...
BUT FOR A NEW YORK GIRL, IT'S A LITTLE *TOO MUCH* GREEN, YA KNOW?
BY THE TIME WE GOT TO TANNER'S I WAS READY FOR SOME *CIVILIZATION*.

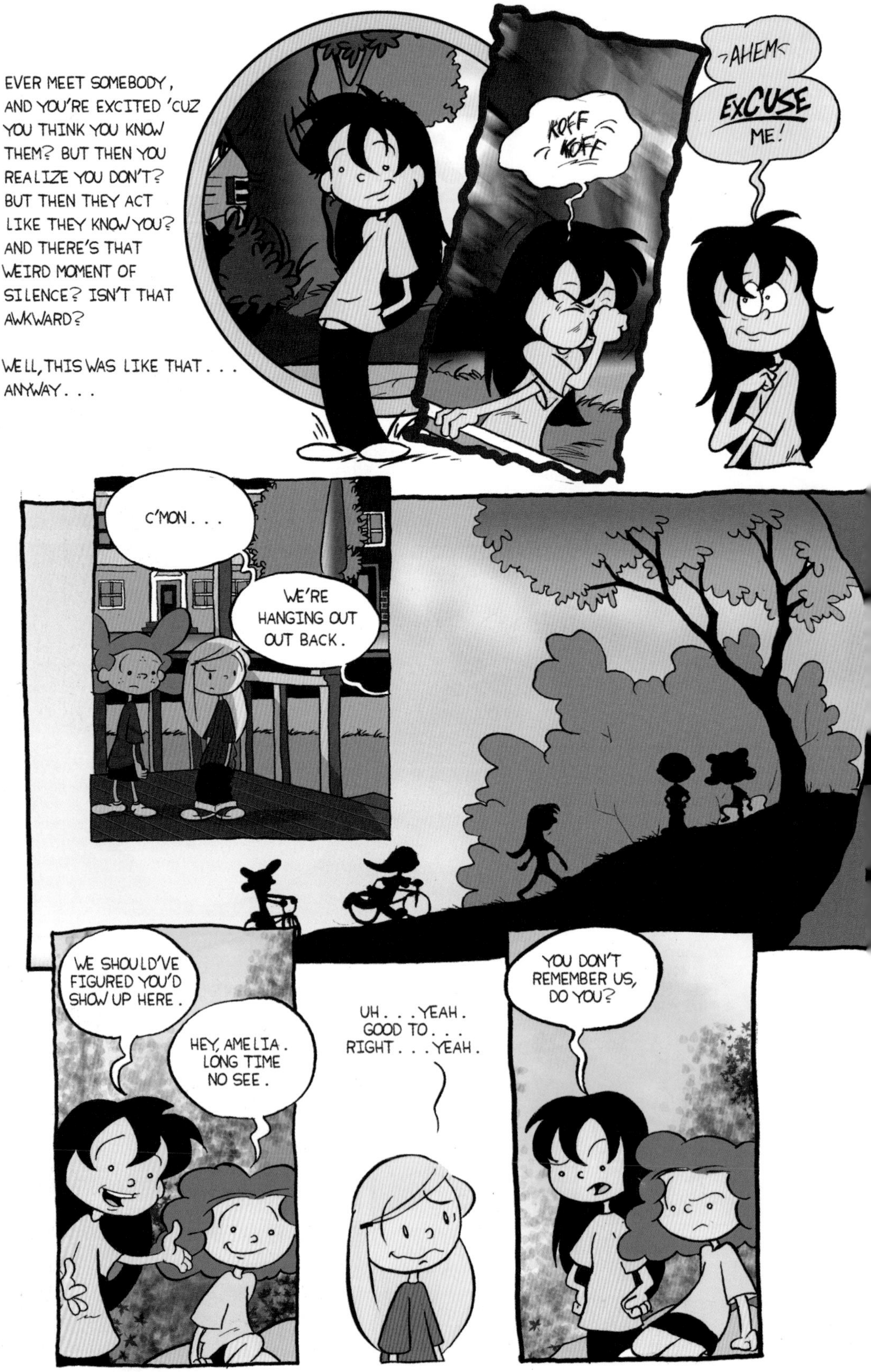
EVER MEET SOMEBODY, AND YOU'RE EXCITED 'CUZ YOU THINK YOU KNOW THEM? BUT THEN YOU REALIZE YOU DON'T? BUT THEN THEY ACT LIKE THEY KNOW YOU? AND THERE'S THAT WEIRD MOMENT OF SILENCE? ISN'T THAT AWKWARD?
WELL, THIS WAS LIKE THAT . . . ANYWAY . . .
KOFF KOFF
AHEM
EXCUSE ME!
C'MON . . .
WE'RE HANGING OUT OUT BACK.
WE SHOULD'VE FIGURED YOU'D SHOW UP HERE.
HEY, AMELIA. LONG TIME NO SEE.
UH. . . YEAH. GOOD TO. . . RIGHT. . . YEAH.
YOU DON'T REMEMBER US, DO YOU?

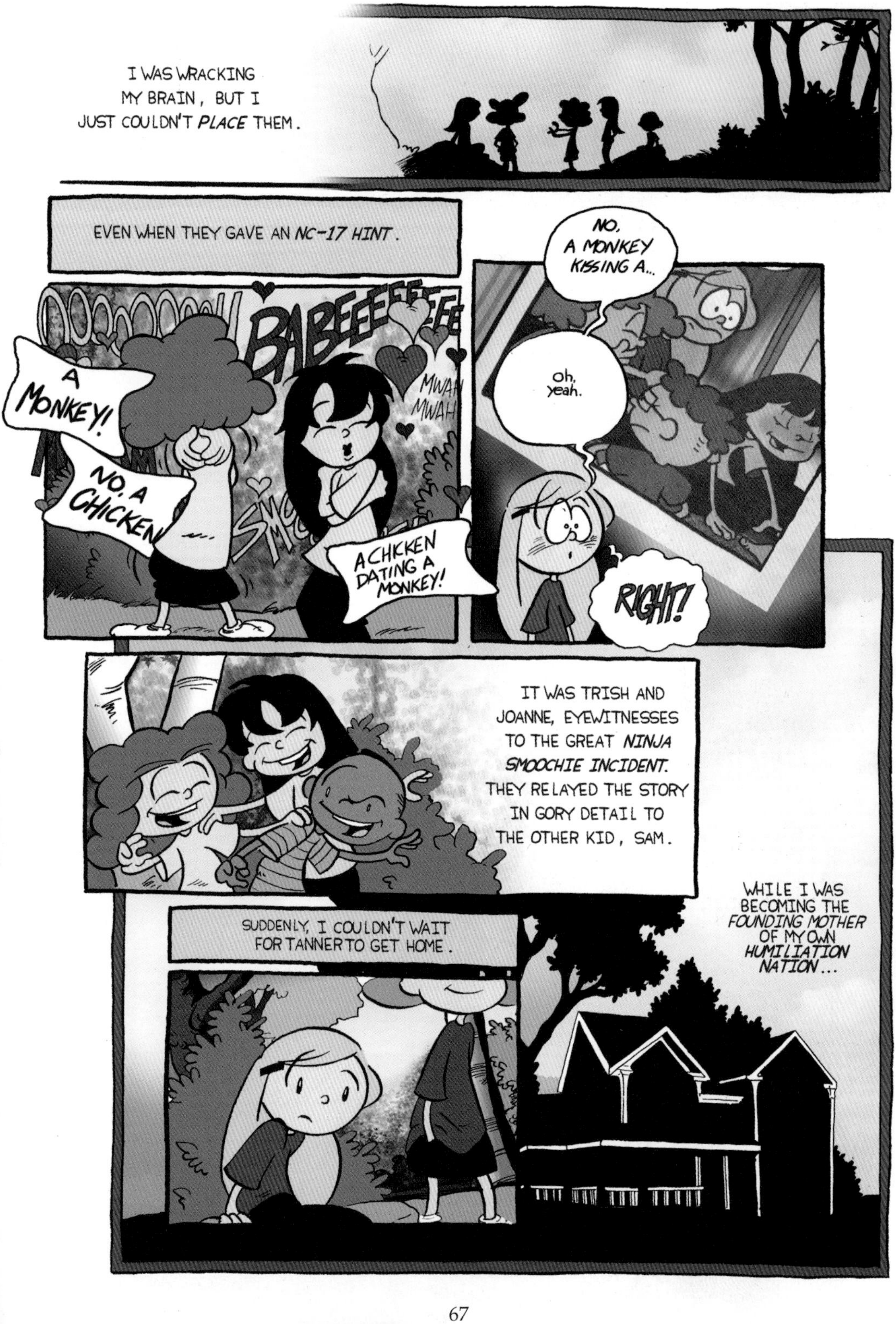
I WAS WRACKING MY BRAIN, BUT I JUST COULDN'T *PLACE* THEM.
EVEN WHEN THEY GAVE AN *NC-17 HINT*.
OOOOOOOOOOU
BABEEEEEEEE
MWAH MWAH
A MONKEY!
NO, A CHICKEN
A CHICKEN DATING A MONKEY!
NO, A MONKEY KISSING A...
Oh, yeah.
RIGHT!
IT WAS TRISH AND JOANNE, EYEWITNESSES TO THE GREAT *NINJA SMOOCHIE INCIDENT*. THEY RELAYED THE STORY IN GORY DETAIL TO THE OTHER KID, SAM.
WHILE I WAS BECOMING THE *FOUNDING MOTHER* OF MY OWN *HUMILIATION NATION*...
SUDDENLY, I COULDN'T WAIT FOR TANNER TO GET HOME.

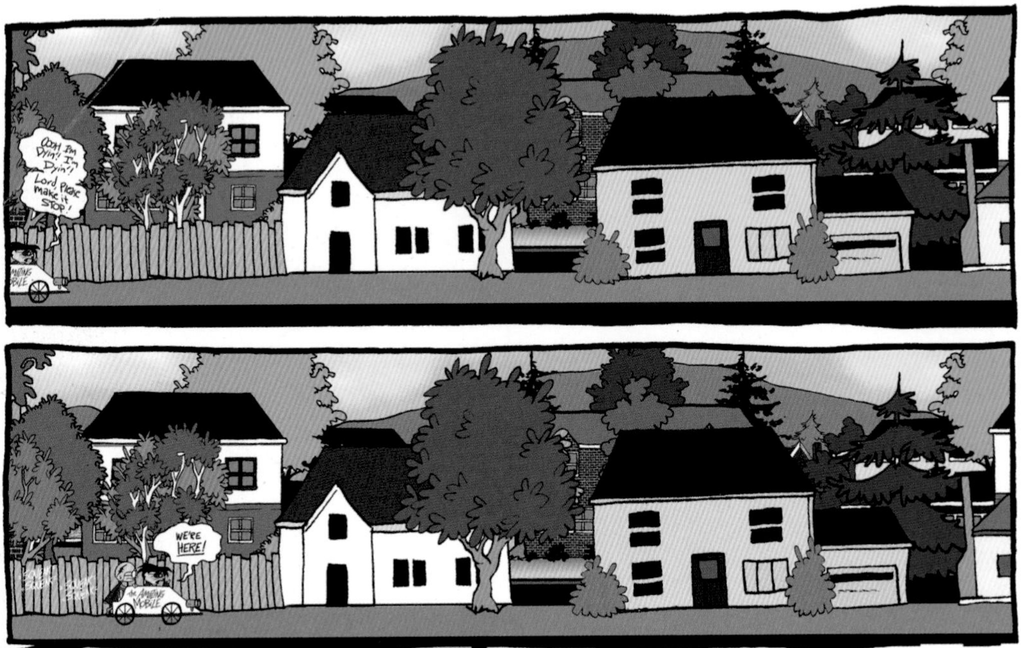
OOOH! I'm Dyin'! I'm Dyin'! Lord Please make it STOP!
WE'RE HERE!
the AMAZING MOBILE

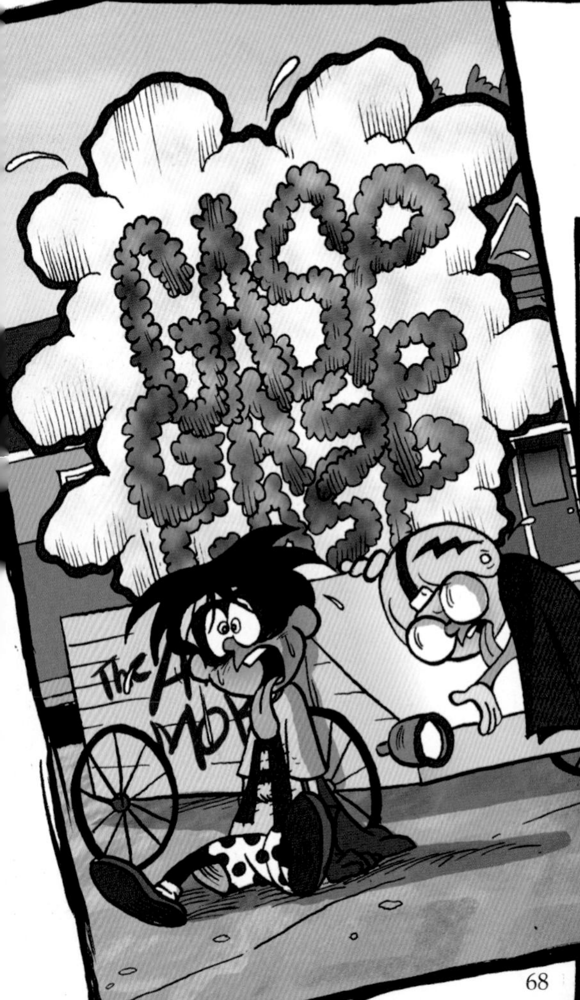
GASP GASP

AND, AFTER TWO MINOR **STROKES**, THEY **REACHED** IT.

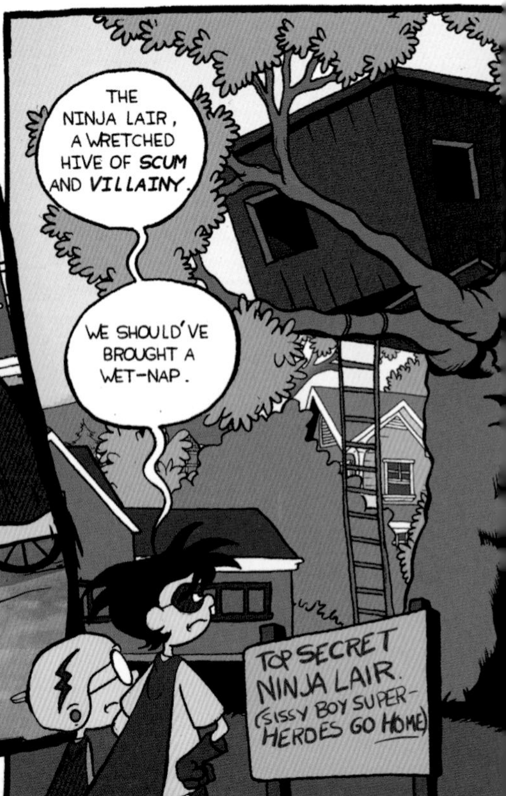
THE NINJA LAIR, A WRETCHED HIVE OF **SCUM** AND ***VILLAINY***.
WE SHOULD'VE BROUGHT A WET-NAP.
TOP SECRET NINJA LAIR. (SISSY BOY SUPER-HEROES GO HOME)

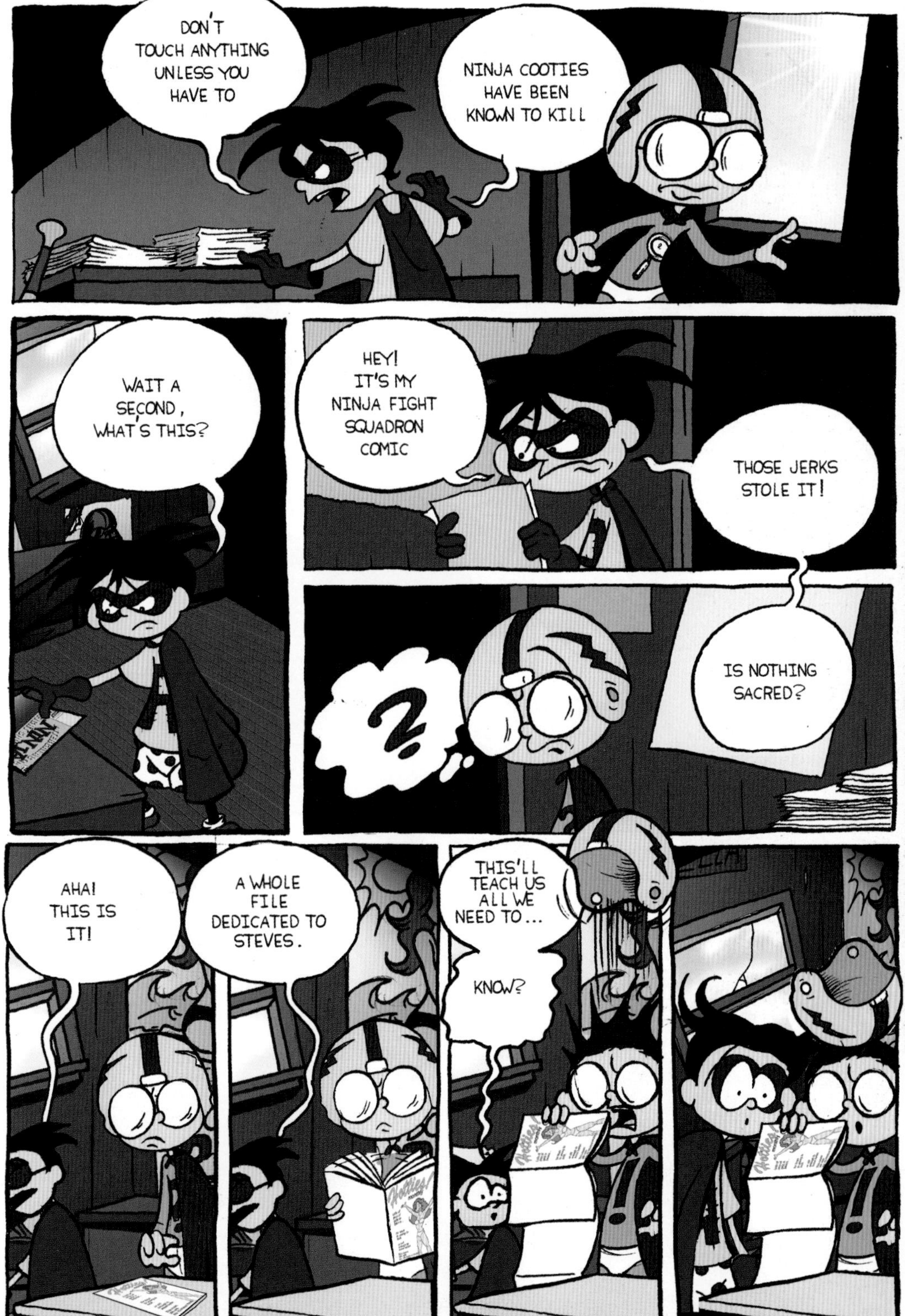

DON'T TOUCH ANYTHING UNLESS YOU HAVE TO
NINJA COOTIES HAVE BEEN KNOWN TO KILL
WAIT A SECOND, WHAT'S THIS?
HEY! IT'S MY NINJA FIGHT SQUADRON COMIC
THOSE JERKS STOLE IT!
?
IS NOTHING SACRED?
AHA! THIS IS IT!
A WHOLE FILE DEDICATED TO STEVES.
THIS'LL TEACH US ALL WE NEED TO...
KNOW?

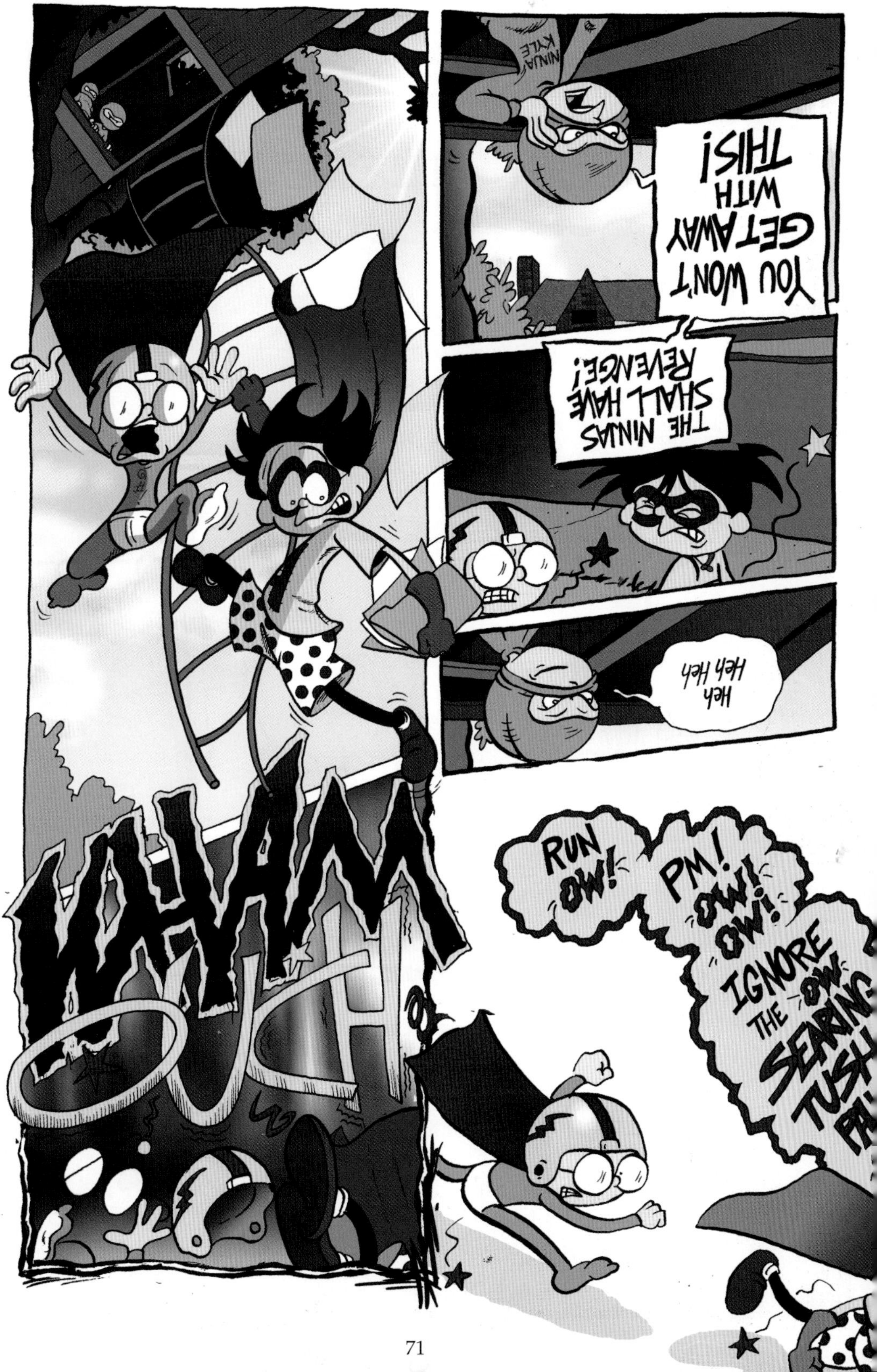
Heh Heh Heh
THE NINJAS SHALL HAVE REVENGE!
YOU WON'T GET AWAY WITH THIS!
NINJA KYLE
WHAM
RUN OW!
PM! OW! OW! OW!
IGNORE THE OW SEARING TUSH

AND SPEAKING OF *PAINS IN THE BUTT*. . .I FIGURED THE BEST WAY TO STOP BEING EMBARRASSED WAS TO START DOING THE EMBARRASSING. SO I TURNED THE SPOTLIGHT ON MY GOOD FRIEND RHONDA.

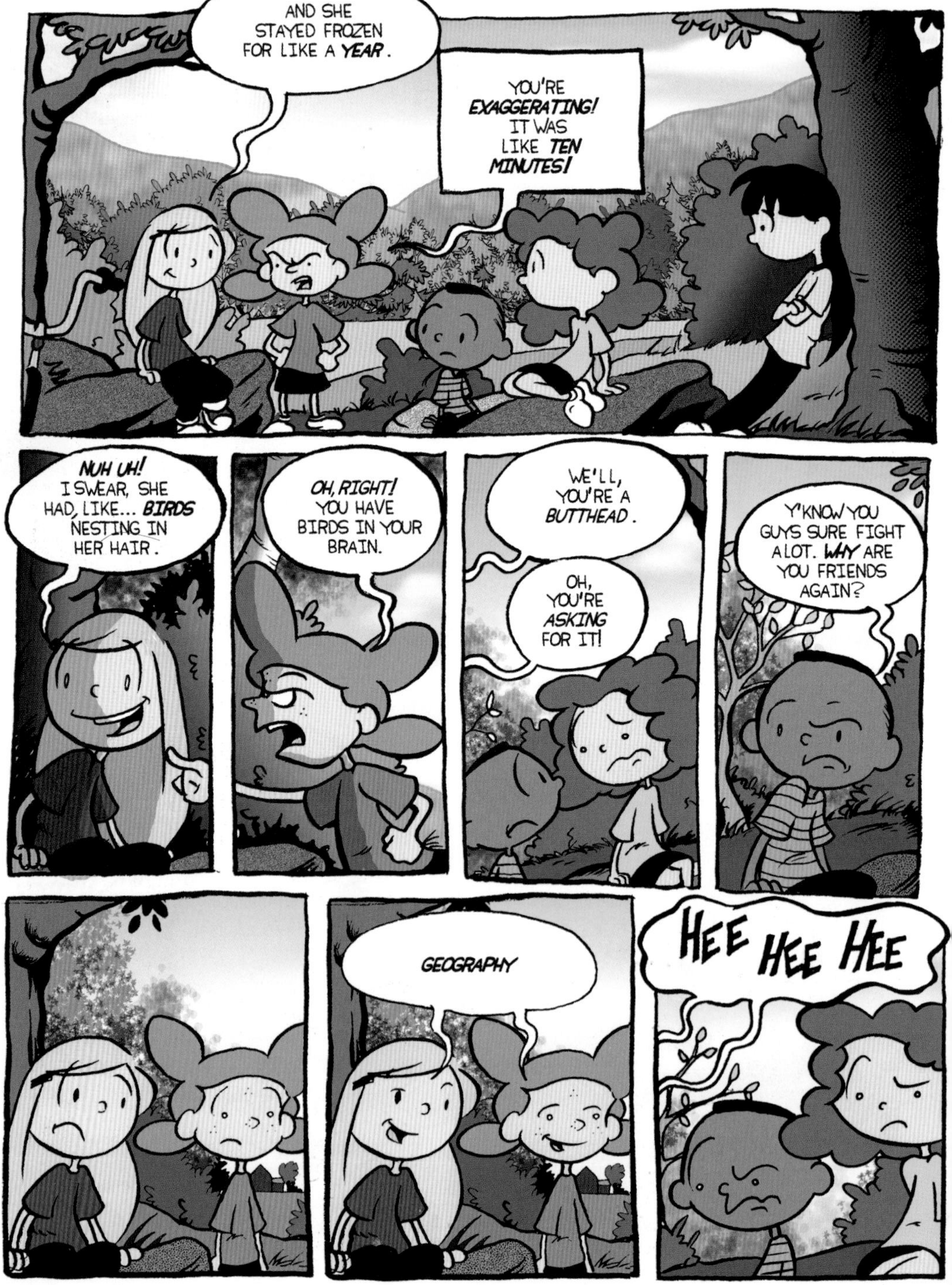
AND SHE STAYED FROZEN FOR LIKE A YEAR.
YOU'RE EXAGGERATING! IT WAS LIKE TEN MINUTES!
NUH UH! I SWEAR, SHE HAD, LIKE... BIRDS NESTING IN HER HAIR.
OH, RIGHT! YOU HAVE BIRDS IN YOUR BRAIN.
WE'LL, YOU'RE A BUTTHEAD.
OH, YOU'RE ASKING FOR IT!
Y'KNOW YOU GUYS SURE FIGHT ALOT. WHY ARE YOU FRIENDS AGAIN?
GEOGRAPHY
HEE HEE HEE

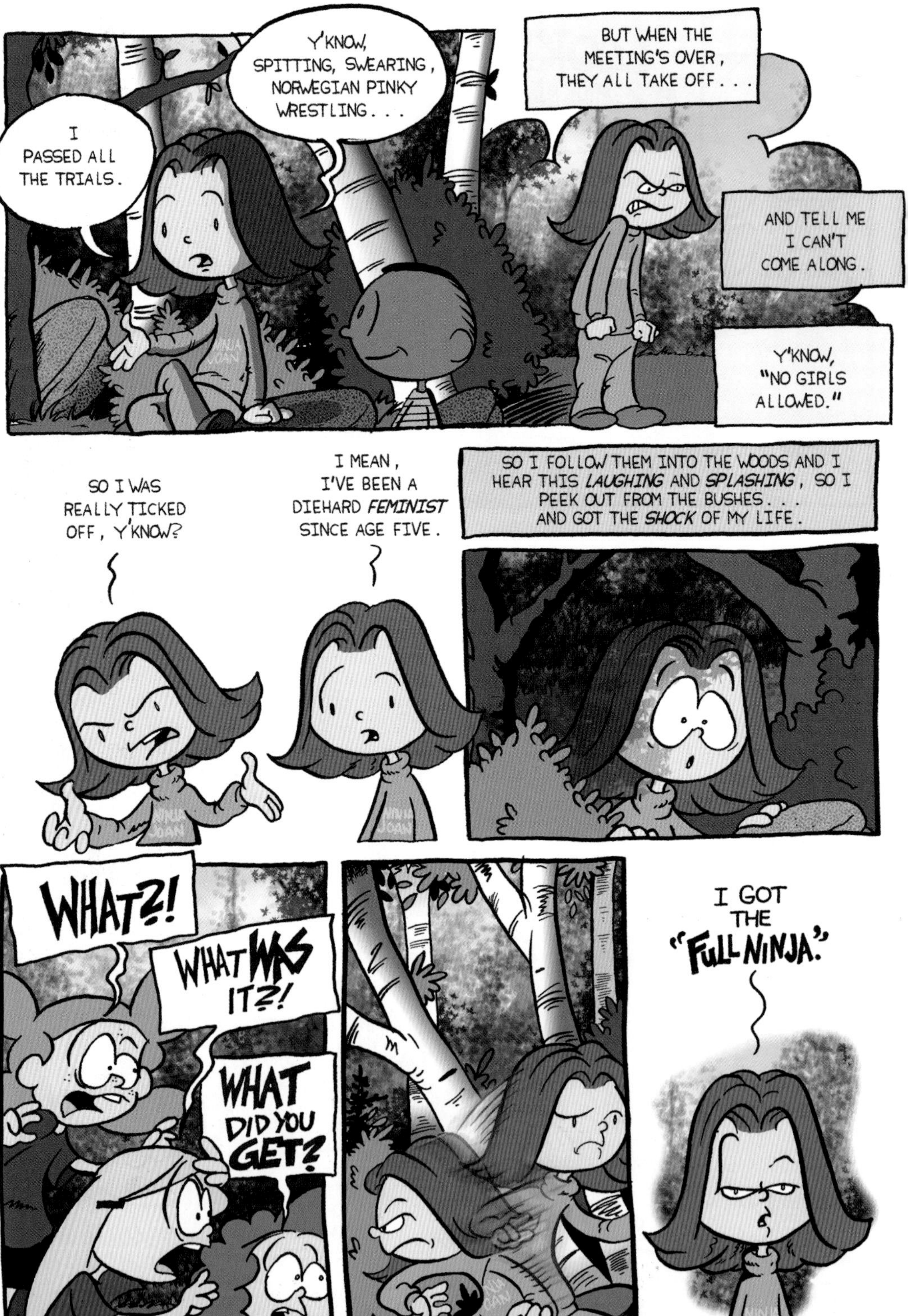
I PASSED ALL THE TRIALS.
Y'KNOW, SPITTING, SWEARING, NORWEGIAN PINKY WRESTLING . . .
BUT WHEN THE MEETING'S OVER, THEY ALL TAKE OFF . . .
AND TELL ME I CAN'T COME ALONG.
Y'KNOW, "NO GIRLS ALLOWED."
SO I WAS REALLY TICKED OFF, Y'KNOW?
I MEAN, I'VE BEEN A DIEHARD *FEMINIST* SINCE AGE FIVE.
SO I FOLLOW THEM INTO THE WOODS AND I HEAR THIS *LAUGHING* AND *SPLASHING*, SO I PEEK OUT FROM THE BUSHES . . . AND GOT THE *SHOCK* OF MY LIFE.
WHAT?!
WHAT WAS IT?!
WHAT DID YOU GET?
I GOT THE "FULL NINJA."

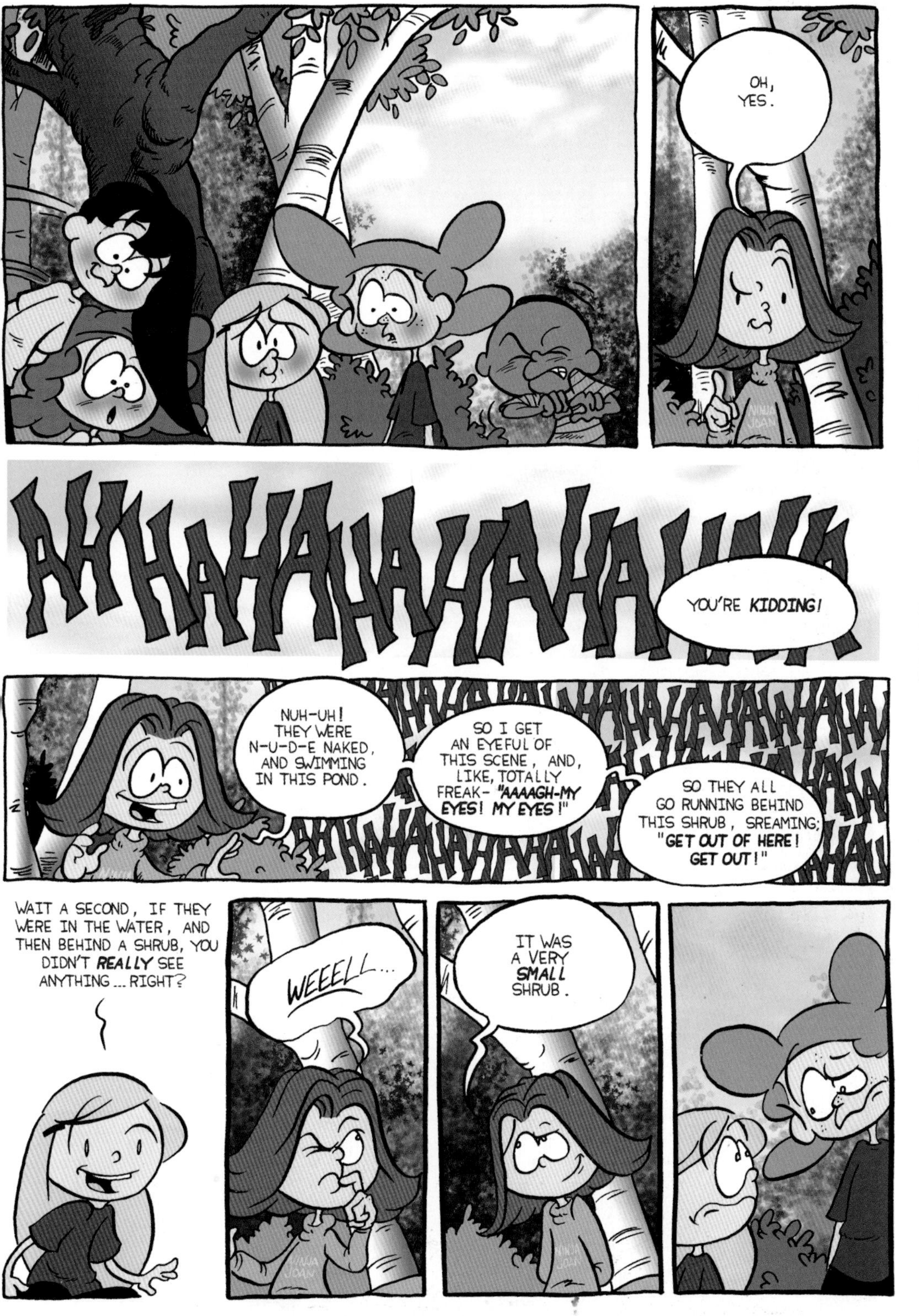

OH, YES.
AHHAHAHAHAHAHAHA
YOU'RE KIDDING!
NUH-UH! THEY WERE N-U-D-E NAKED, AND SWIMMING IN THIS POND.
SO I GET AN EYEFUL OF THIS SCENE, AND, LIKE, TOTALLY FREAK- "AAAAGH-MY EYES! MY EYES!"
SO THEY ALL GO RUNNING BEHIND THIS SHRUB, SREAMING; "GET OUT OF HERE! GET OUT!"
WAIT A SECOND, IF THEY WERE IN THE WATER, AND THEN BEHIND A SHRUB, YOU DIDN'T REALLY SEE ANYTHING... RIGHT?
WEEELL...
IT WAS A VERY SMALL SHRUB.

WHY DON'T I GIVE YOU A MINUTE TO ERASE THAT HORRIBLE IMAGE. OKAY, READY? LET'S CONTINUE.

WE ENDED UP HANGING OUT FOR A LONG TIME, AND IT WAS KINDA COOL. JOAN WAS EASILY THE MOST NORMAL NINJA I'D MET YET, AND EVERYONE ELSE SEEMED NICE, TOO. SO WHEN NINJA JOAN HAD TO GO HOME, WE DIDN'T MIND BEING HIJACKED OVER TO JOANNE'S HOUSE.

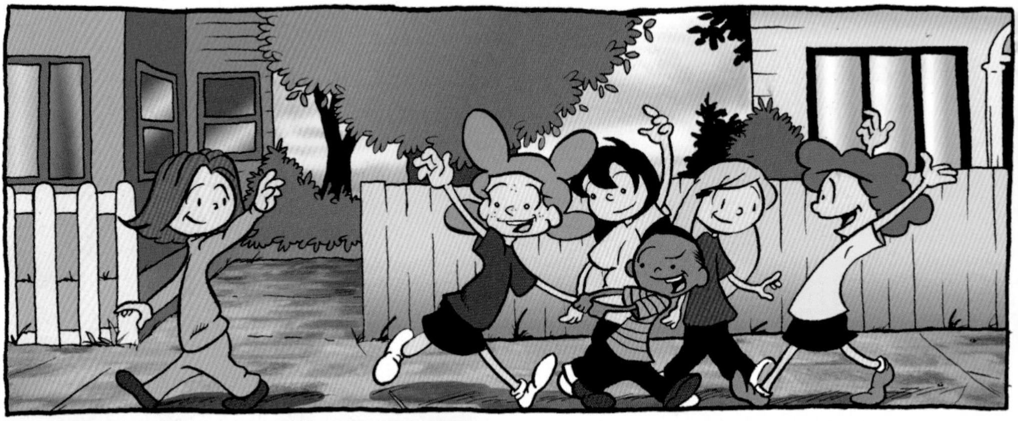

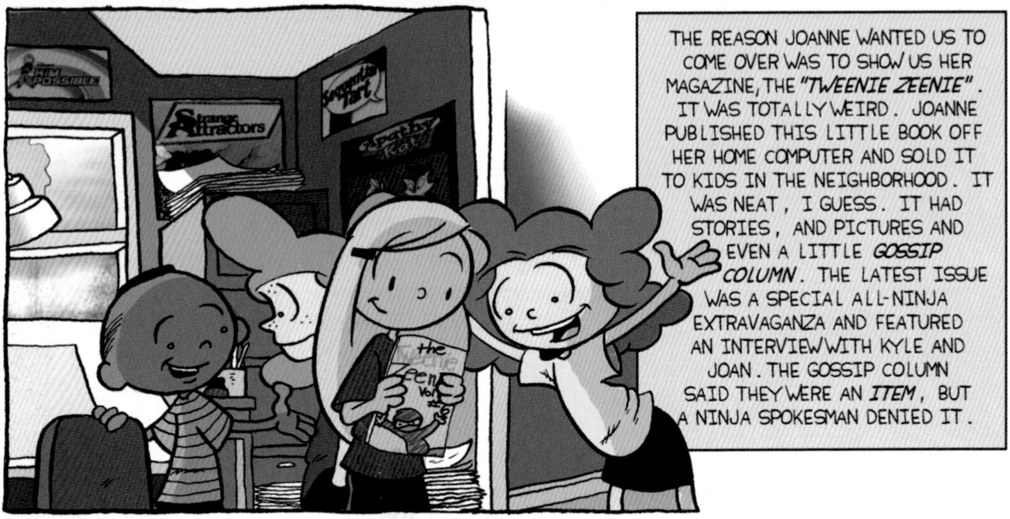
Strange Attractors
THE REASON JOANNE WANTED US TO COME OVER WAS TO SHOW US HER MAGAZINE, THE "TWEENIE ZEENIE". IT WAS TOTALLY WEIRD. JOANNE PUBLISHED THIS LITTLE BOOK OFF HER HOME COMPUTER AND SOLD IT TO KIDS IN THE NEIGHBORHOOD. IT WAS NEAT, I GUESS. IT HAD STORIES, AND PICTURES AND EVEN A LITTLE GOSSIP COLUMN. THE LATEST ISSUE WAS A SPECIAL ALL-NINJA EXTRAVAGANZA AND FEATURED AN INTERVIEW WITH KYLE AND JOAN. THE GOSSIP COLUMN SAID THEY WERE AN ITEM, BUT A NINJA SPOKESMAN DENIED IT.

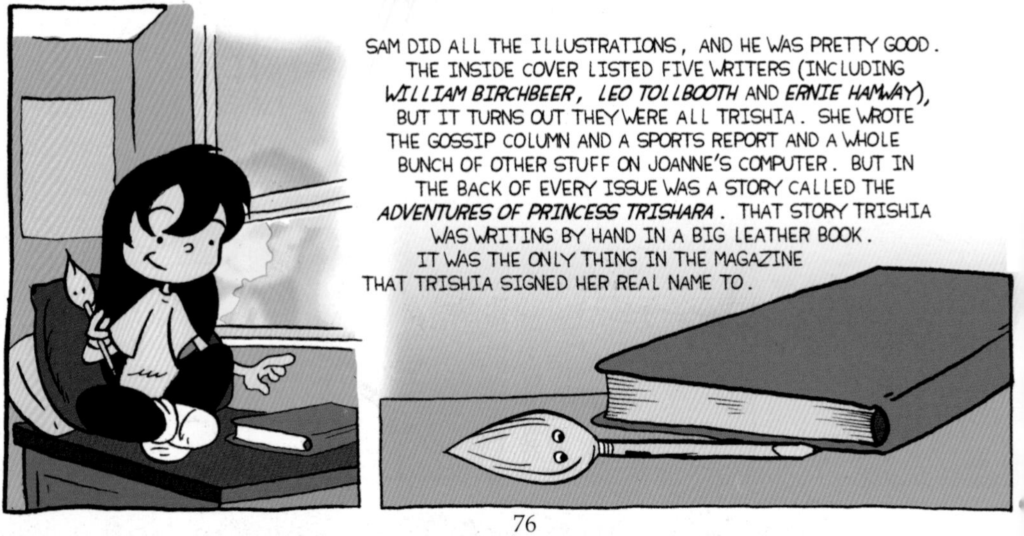
SAM DID ALL THE ILLUSTRATIONS, AND HE WAS PRETTY GOOD. THE INSIDE COVER LISTED FIVE WRITERS (INCLUDING WILLIAM BIRCHBEER, LEO TOLLBOOTH AND ERNIE HAMWAY), BUT IT TURNS OUT THEY WERE ALL TRISHIA. SHE WROTE THE GOSSIP COLUMN AND A SPORTS REPORT AND A WHOLE BUNCH OF OTHER STUFF ON JOANNE'S COMPUTER. BUT IN THE BACK OF EVERY ISSUE WAS A STORY CALLED THE ADVENTURES OF PRINCESS TRISHARA. THAT STORY TRISHIA WAS WRITING BY HAND IN A BIG LEATHER BOOK. IT WAS THE ONLY THING IN THE MAGAZINE THAT TRISHIA SIGNED HER REAL NAME TO.

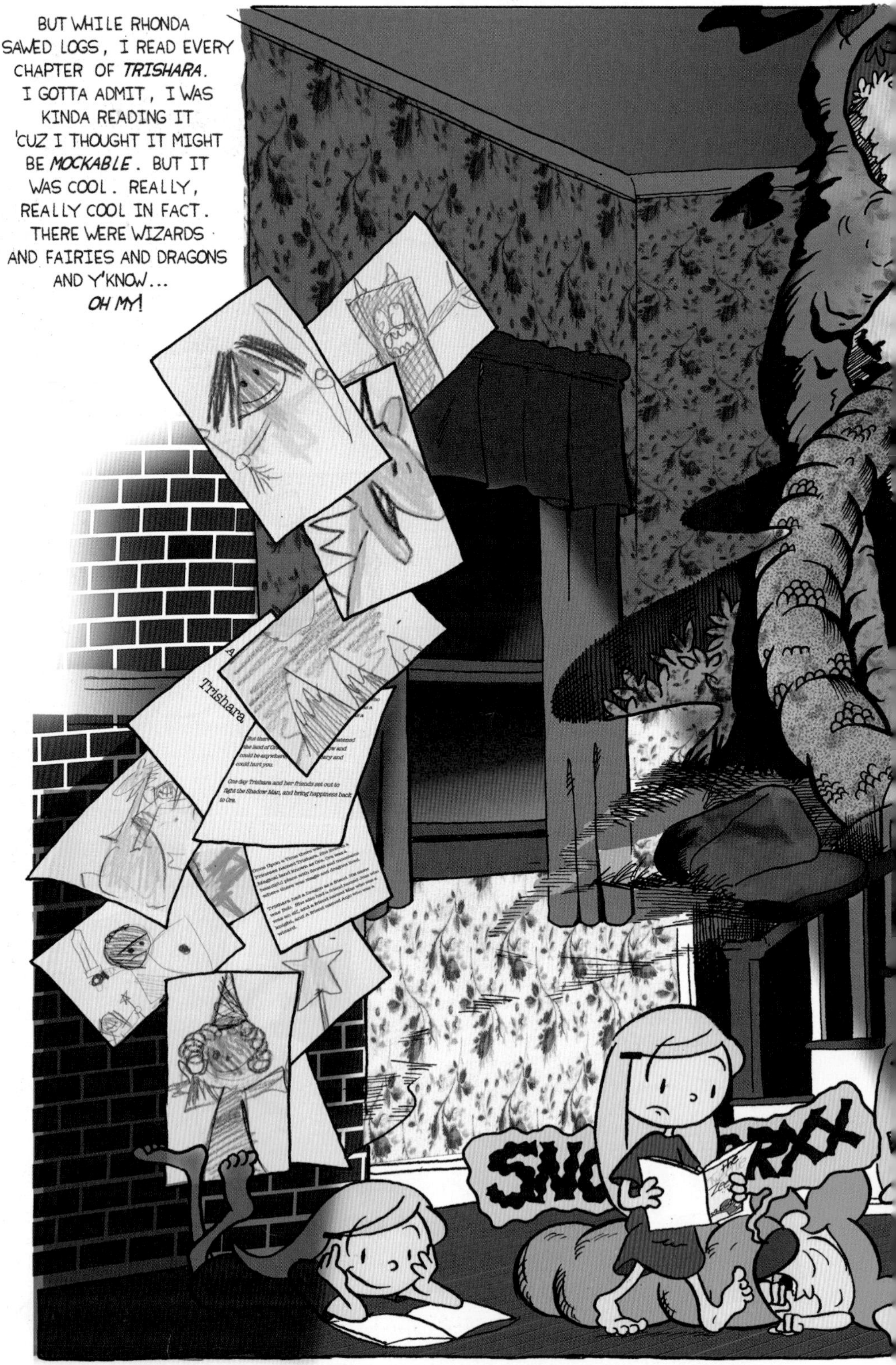
BUT WHILE RHONDA SAWED LOGS, I READ EVERY CHAPTER OF *TRISHARA*. I GOTTA ADMIT, I WAS KINDA READING IT 'CUZ I THOUGHT IT MIGHT BE *MOCKABLE*. BUT IT WAS COOL. REALLY, REALLY COOL IN FACT. THERE WERE WIZARDS AND FAIRIES AND DRAGONS AND Y'KNOW... *OH MY!*
Trishara
could hurt you.
One day Trishara and her friends set out to fight the Shadow Man, and bring happiness back to Ora.

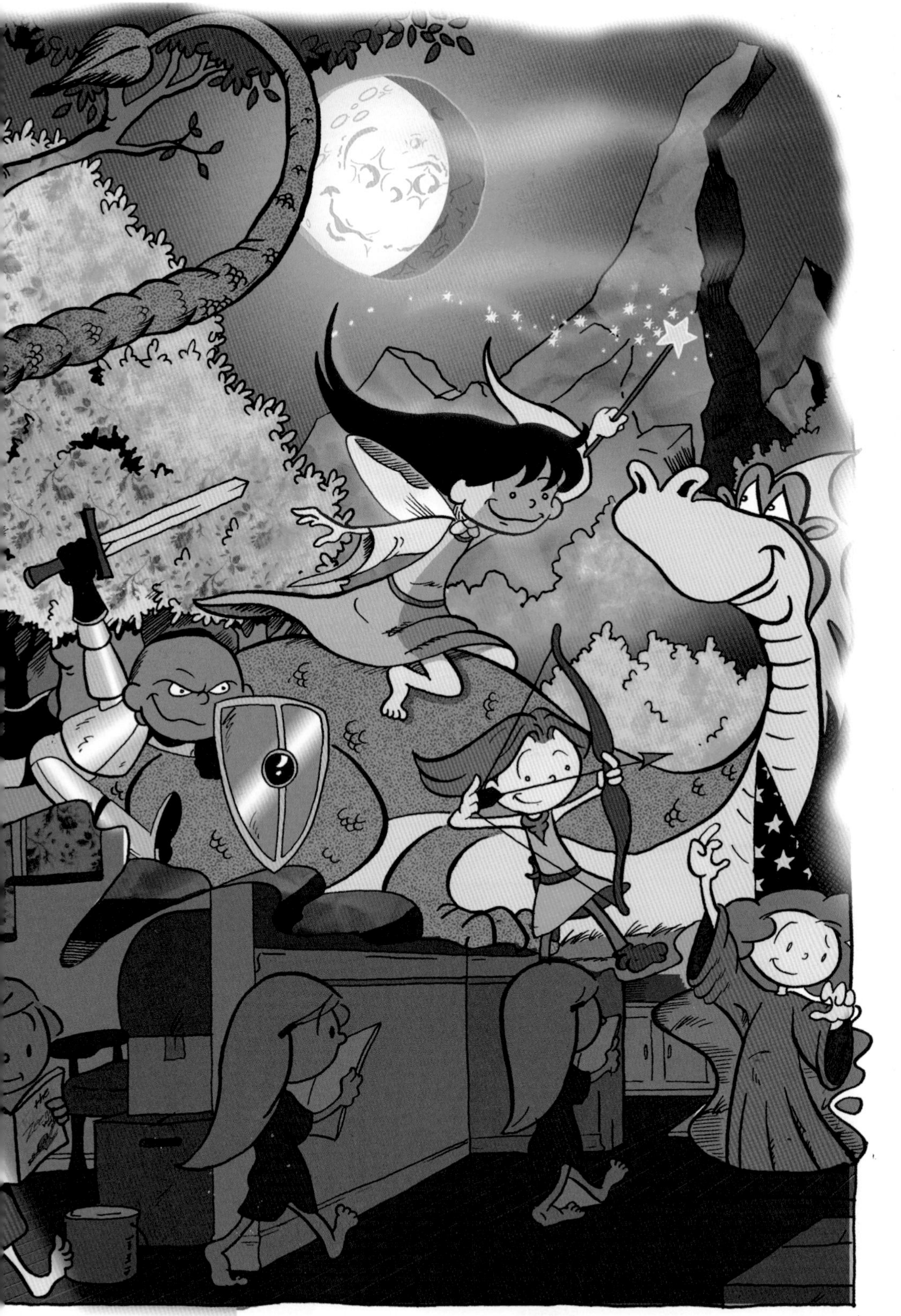

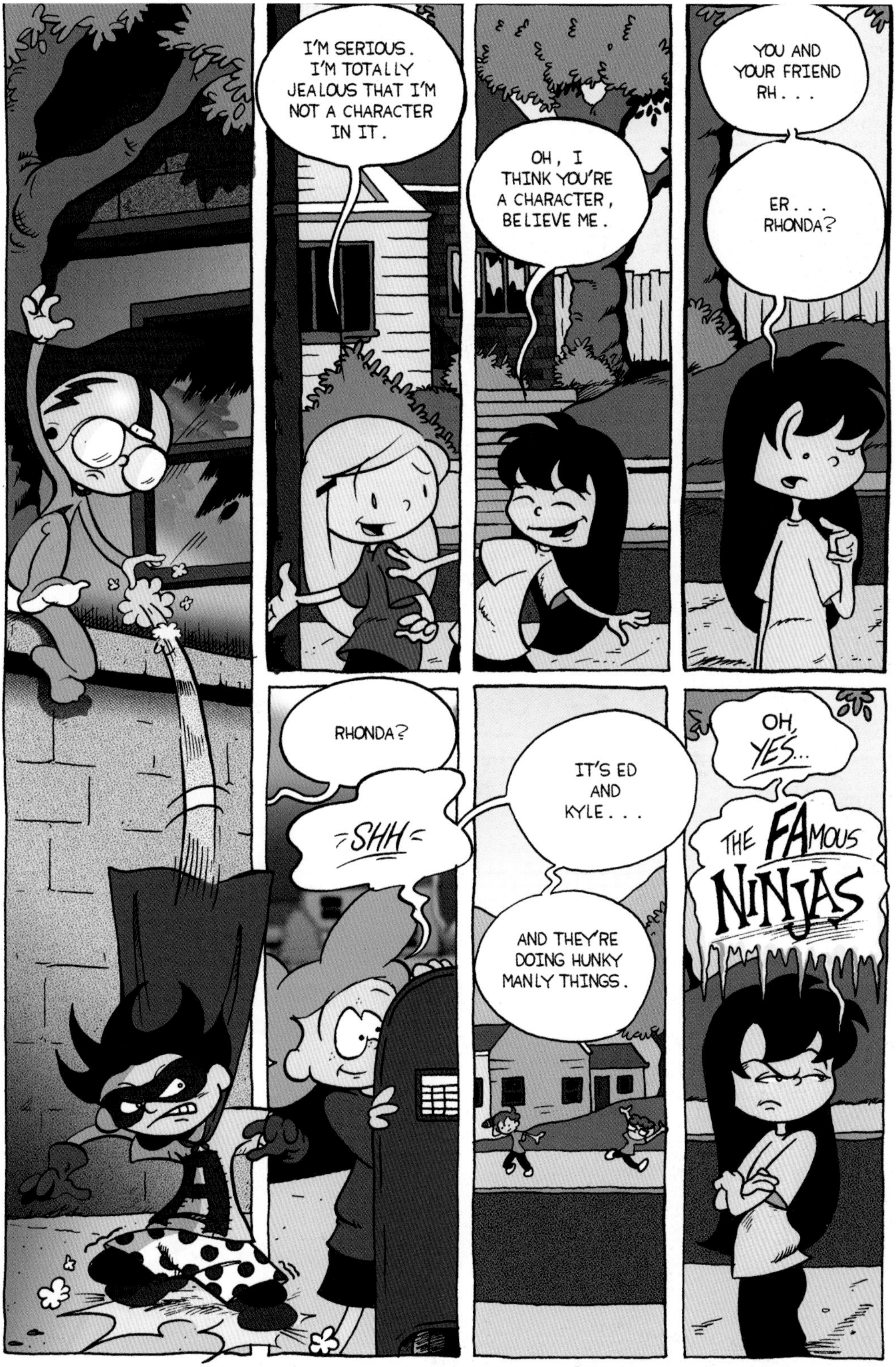
I'M SERIOUS. I'M TOTALLY JEALOUS THAT I'M NOT A CHARACTER IN IT.
OH, I THINK YOU'RE A CHARACTER, BELIEVE ME.
YOU AND YOUR FRIEND RH...
ER... RHONDA?
RHONDA?
SHH
IT'S ED AND KYLE...
AND THEY'RE DOING HUNKY MANLY THINGS.
OH, YES...
THE FAMOUS NINJAS

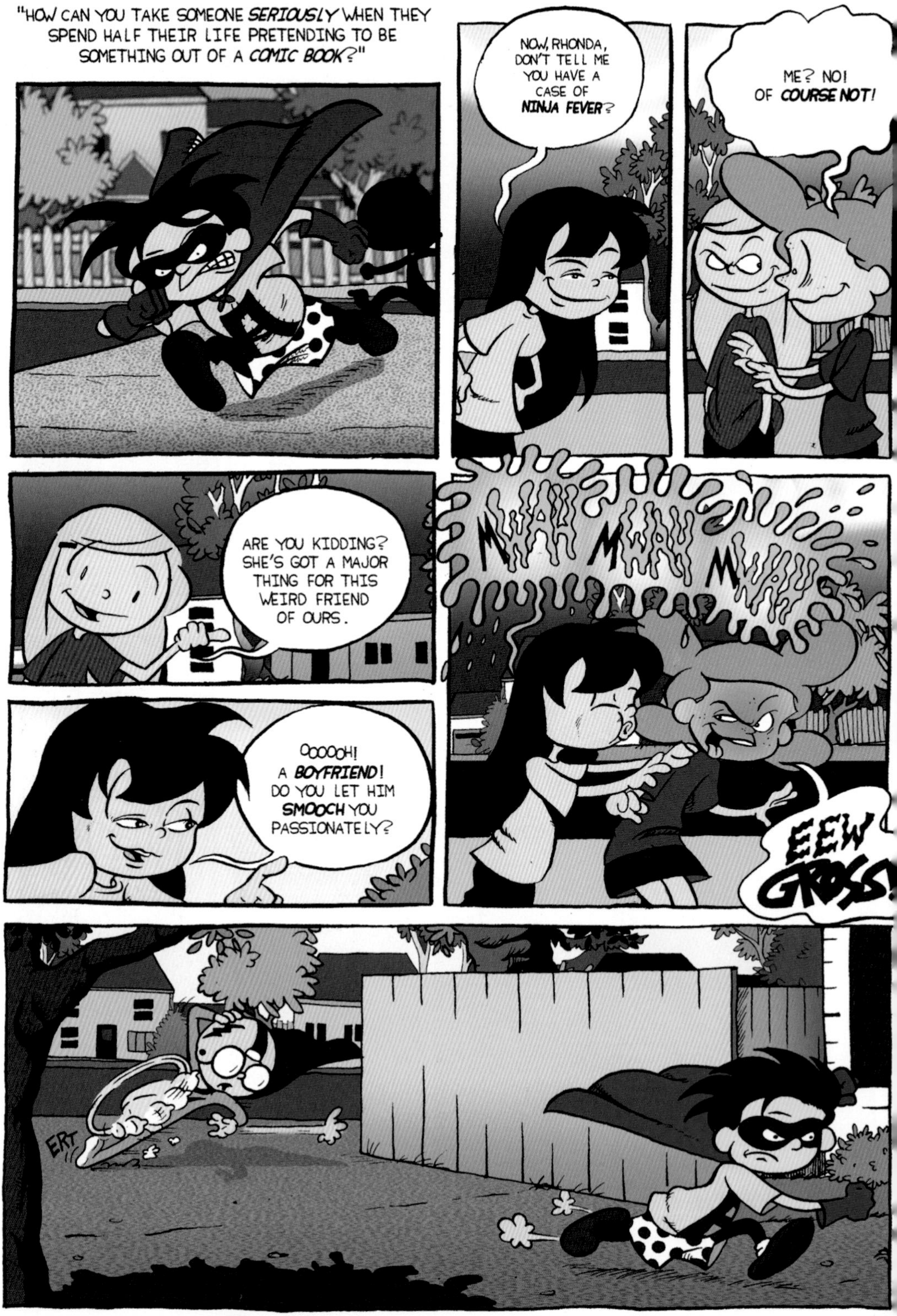
"HOW CAN YOU TAKE SOMEONE SERIOUSLY WHEN THEY SPEND HALF THEIR LIFE PRETENDING TO BE SOMETHING OUT OF A COMIC BOOK?"
NOW, RHONDA, DON'T TELL ME YOU HAVE A CASE OF NINJA FEVER?
ME? NO! OF COURSE NOT!
ARE YOU KIDDING? SHE'S GOT A MAJOR THING FOR THIS WEIRD FRIEND OF OURS.
OOOOOH! A BOYFRIEND! DO YOU LET HIM SMOOCH YOU PASSIONATELY?
MWAH MWAH MWAH
EEW GROSS!
ERT

83

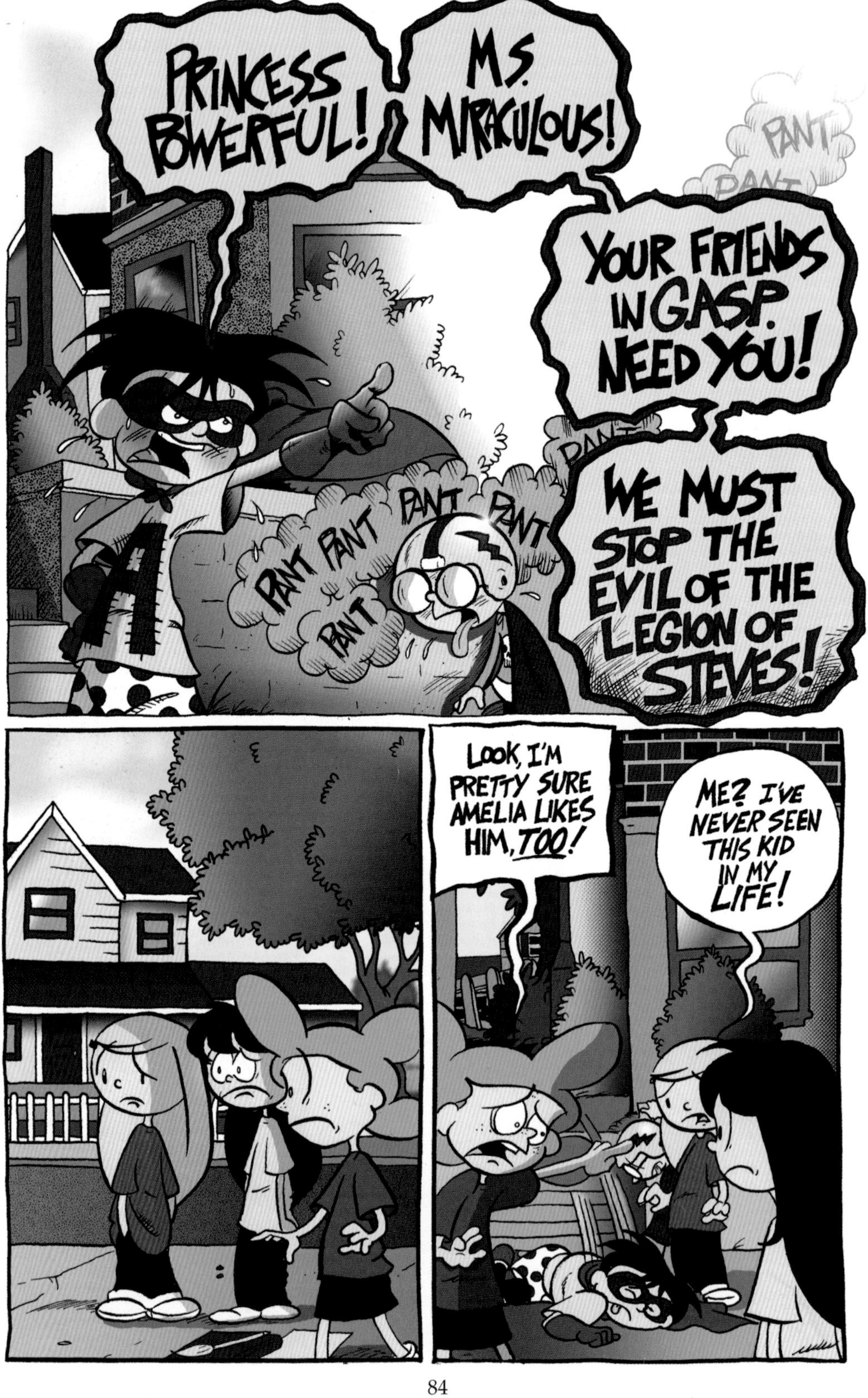

PRINCESS POWERFUL!
M.S. MIRACULOUS!
PANT PANT
YOUR FRIENDS IN G.A.S.P. NEED YOU!
PANT PANT PANT PANT & PANT
WE MUST STOP THE EVIL OF THE LEGION OF STEVES!
LOOK, I'M PRETTY SURE AMELIA LIKES HIM, TOO!
ME? I'VE NEVER SEEN THIS KID IN MY LIFE!

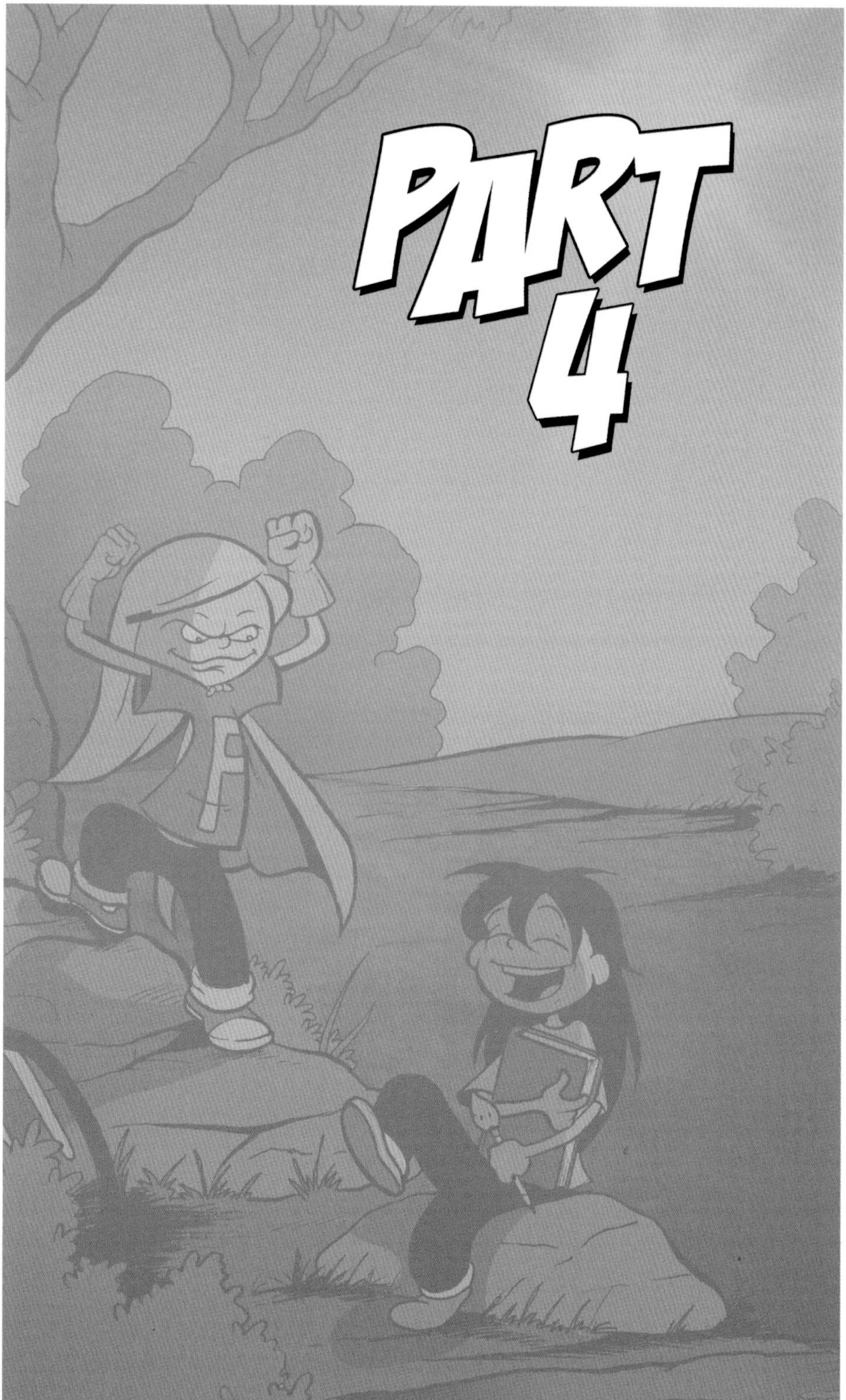
PART 4

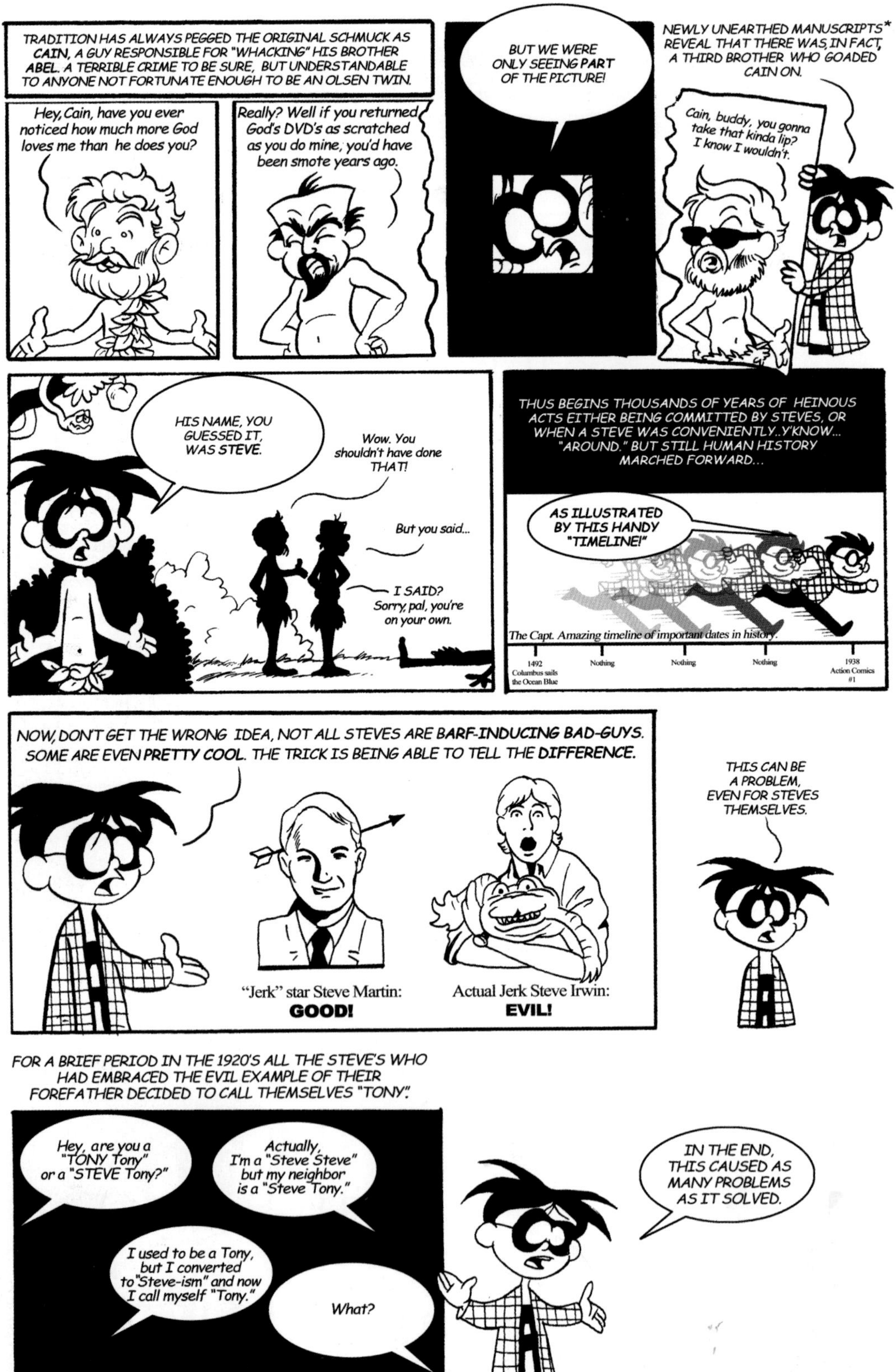

TRADITION HAS ALWAYS PEGGED THE ORIGINAL SCHMUCK AS CAIN, A GUY RESPONSIBLE FOR "WHACKING" HIS BROTHER ABEL. A TERRIBLE CRIME TO BE SURE, BUT UNDERSTANDABLE TO ANYONE NOT FORTUNATE ENOUGH TO BE AN OLSEN TWIN.
Hey, Cain, have you ever noticed how much more God loves me than he does you?
Really? Well if you returned God's DVD's as scratched as you do mine, you'd have been smote years ago.
BUT WE WERE ONLY SEEING PART OF THE PICTURE!
NEWLY UNEARTHED MANUSCRIPTS* REVEAL THAT THERE WAS, IN FACT, A THIRD BROTHER WHO GOADED CAIN ON.
Cain, buddy, you gonna take that kinda lip? I know I wouldn't.
HIS NAME, YOU GUESSED IT, WAS STEVE.
Wow. You shouldn't have done THAT!
But you said...
I SAID? Sorry, pal, you're on your own.
THUS BEGINS THOUSANDS OF YEARS OF HEINOUS ACTS EITHER BEING COMMITTED BY STEVES, OR WHEN A STEVE WAS CONVENIENTLY..Y'KNOW... "AROUND." BUT STILL HUMAN HISTORY MARCHED FORWARD...
AS ILLUSTRATED BY THIS HANDY "TIMELINE!"
The Capt. Amazing timeline of important dates in history.
1492 Columbus sails the Ocean Blue
Nothing
Nothing
Nothing
1938 Action Comics #1
NOW, DON'T GET THE WRONG IDEA, NOT ALL STEVES ARE BARF-INDUCING BAD-GUYS. SOME ARE EVEN PRETTY COOL. THE TRICK IS BEING ABLE TO TELL THE DIFFERENCE.
"Jerk" star Steve Martin: GOOD!
Actual Jerk Steve Irwin: EVIL!
THIS CAN BE A PROBLEM, EVEN FOR STEVES THEMSELVES.
FOR A BRIEF PERIOD IN THE 1920'S ALL THE STEVE'S WHO HAD EMBRACED THE EVIL EXAMPLE OF THEIR FOREFATHER DECIDED TO CALL THEMSELVES "TONY".
Hey, are you a "TONY Tony" or a "STEVE Tony?"
Actually, I'm a "Steve Steve" but my neighbor is a "Steve Tony."
I used to be a Tony, but I converted to "Steve-ism" and now I call myself "Tony."
What?
IN THE END, THIS CAUSED AS MANY PROBLEMS AS IT SOLVED.

*Some experts doubt the authenticity of these documents, citing the fact that they were written on "Post-its", and contain several oblique references to "Chicken McNuggets."

*Actually, this chart makes no sense, but it always looks more official when you have a chart.

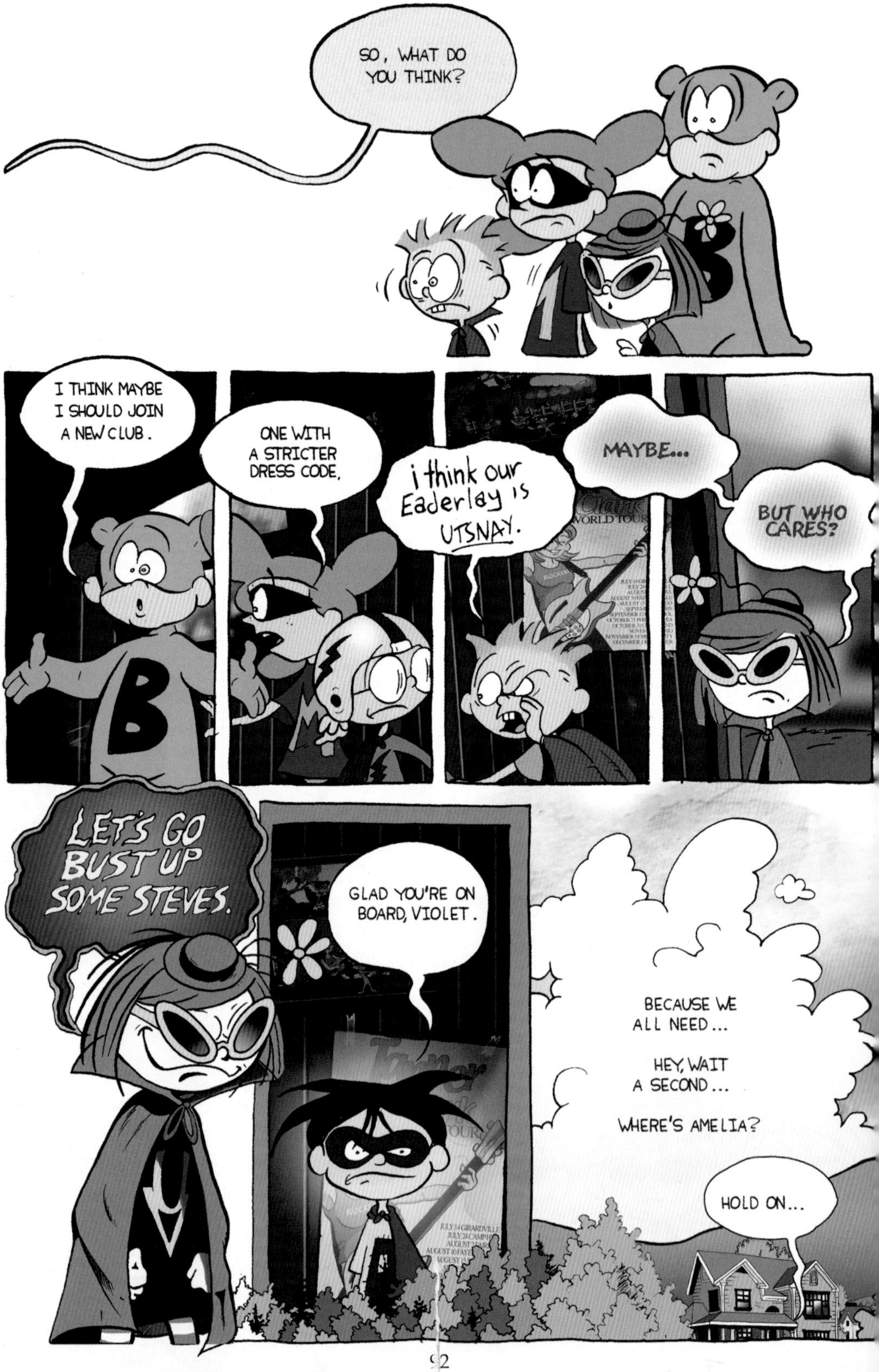
SO, WHAT DO YOU THINK?
I THINK MAYBE I SHOULD JOIN A NEW CLUB.
ONE WITH A STRICTER DRESS CODE.
i think our Eaderlay is UTSNAY.
MAYBE...
BUT WHO CARES?
LET'S GO BUST UP SOME STEVES.
GLAD YOU'RE ON BOARD, VIOLET.
BECAUSE WE ALL NEED...
HEY, WAIT A SECOND...
WHERE'S AMELIA?
HOLD ON...

93

See, the thing about Sarah is she was, well, very Sarah-ish, you know? She totally was her own person. She wanted to be a writer, so she wrote. And those *Lucy and Mew* books were super-popular. When I was a kid, they made *Softee Chicken* look pretty much like...well, like *Softee Chicken*. But Sarah didn't want to be famous, that's why she used the pen name. Some people knew her for years and never knew what she did.

Now here's the interesting part. When she was just 20 and living in New York City, Sarah met her one true love, another aspiring writer named Hugh S. Travers. They were inseparable. Everything was perfect except that the better Sarah's career went, the worse Hugh's did. Still, that didn't stop their love. They lived a very New York life, same street, different buildings. Together when they wanted, apart when they needed.

And they vowed never to get married.

So everything's going along normally. Sarah's selling zillions of books. Hugh's collecting rejection slips. Then one day, Hugh's mother gets sick. Really sick. Hugh needs to go back to Pennsylvania, to the town where he grew up, to take care of her. So, on the night before he leaves, he does the unthinkable and asks Sarah to marry him. Of course, she says no. Hugh is heartbroken, but he has responsibilities and leaves New York, never to return.

Five years pass. Sarah has no contact with Hugh, but she never forgets him. She writes another book called *Lucy and Mew: Against Unbelievable Odds.* It's totally a mash note to Hugh, but written so that only he would understand. Sarah has no idea if he'll ever see it. He does. He gets it. They reconnect, and it's still magic.

She moves to Pennsylvania. To Hugh's hometown. To THIS town. She buys this house, and they live happily ever after. Unmarried, on the same street, and in two different houses.

When Hugh died, Sarah didn't spend much time here, but she kept the house.

I moved here, in large part to be near Sarah. My sister moved here to stay with me, and she brought Amelia along with her.

AND NOW, HERE WE ARE.

DID HUGH EVER GET ANY BOOKS PUBLISHED?

YEAH, EVENTUALLY. HE WROTE THE 'SPOINGLE' BOOKS UNDER THE NAME *PROFESSOR SCHMUTZ.*

CREAM-O
MINT CHOC CHIP

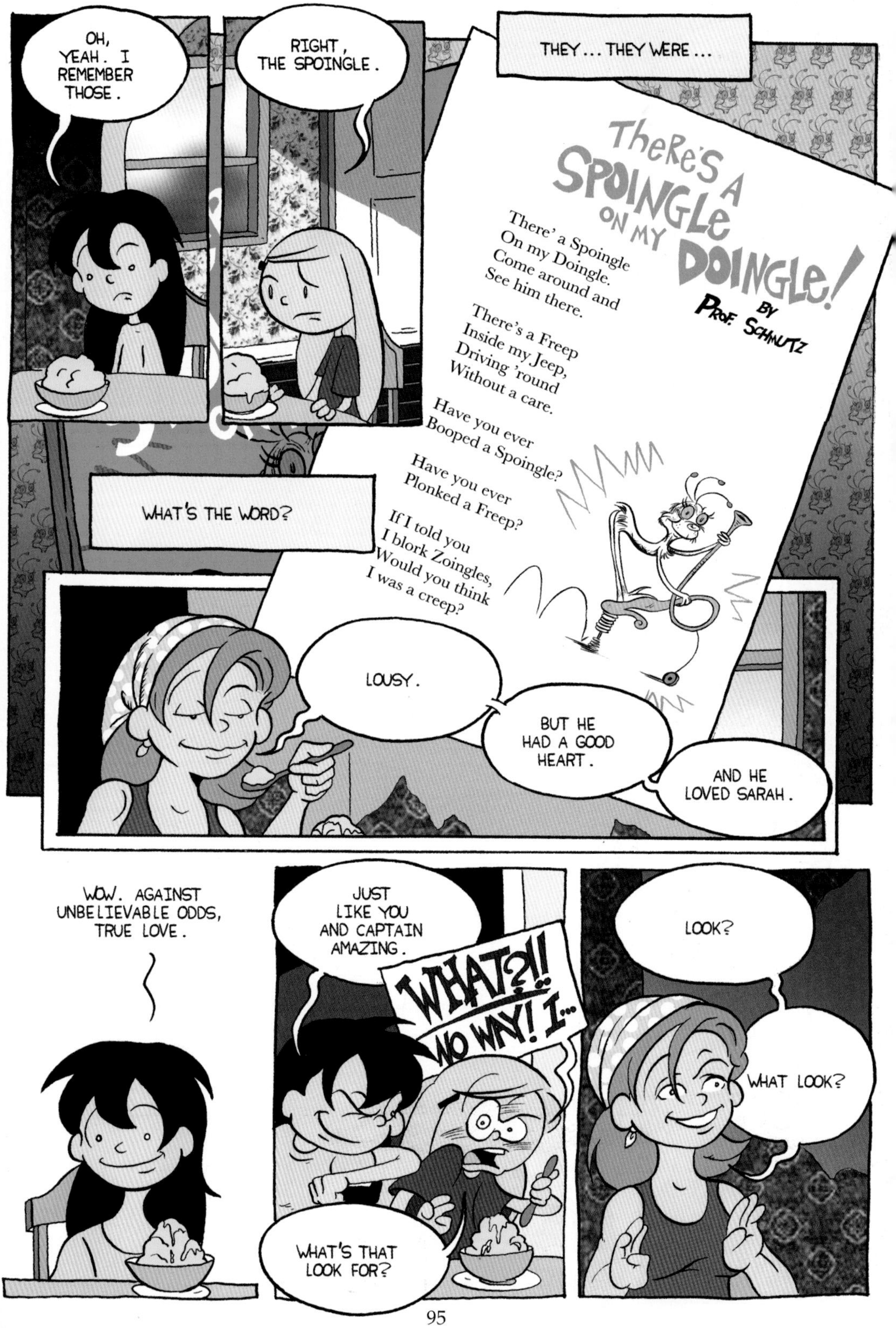
OH, YEAH. I REMEMBER THOSE.
RIGHT, THE SPOINGLE.
THEY... THEY WERE...
There's a SPOINGLE ON MY DOINGLE! BY PROF. SCHMUTZ
There' a Spoingle
On my Doingle.
Come around and
See him there.
There's a Freep
Inside my Jeep,
Driving 'round
Without a care.
Have you ever
Booped a Spoingle?
Have you ever
Plonked a Freep?
If I told you
I blork Zoingles,
Would you think
I was a creep?
WHAT'S THE WORD?
LOUSY.
BUT HE HAD A GOOD HEART.
AND HE LOVED SARAH.
WOW. AGAINST UNBELIEVABLE ODDS, TRUE LOVE.
JUST LIKE YOU AND CAPTAIN AMAZING.
WHAT?!! NO WAY! I...
WHAT'S THAT LOOK FOR?
LOOK?
WHAT LOOK?

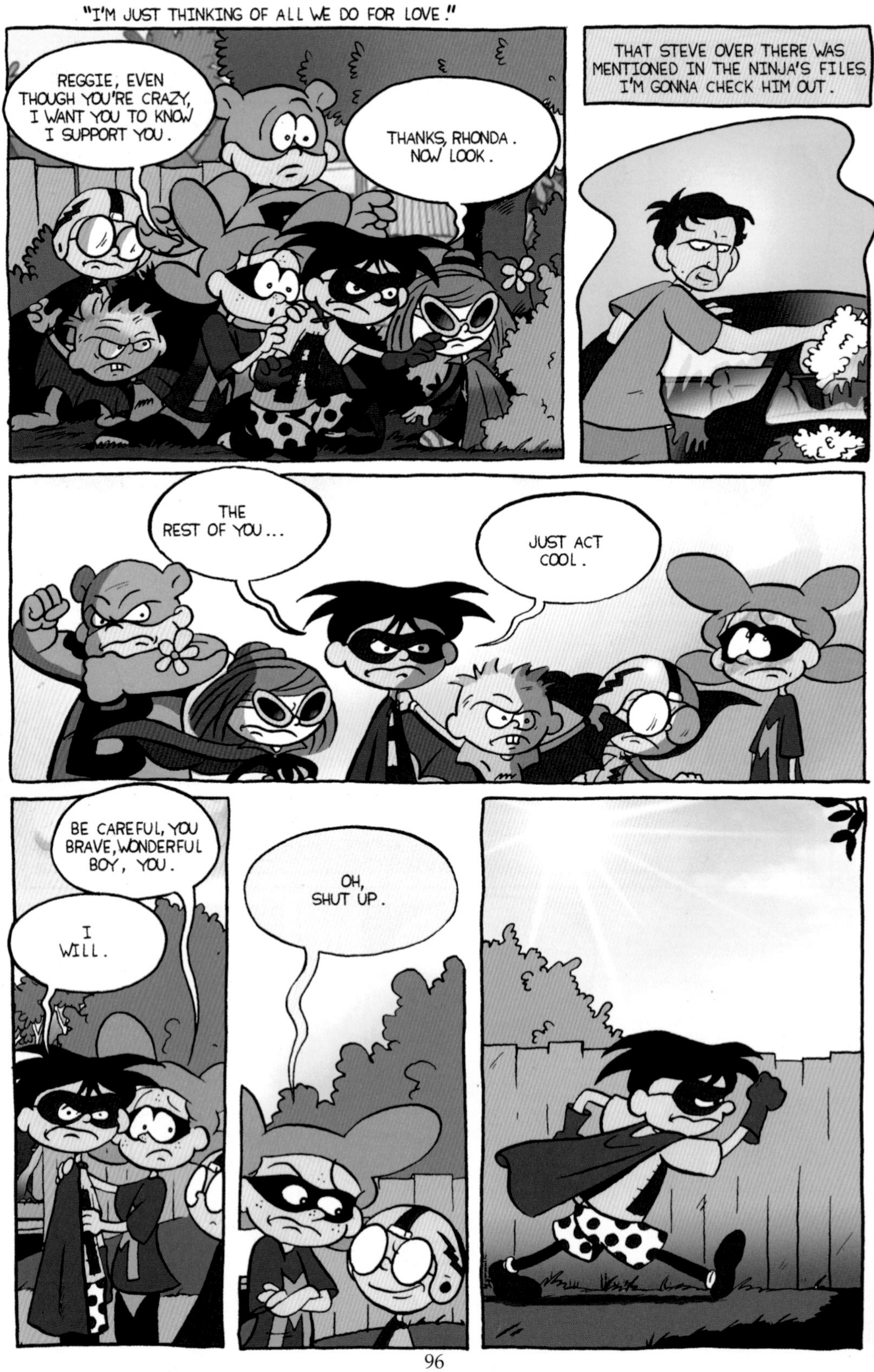
"I'M JUST THINKING OF ALL WE DO FOR LOVE."
REGGIE, EVEN THOUGH YOU'RE CRAZY, I WANT YOU TO KNOW I SUPPORT YOU.
THANKS, RHONDA. NOW LOOK.
THAT STEVE OVER THERE WAS MENTIONED IN THE NINJA'S FILES. I'M GONNA CHECK HIM OUT.
THE REST OF YOU...
JUST ACT COOL.
BE CAREFUL, YOU BRAVE, WONDERFUL BOY, YOU.
I WILL.
OH, SHUT UP.

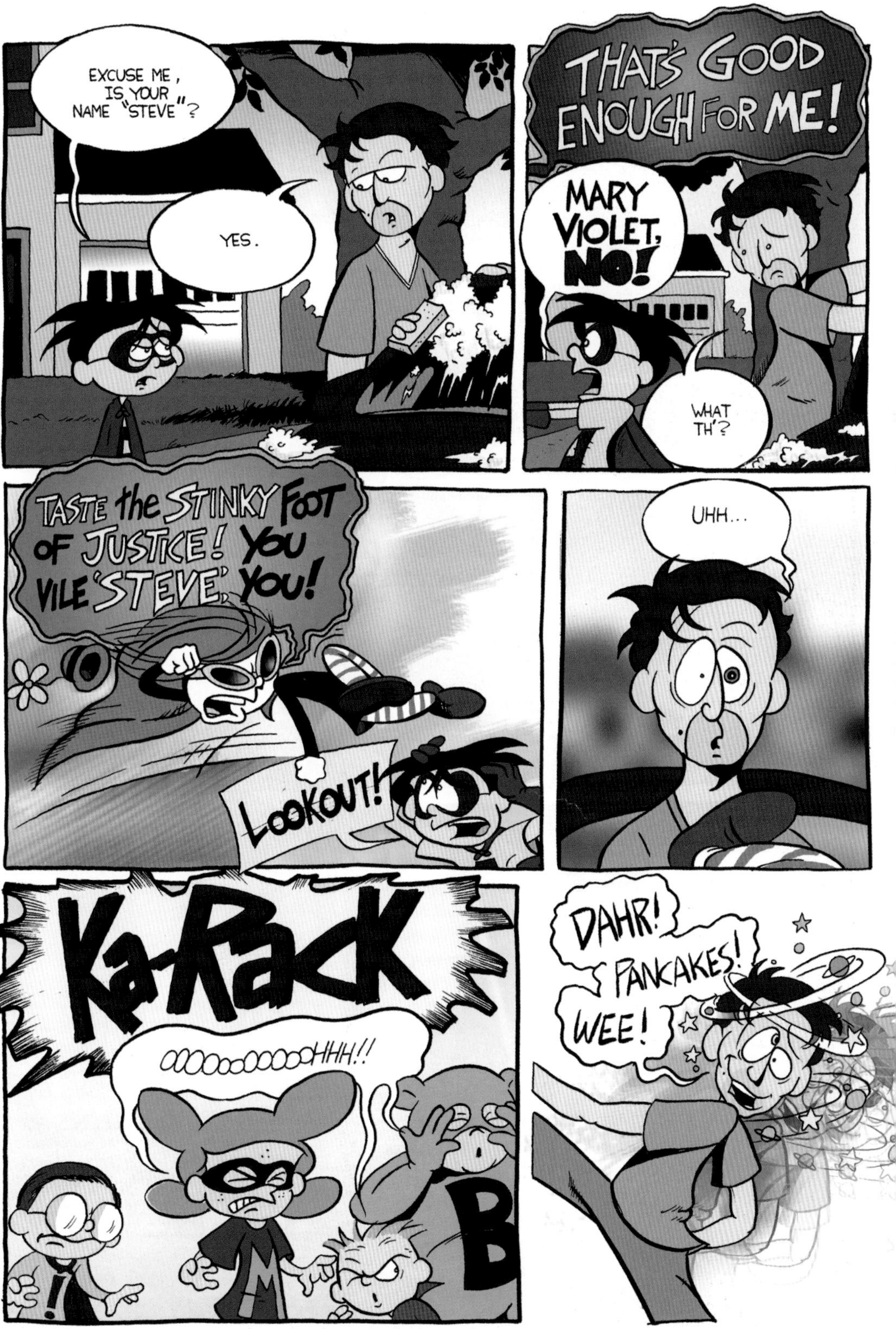
EXCUSE ME, IS YOUR NAME "STEVE"?
YES.
THAT'S GOOD ENOUGH FOR ME!
MARY VIOLET, NO!
WHAT TH'?
TASTE the STINKY FOOT OF JUSTICE! YOU VILE 'STEVE', YOU!
LOOKOUT!
UHH...
KA-RACK
OOOOooOOOOOHHH!!
B
DAHR!
PANKAKES!
WEE!

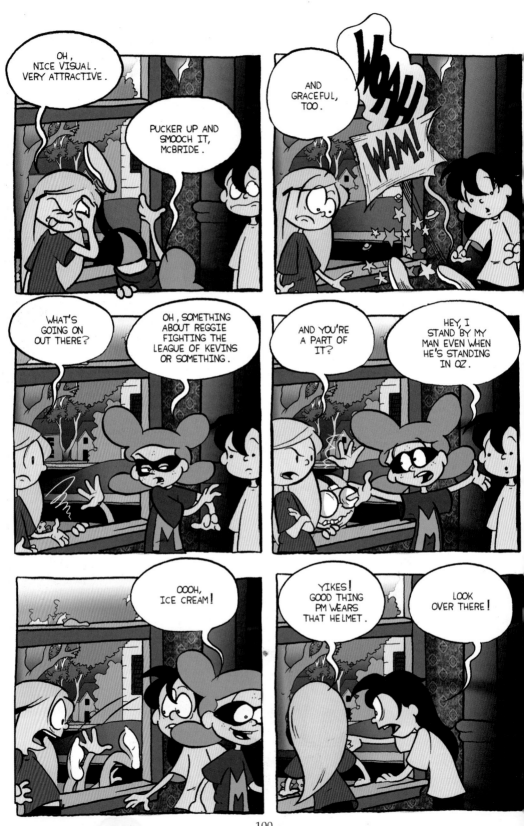

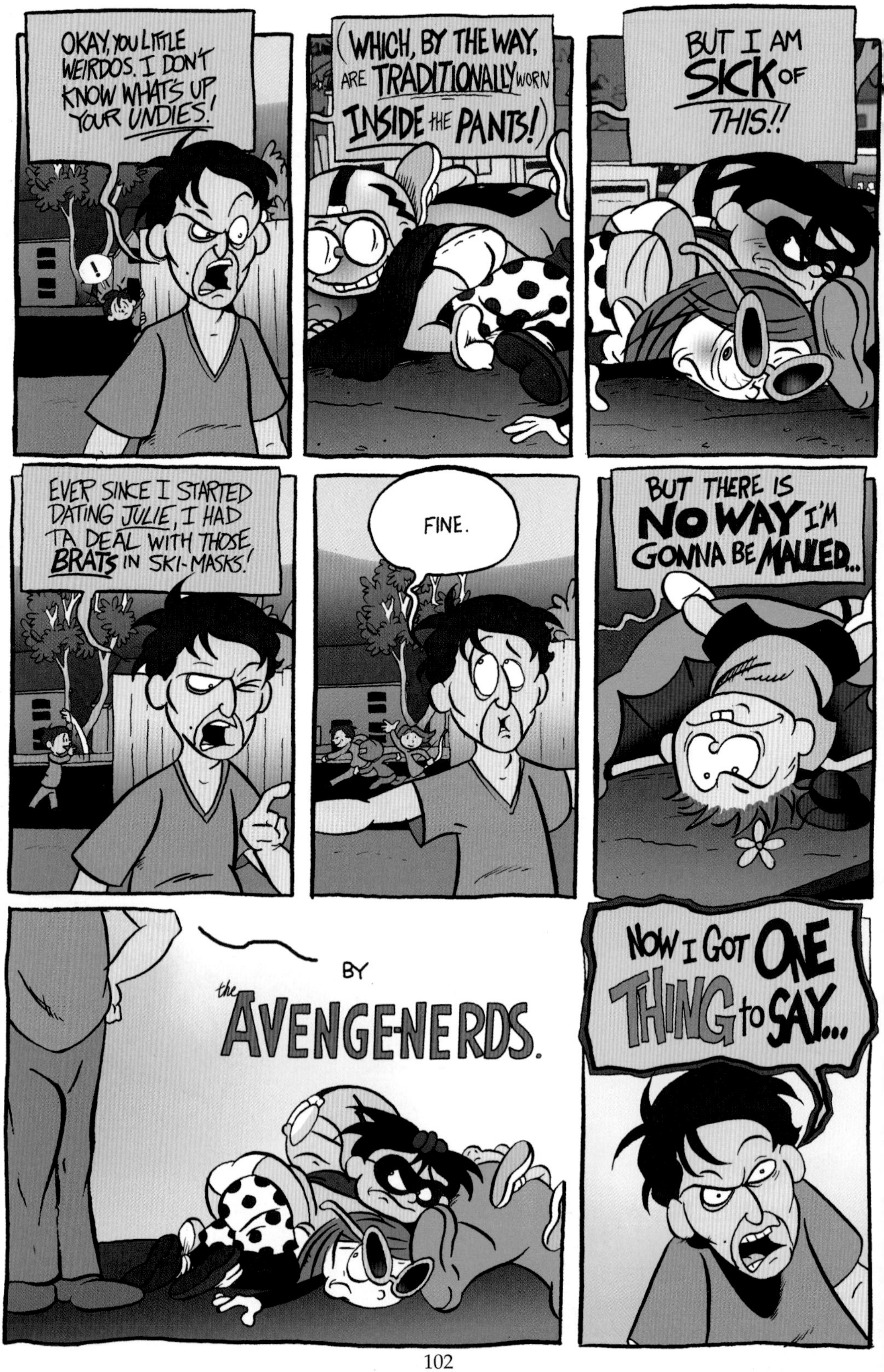
OKAY, YOU LITTLE WEIRDOS. I DON'T KNOW WHAT'S UP YOUR UNDIES!
(WHICH, BY THE WAY, ARE TRADITIONALLY WORN INSIDE THE PANTS!)
BUT I AM SICK OF THIS!!
EVER SINCE I STARTED DATING JULIE, I HAD TA DEAL WITH THOSE BRATS IN SKI-MASKS!
FINE.
BUT THERE IS NO WAY I'M GONNA BE MAULED...
BY the AVENGE-NERDS.
NOW I GOT ONE THING to SAY...

103

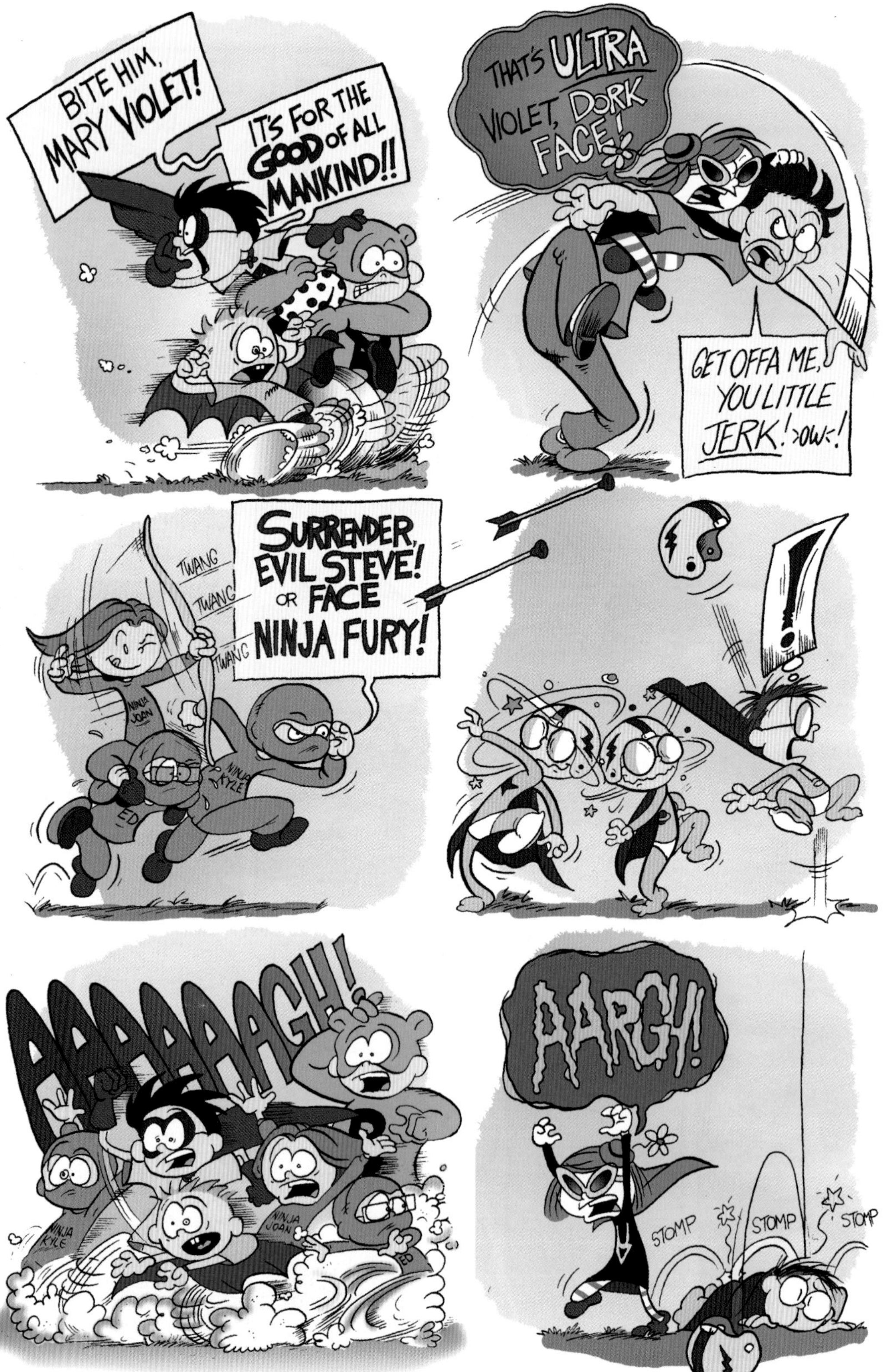
BITE HIM, MARY VIOLET!
IT'S FOR THE GOOD OF ALL MANKIND!!
THAT'S ULTRA VIOLET, DORK FACE!
GET OFFA ME, YOU LITTLE JERK! >OW<!
TWANG
TWANG
TWANG
SURRENDER, EVIL STEVE! OR FACE NINJA FURY!
NINJA JOAN
NINJA KYLE
ED
!
AAAAAAGH!
NINJA KYLE
NINJA JOAN
ED
AARGH!
STOMP
STOMP
STOMP

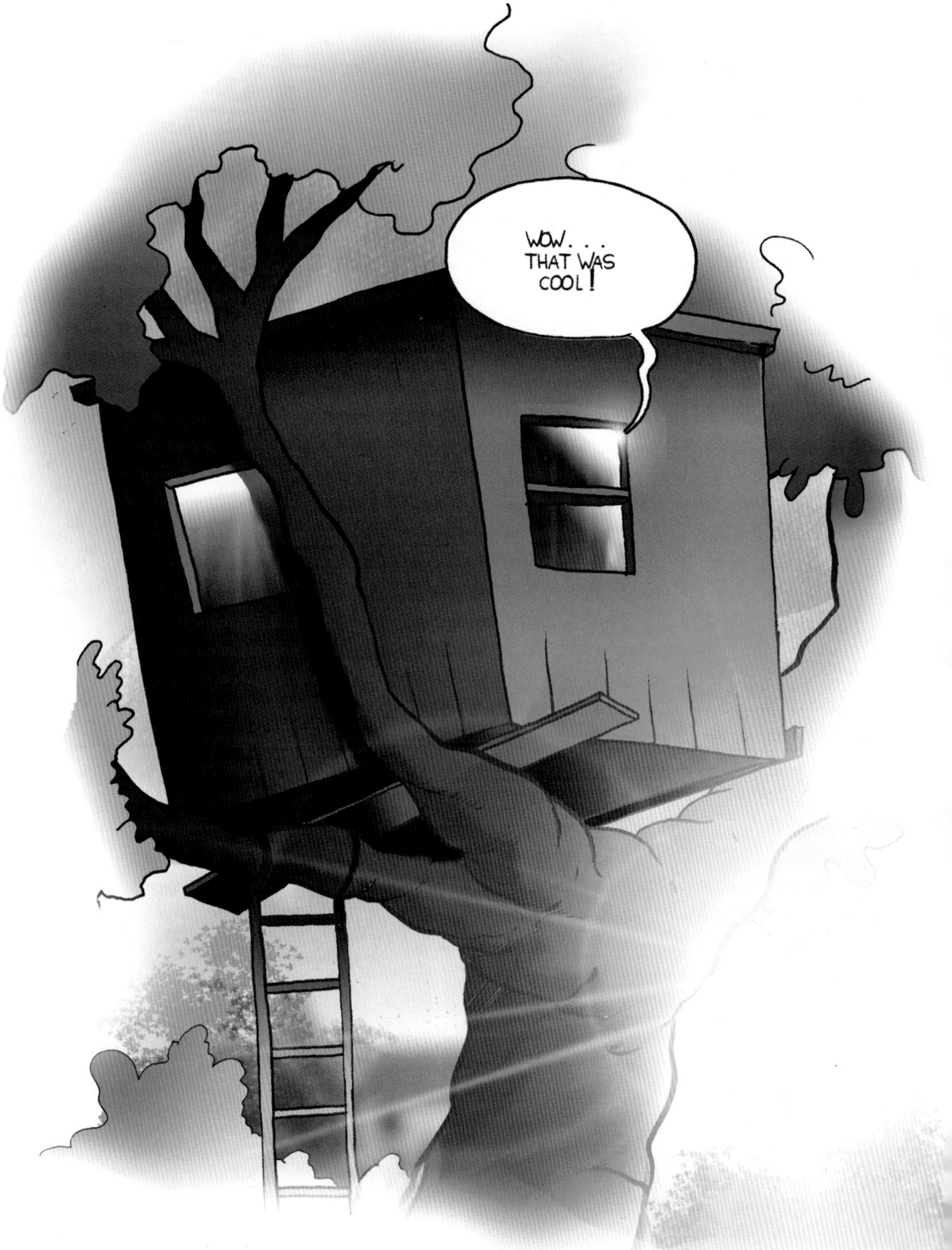
WOW. . . THAT WAS COOL!

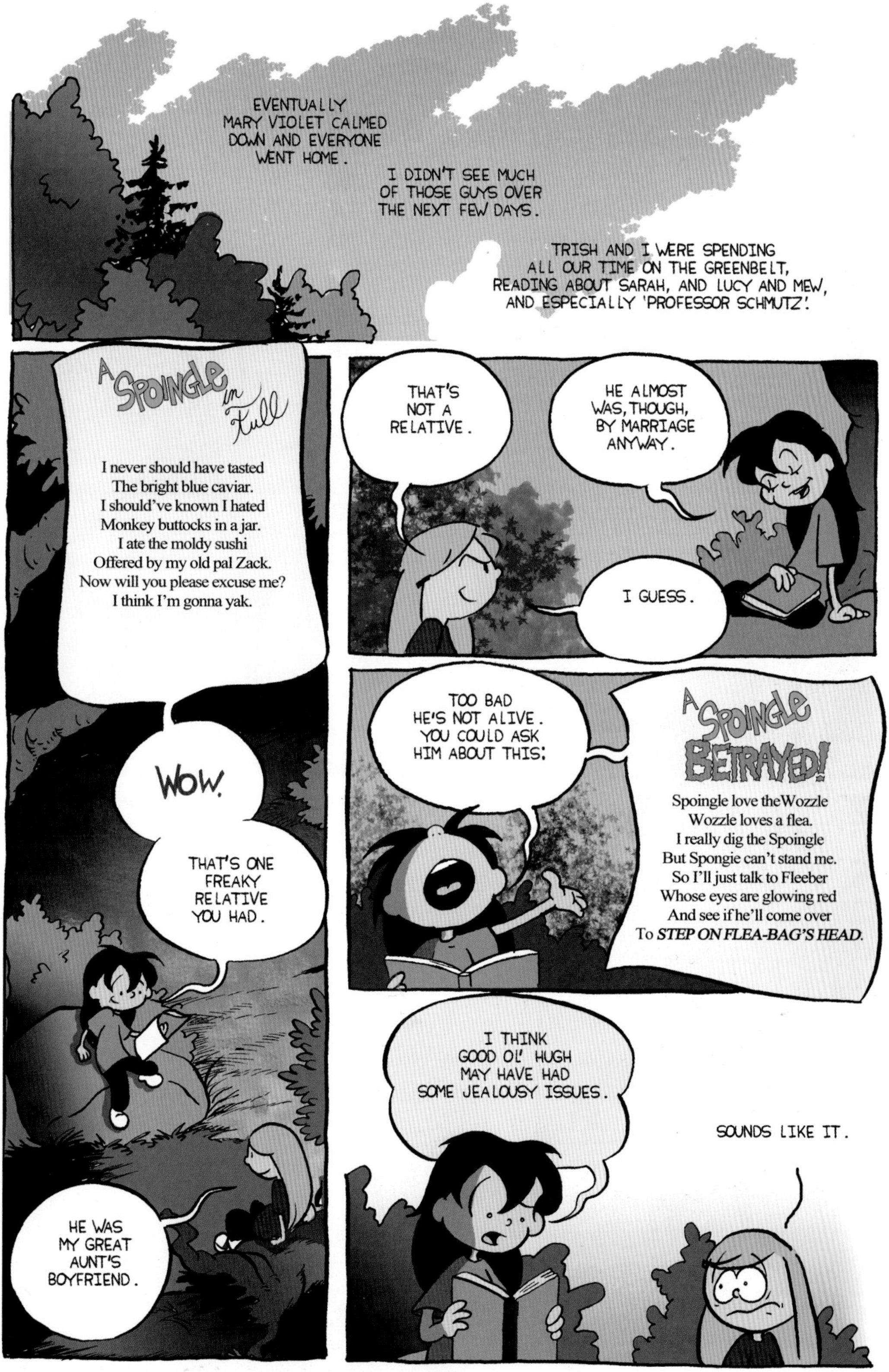
EVENTUALLY MARY VIOLET CALMED DOWN AND EVERYONE WENT HOME.
I DIDN'T SEE MUCH OF THOSE GUYS OVER THE NEXT FEW DAYS.
TRISH AND I WERE SPENDING ALL OUR TIME ON THE GREENBELT, READING ABOUT SARAH, AND LUCY AND MEW, AND ESPECIALLY 'PROFESSOR SCHMUTZ'.
A Spoingle in Full
I never should have tasted
The bright blue caviar.
I should've known I hated
Monkey buttocks in a jar.
I ate the moldy sushi
Offered by my old pal Zack.
Now will you please excuse me?
I think I'm gonna yak.
WOW.
THAT'S ONE FREAKY RELATIVE YOU HAD.
HE WAS MY GREAT AUNT'S BOYFRIEND.
THAT'S NOT A RELATIVE.
HE ALMOST WAS, THOUGH, BY MARRIAGE ANYWAY.
I GUESS.
TOO BAD HE'S NOT ALIVE. YOU COULD ASK HIM ABOUT THIS:
A Spoingle BETRAYED!
Spoingle love theWozzle
Wozzle loves a flea.
I really dig the Spoingle
But Spongie can't stand me.
So I'll just talk to Fleeber
Whose eyes are glowing red
And see if he'll come over
To STEP ON FLEA-BAG'S HEAD.
I THINK GOOD OL' HUGH MAY HAVE HAD SOME JEALOUSY ISSUES.
SOUNDS LIKE IT.

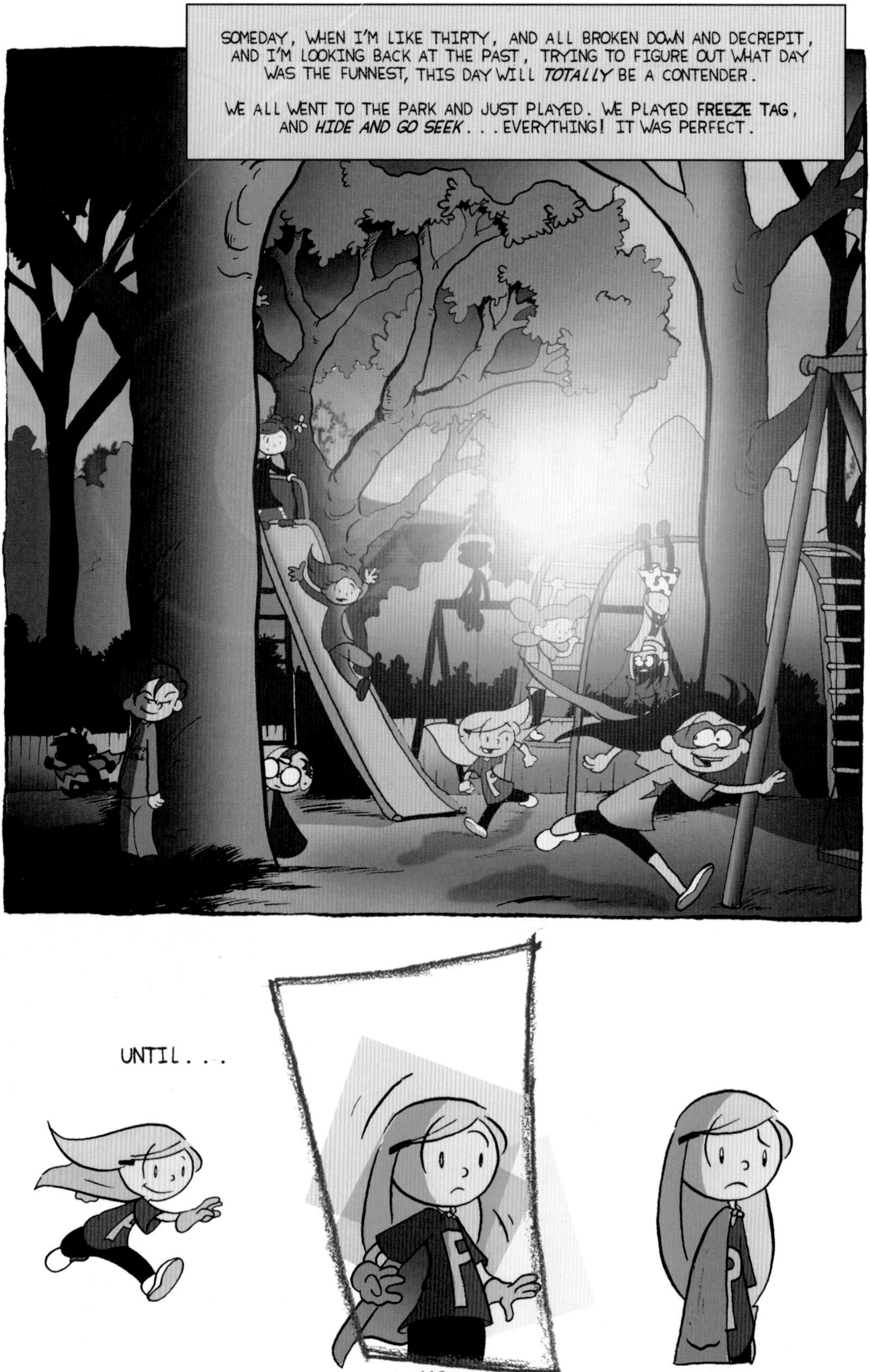
SOMEDAY, WHEN I'M LIKE THIRTY, AND ALL BROKEN DOWN AND DECREPIT, AND I'M LOOKING BACK AT THE PAST, TRYING TO FIGURE OUT WHAT DAY WAS THE FUNNEST, THIS DAY WILL *TOTALLY* BE A CONTENDER.
WE ALL WENT TO THE PARK AND JUST PLAYED. WE PLAYED **FREEZE** TAG, AND ***HIDE AND GO SEEK***. . . EVERYTHING! IT WAS PERFECT.
UNTIL. . . .

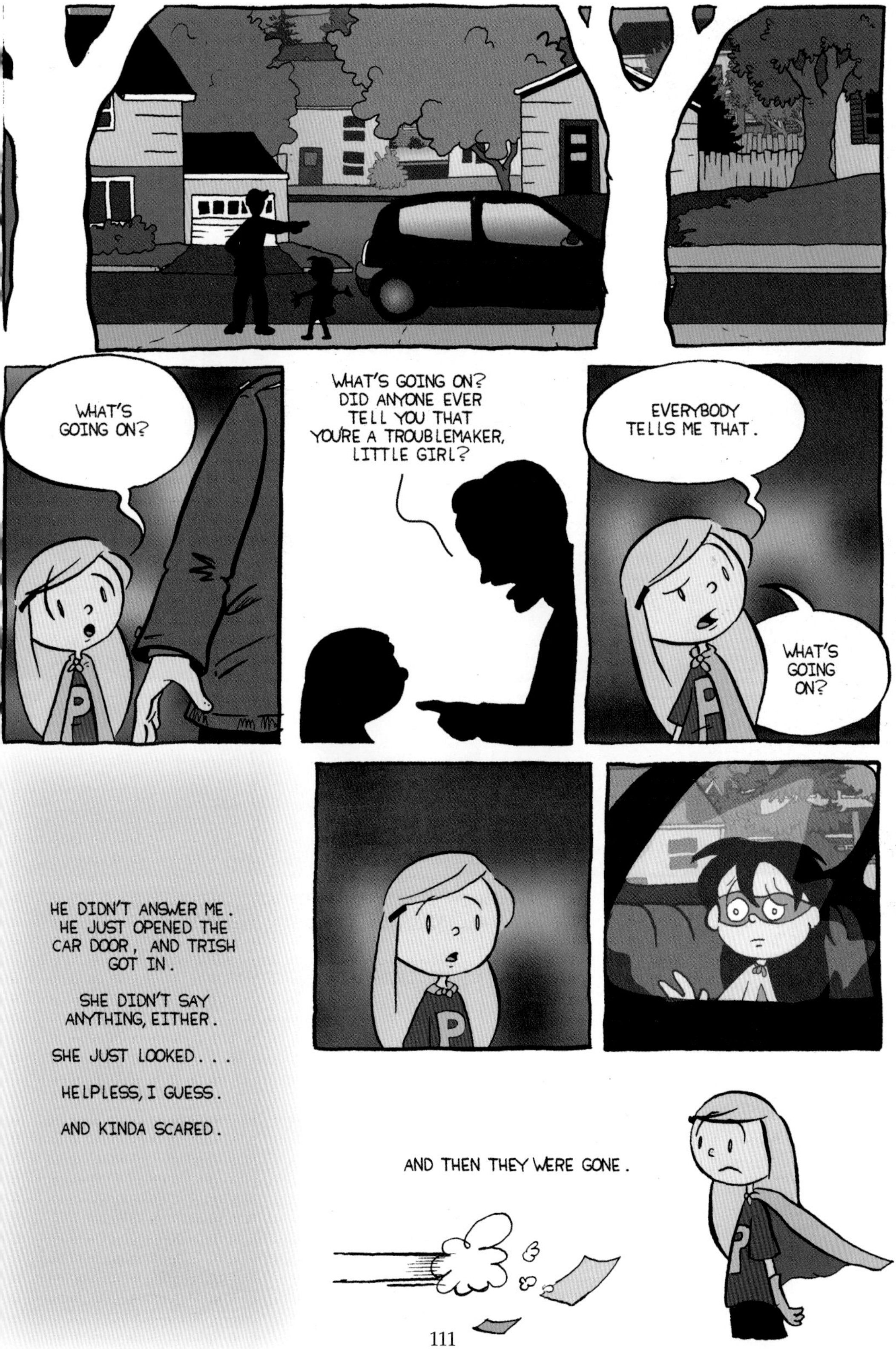
WHAT'S GOING ON?
WHAT'S GOING ON? DID ANYONE EVER TELL YOU THAT YOU'RE A TROUBLEMAKER, LITTLE GIRL?
EVERYBODY TELLS ME THAT.
WHAT'S GOING ON?
HE DIDN'T ANSWER ME. HE JUST OPENED THE CAR DOOR, AND TRISH GOT IN.
SHE DIDN'T SAY ANYTHING, EITHER.
SHE JUST LOOKED...
HELPLESS, I GUESS.
AND KINDA SCARED.
AND THEN THEY WERE GONE.

AFTER THAT, NO ONE SAW TRISHIA FOR WEEKS.

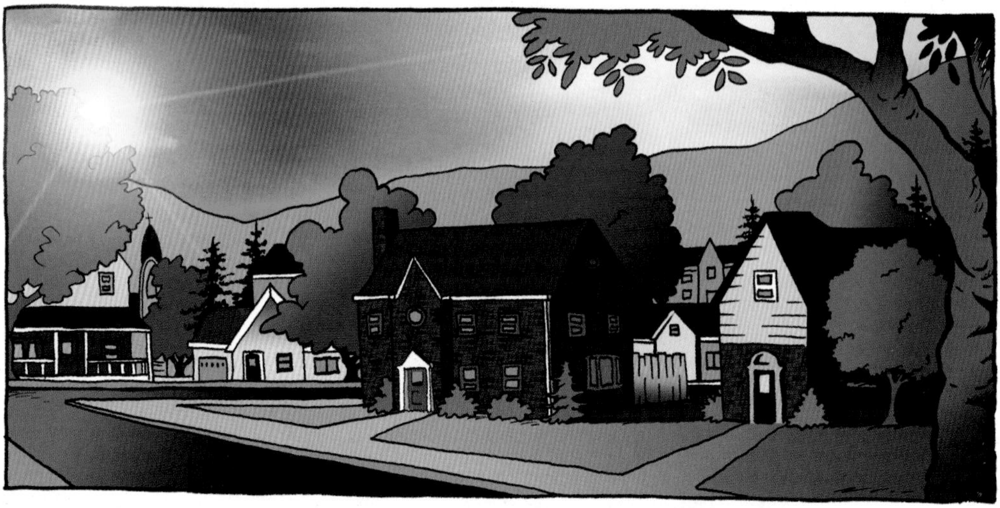

IT RAINED OFF AND ON, WHICH ALWAYS STINKS DURING SUMMER VACATION.

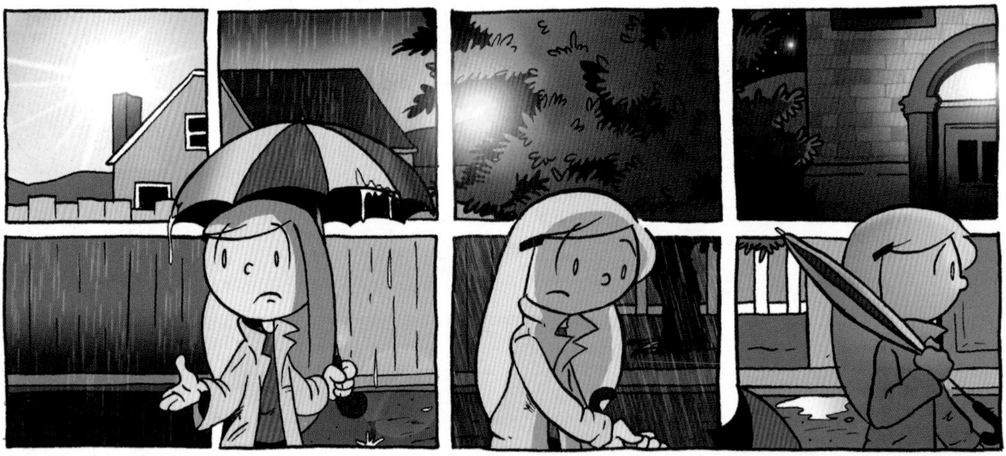

ONE DAY JOANNE SHOWED UP WITH THE NEW TWEENIE ZEENIE. EVERYONE WANTED TO KNOW WHAT HAPPENED TO PRINCESS TRISHARA.

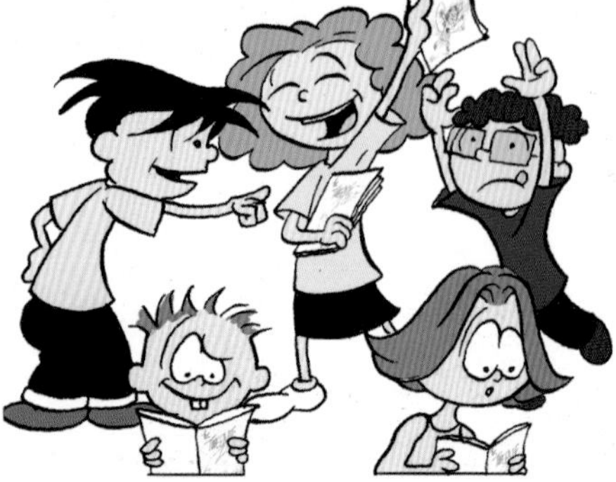

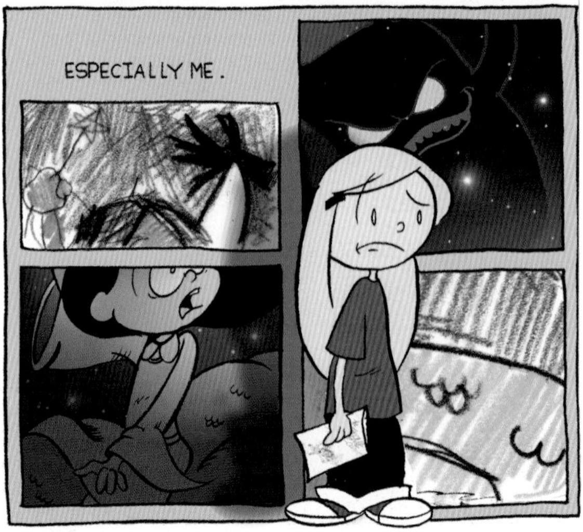
ESPECIALLY ME.

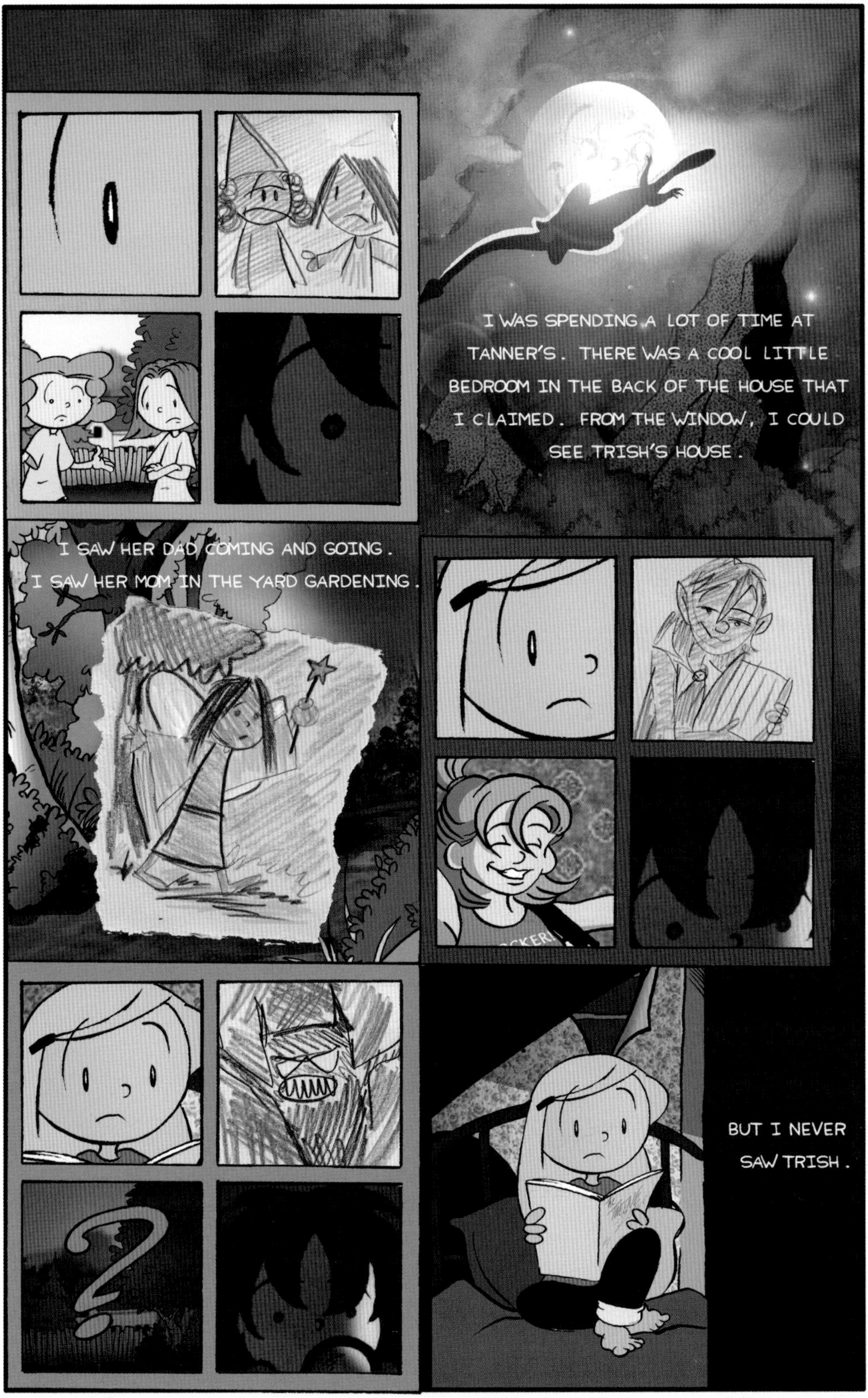
I WAS SPENDING A LOT OF TIME AT TANNER'S. THERE WAS A COOL LITTLE BEDROOM IN THE BACK OF THE HOUSE THAT I CLAIMED. FROM THE WINDOW, I COULD SEE TRISH'S HOUSE.
I SAW HER DAD COMING AND GOING.
I SAW HER MOM IN THE YARD GARDENING.
BUT I NEVER SAW TRISH.

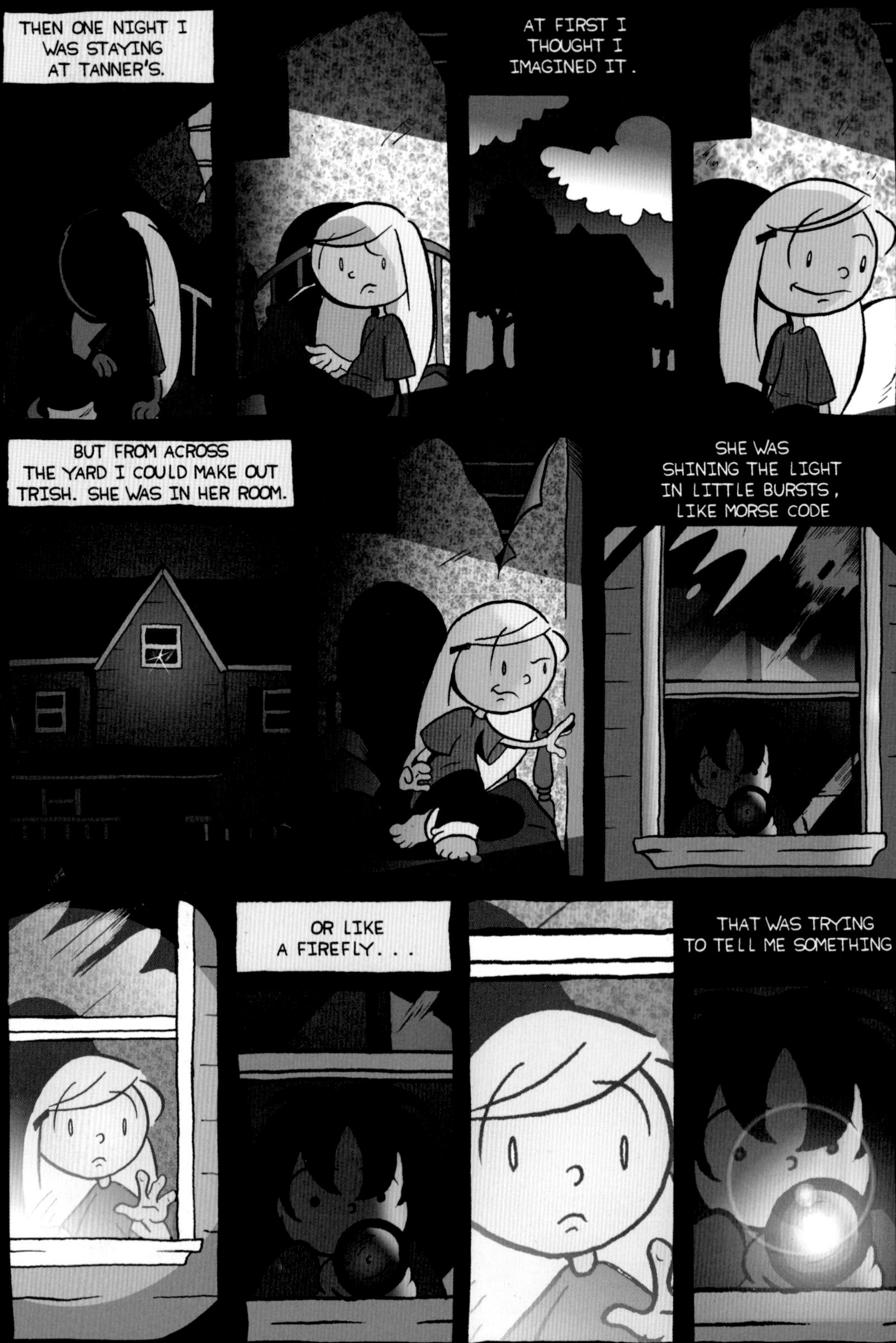
THEN ONE NIGHT I WAS STAYING AT TANNER'S.
AT FIRST I THOUGHT I IMAGINED IT.
BUT FROM ACROSS THE YARD I COULD MAKE OUT TRISH. SHE WAS IN HER ROOM.
SHE WAS SHINING THE LIGHT IN LITTLE BURSTS, LIKE MORSE CODE
OR LIKE A FIREFLY...
THAT WAS TRYING TO TELL ME SOMETHING

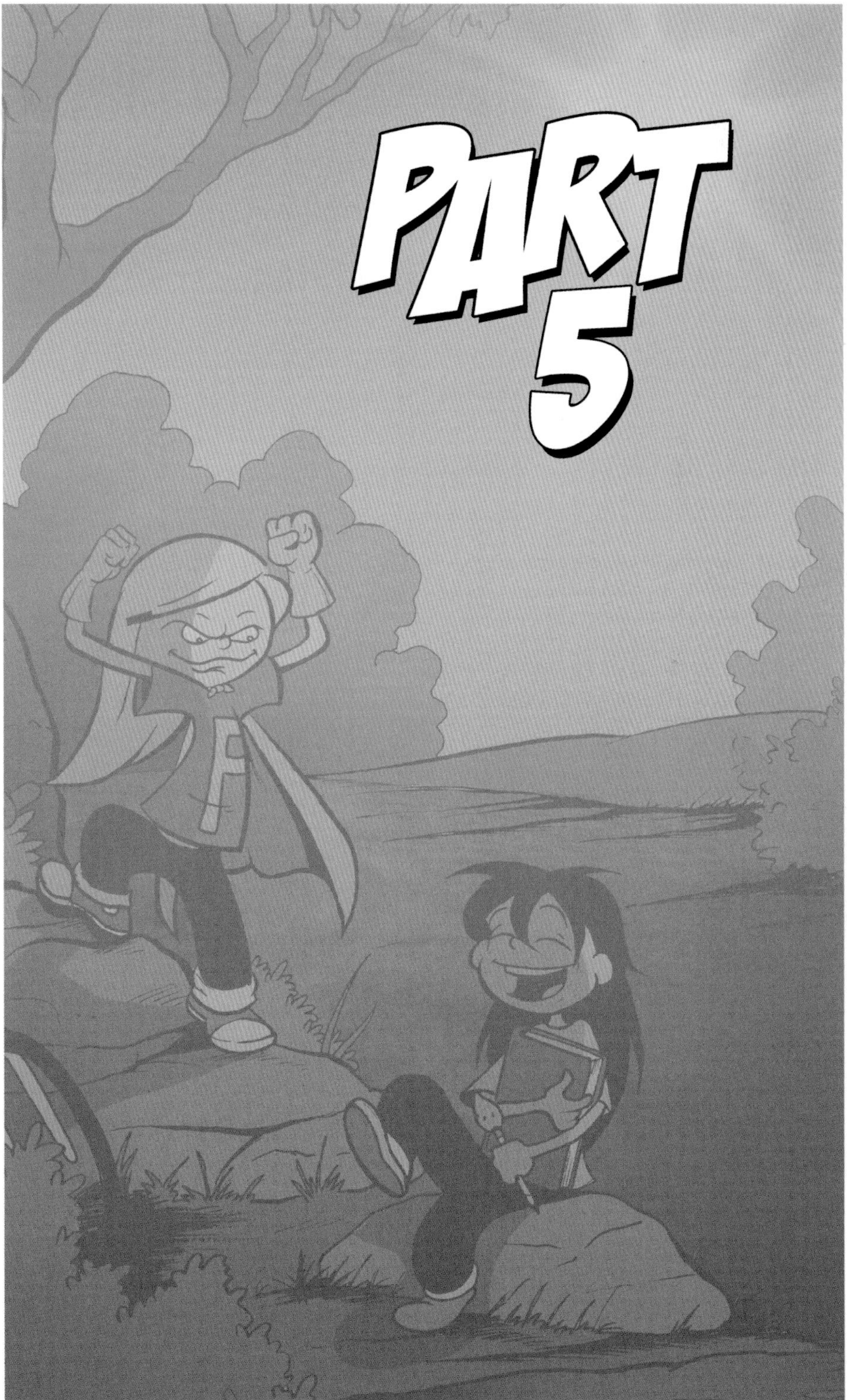
PART
5

BEFORE SCHOOL STARTED UP AGAIN, TANNER DECIDED TO LET ME HAVE A SLEEPOVER AT HER HOUSE. ALL THE GIRLS WERE COMING, EVEN TRISHIA. I WAS SUPER-EXCITED. THEN, ON THE DAY BEFORE THE PARTY, TANNER SAT ME DOWN.

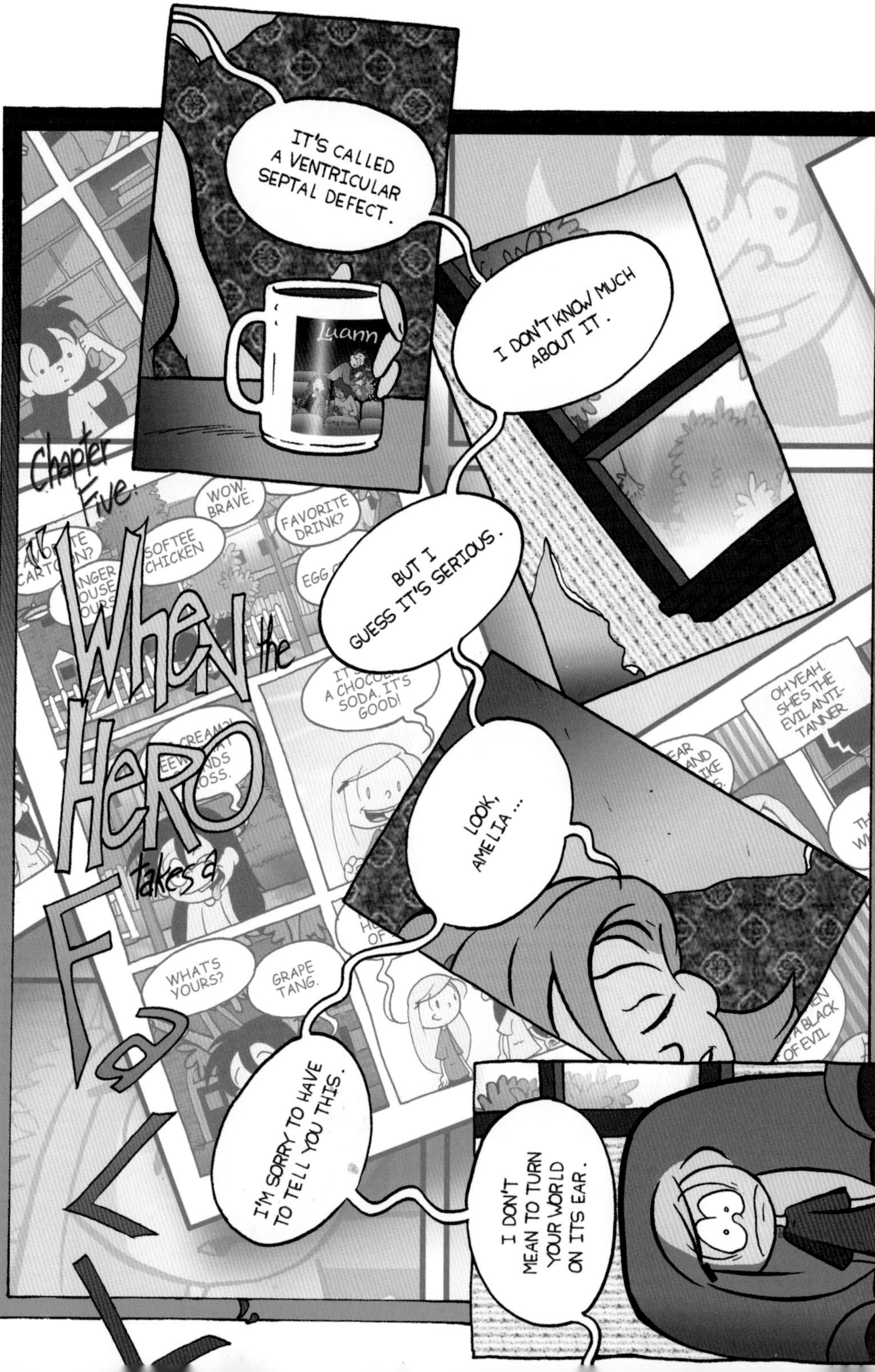

IT'S CALLED A VENTRICULAR SEPTAL DEFECT.
Luann
I DON'T KNOW MUCH ABOUT IT.
Chapter Five:
When the HERO takes a Fall
WOW. BRAVE.
FAVORITE DRINK?
SOFTEE CHICKEN
BUT I GUESS IT'S SERIOUS.
OH YEAH. SHE'S THE EVIL ANTI-TANNER.
LOOK, AMELIA...
WHAT'S YOURS?
GRAPE TANG.
I'M SORRY TO HAVE TO TELL YOU THIS.
I DON'T MEAN TO TURN YOUR WORLD ON ITS EAR.

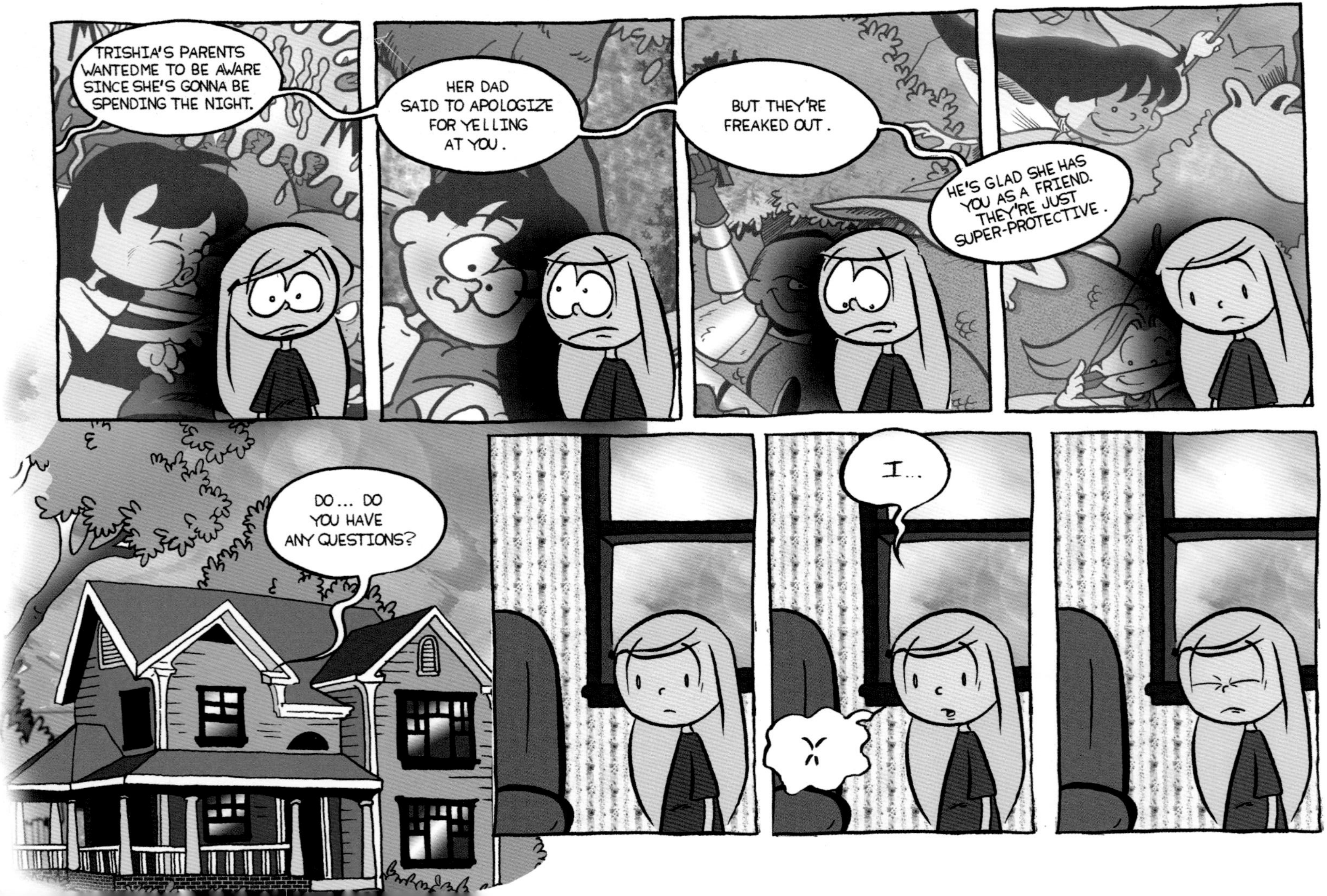
TRISHIA'S PARENTS WANTEDME TO BE AWARE SINCE SHE'S GONNA BE SPENDING THE NIGHT.
HER DAD SAID TO APOLOGIZE FOR YELLING AT YOU.
BUT THEY'RE FREAKED OUT.
HE'S GLAD SHE HAS YOU AS A FRIEND. THEY'RE JUST SUPER-PROTECTIVE.
DO... DO YOU HAVE ANY QUESTIONS?
I...

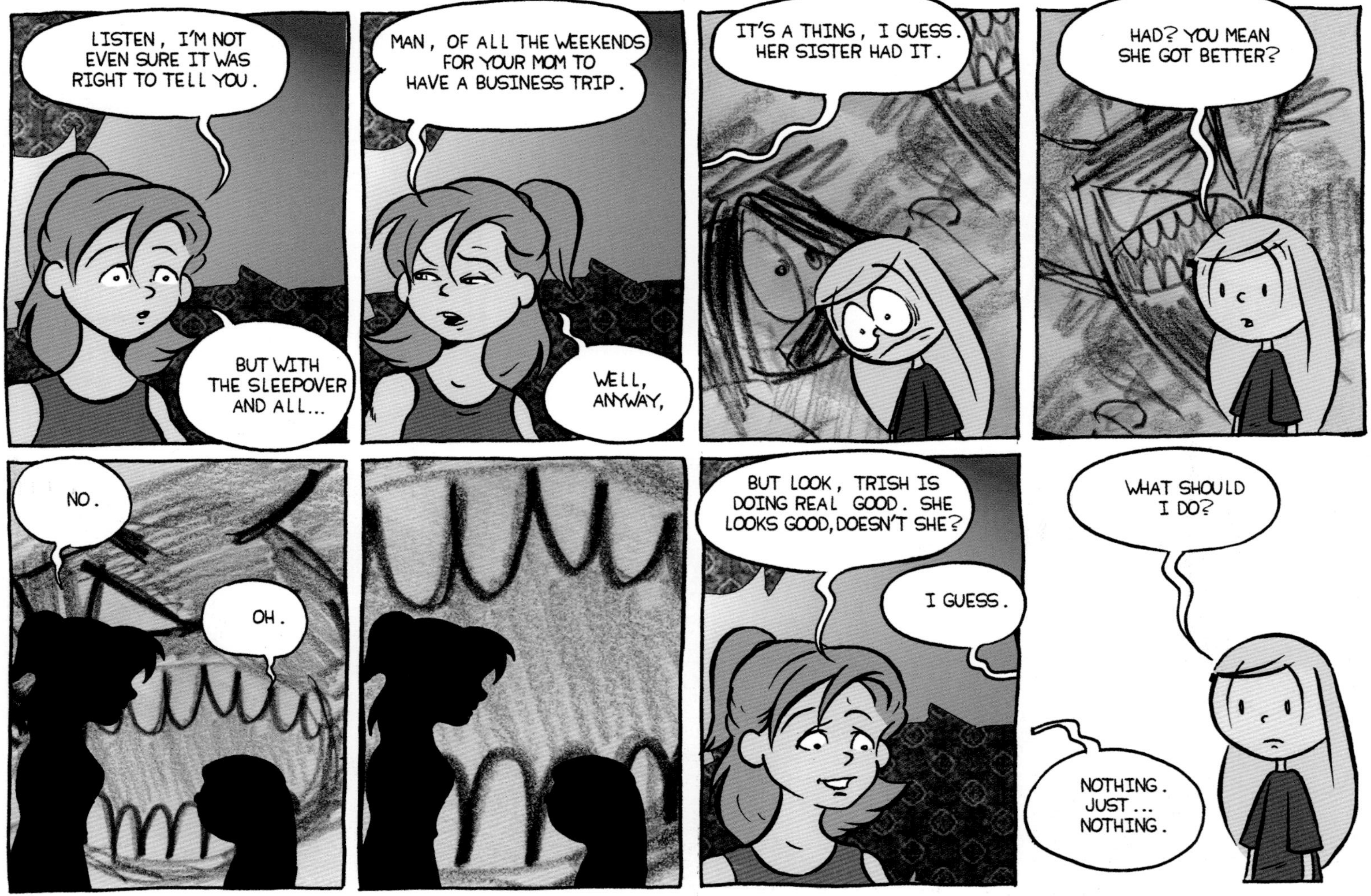
LISTEN, I'M NOT EVEN SURE IT WAS RIGHT TO TELL YOU.
BUT WITH THE SLEEPOVER AND ALL...
MAN, OF ALL THE WEEKENDS FOR YOUR MOM TO HAVE A BUSINESS TRIP.
WELL, ANYWAY,
IT'S A THING, I GUESS. HER SISTER HAD IT.
HAD? YOU MEAN SHE GOT BETTER?
NO.
OH.
BUT LOOK, TRISH IS DOING REAL GOOD. SHE LOOKS GOOD, DOESN'T SHE?
I GUESS.
WHAT SHOULD I DO?
NOTHING. JUST... NOTHING.

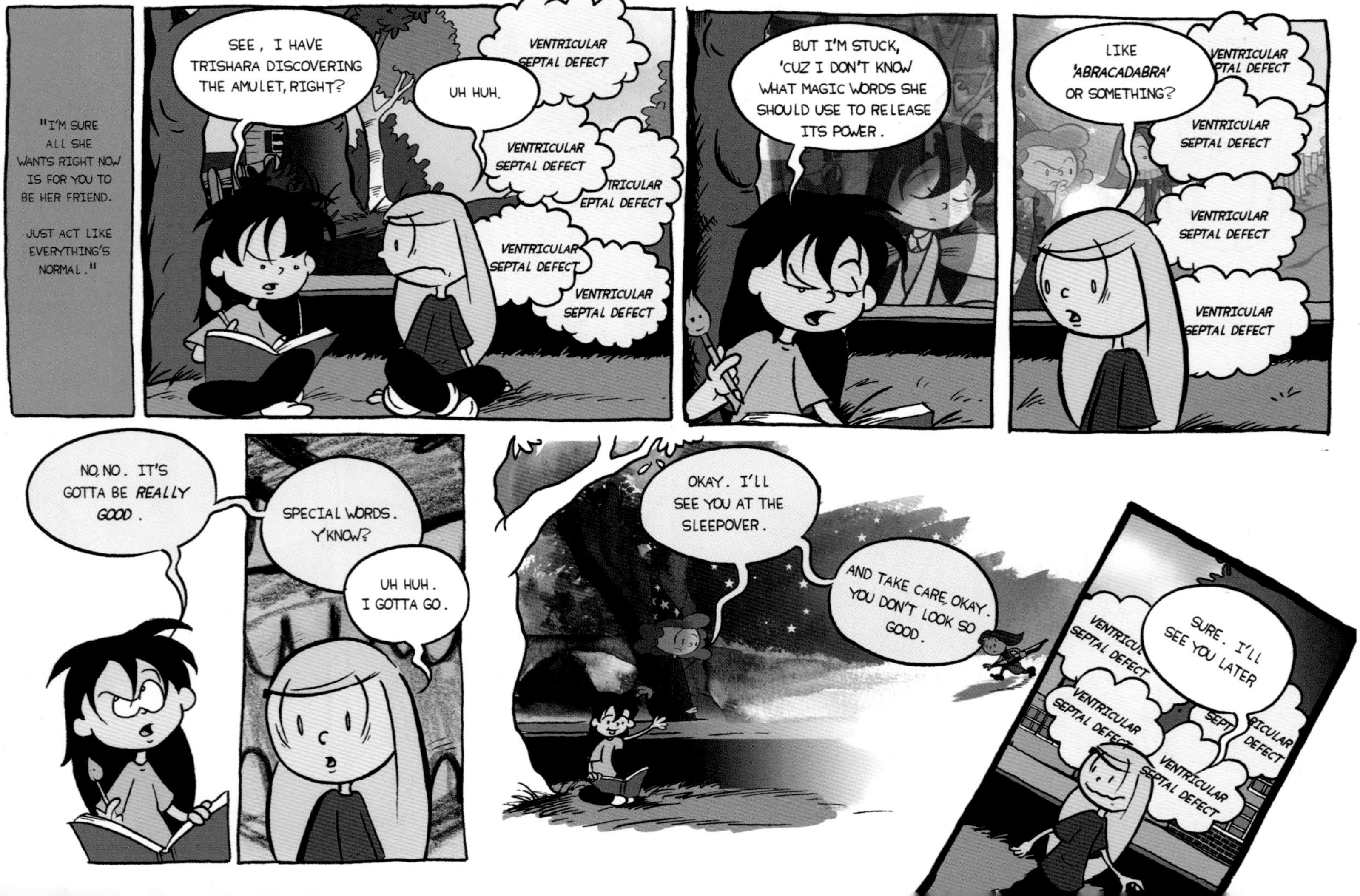
"I'M SURE ALL SHE WANTS RIGHT NOW IS FOR YOU TO BE HER FRIEND.
JUST ACT LIKE EVERYTHING'S NORMAL."
SEE, I HAVE TRISHARA DISCOVERING THE AMULET, RIGHT?
VENTRICULAR SEPTAL DEFECT
UH HUH.
VENTRICULAR SEPTAL DEFECT
VENTRICULAR SEPTAL DEFECT
VENTRICULAR SEPTAL DEFECT
BUT I'M STUCK, 'CUZ I DON'T KNOW WHAT MAGIC WORDS SHE SHOULD USE TO RELEASE ITS POWER.
LIKE *'ABRACADABRA'* OR SOMETHING?
VENTRICULAR SEPTAL DEFECT
VENTRICULAR SEPTAL DEFECT
VENTRICULAR SEPTAL DEFECT
NO, NO. IT'S GOTTA BE *REALLY GOOD*.
SPECIAL WORDS. Y'KNOW?
UH HUH. I GOTTA GO.
OKAY. I'LL SEE YOU AT THE SLEEPOVER.
AND TAKE CARE, OKAY. YOU DON'T LOOK SO GOOD.
SURE. I'LL SEE YOU LATER
VENTRICULAR SEPTAL DEFECT
VENTRICULAR SEPTAL DEFECT

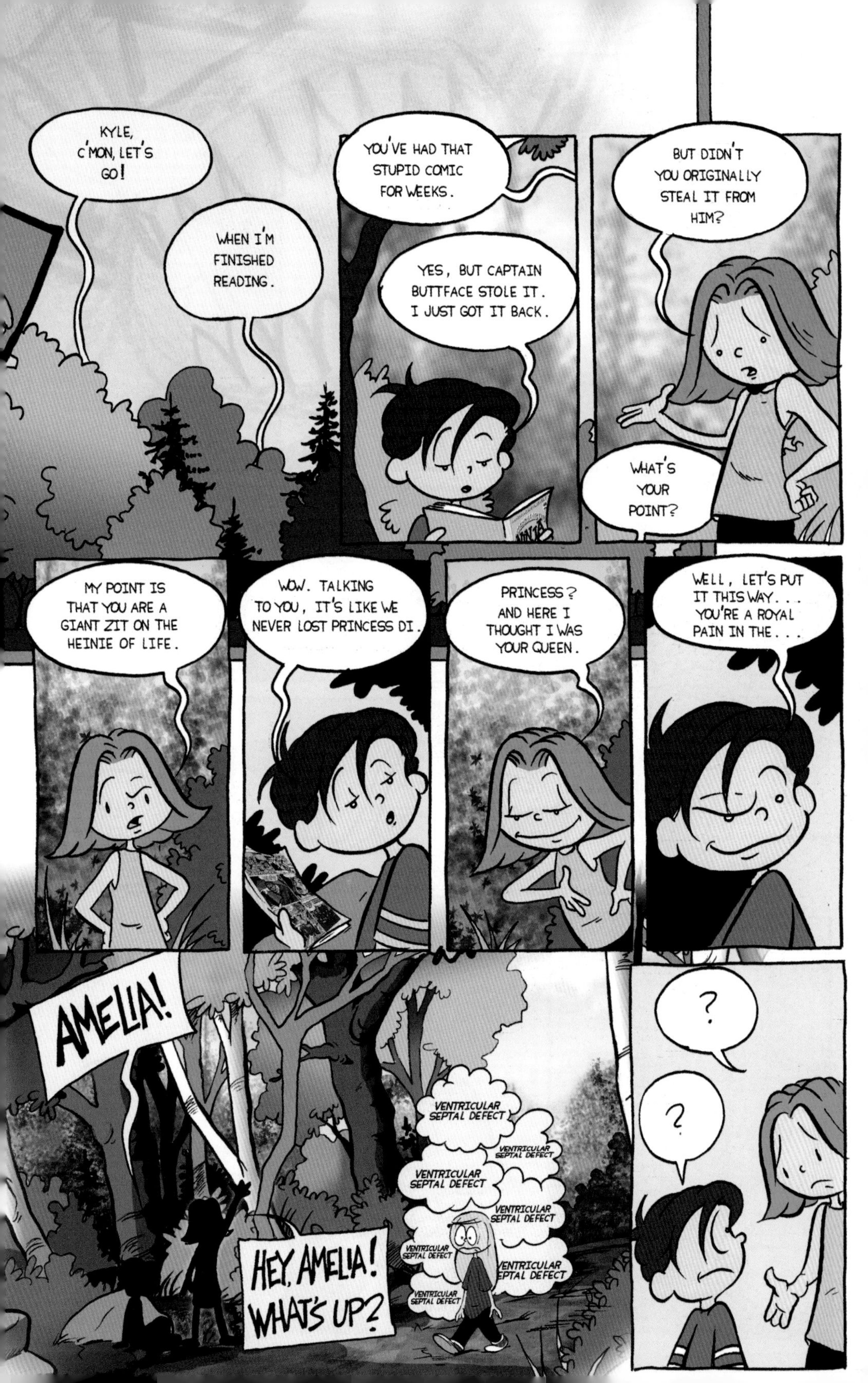
KYLE, C'MON, LET'S GO!
WHEN I'M FINISHED READING.
YOU'VE HAD THAT STUPID COMIC FOR WEEKS.
YES, BUT CAPTAIN BUTTFACE STOLE IT. I JUST GOT IT BACK.
BUT DIDN'T YOU ORIGINALLY STEAL IT FROM HIM?
WHAT'S YOUR POINT?
MY POINT IS THAT YOU ARE A GIANT ZIT ON THE HEINIE OF LIFE.
WOW. TALKING TO YOU, IT'S LIKE WE NEVER LOST PRINCESS DI.
PRINCESS? AND HERE I THOUGHT I WAS YOUR QUEEN.
WELL, LET'S PUT IT THIS WAY... YOU'RE A ROYAL PAIN IN THE...
AMELIA!
HEY, AMELIA! WHAT'S UP?
VENTRICULAR SEPTAL DEFECT
VENTRICULAR SEPTAL DEFECT
VENTRICULAR SEPTAL DEFECT
VENTRICULAR SEPTAL DEFECT
VENTRICULAR SEPTAL DEFECT
VENTRICULAR SEPTAL DEFECT
VENTRICULAR SEPTAL DEFECT
?
?

125

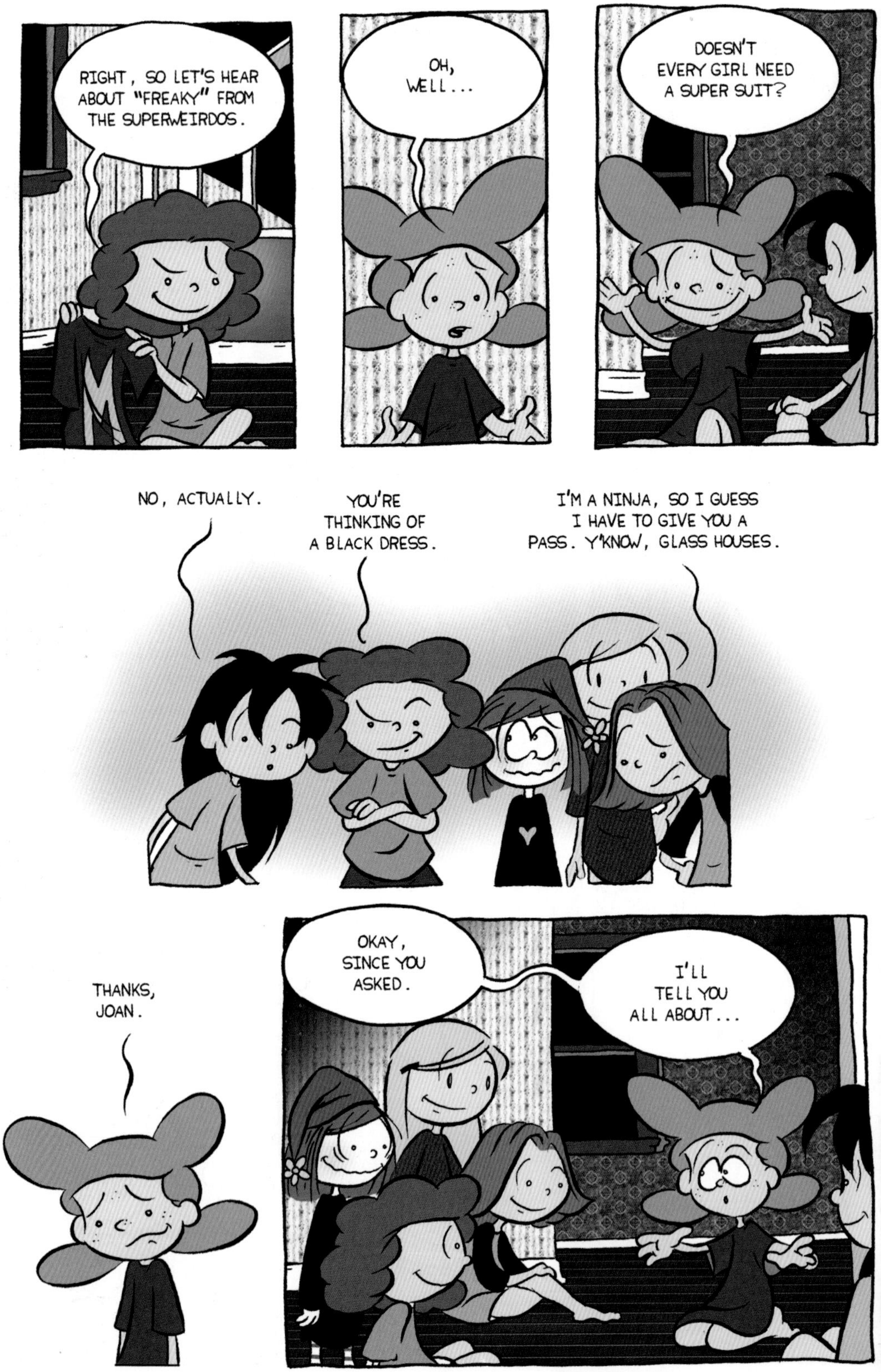
RIGHT, SO LET'S HEAR ABOUT "FREAKY" FROM THE SUPERWEIRDOS.
OH, WELL...
DOESN'T EVERY GIRL NEED A SUPER SUIT?
NO, ACTUALLY.
YOU'RE THINKING OF A BLACK DRESS.
I'M A NINJA, SO I GUESS I HAVE TO GIVE YOU A PASS. Y'KNOW, GLASS HOUSES.
THANKS, JOAN.
OKAY, SINCE YOU ASKED.
I'LL TELL YOU ALL ABOUT...

"THE SECRET ORIGIN OF CAPTAIN AMAZING."

IT WAS THE BEGINNING OF FIRST GRADE AND I WAS THE LONELIEST GIRL IN THE WORLD.

THEN, ACROSS THE SCHOOL YARD, I SAW THE CUTEST BOY I'D EVER SEEN.

HE NEVER SAID MUCH IN CLASS. AND AT LUNCH HE WAS EITHER EATING BY HIMSELF, OR GETTING PICKED ON BY BIGGER BOYS.

BUT WHEN HE WAS ALONE, EVERY DAY WAS THE SAME. AFTER HE ATE HIS LUNCH, HE PULLED A LITTLE SLIP OF PAPER OUT OF HIS BAG AND READ IT.

ONE DAY, HE DROPPED THE PAPER WITHOUT NOTICING.

IT WAS SOOO CUTE. I FELL IN TOTAL, SERIOUS LIKE, Y'KNOW?

TOTAL LIKE. CAN YOU IMAGINE THAT, AMELIA?

NO. I. CAN'T.

I MADE IT MY MISSION TO BECOME HIS FRIEND.

AND I WASN'T LONELY ANYMORE.

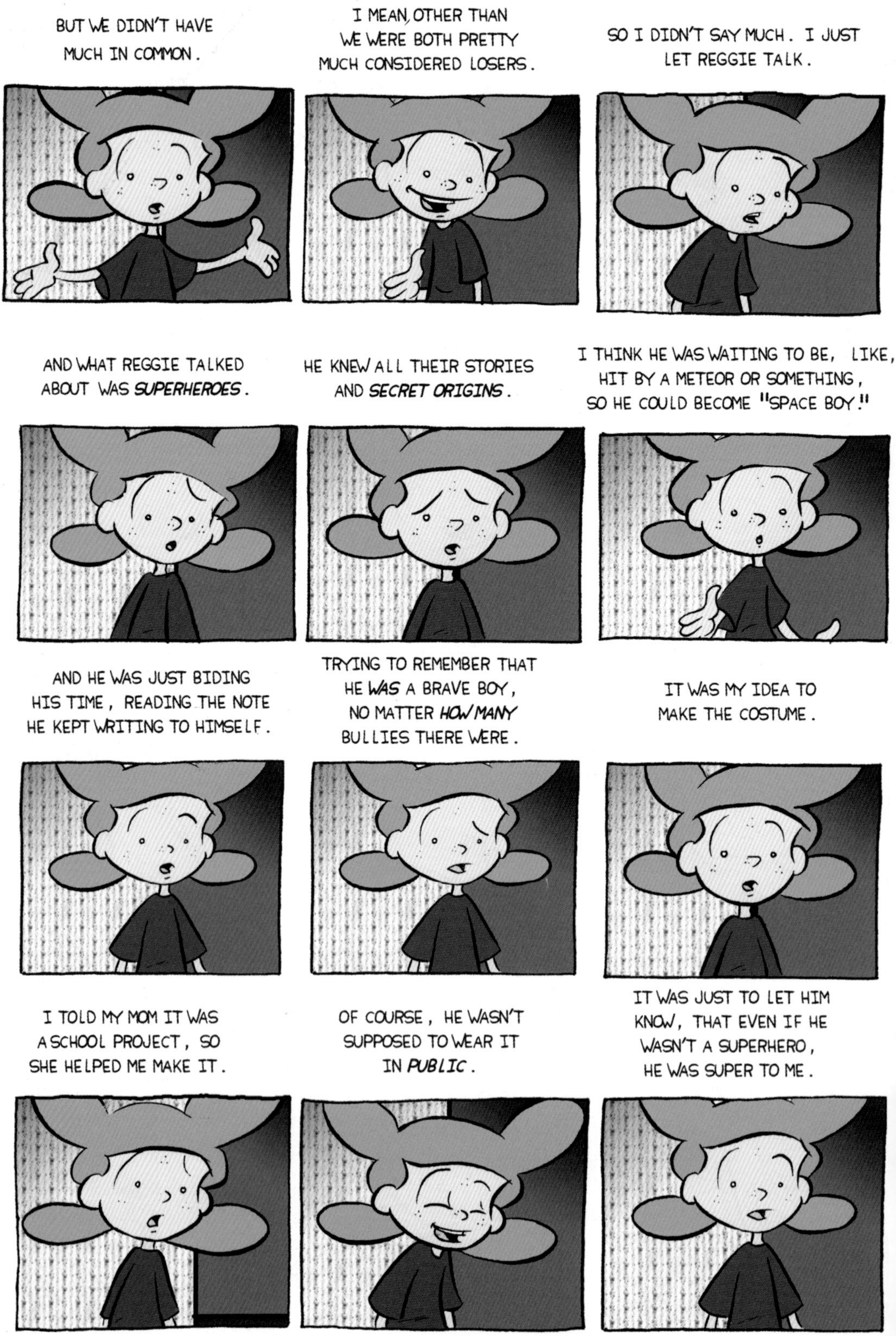
BUT WE DIDN'T HAVE MUCH IN COMMON.
I MEAN, OTHER THAN WE WERE BOTH PRETTY MUCH CONSIDERED LOSERS.
SO I DIDN'T SAY MUCH. I JUST LET REGGIE TALK.
AND WHAT REGGIE TALKED ABOUT WAS *SUPERHEROES*.
HE KNEW ALL THEIR STORIES AND *SECRET ORIGINS*.
I THINK HE WAS WAITING TO BE, LIKE, HIT BY A METEOR OR SOMETHING, SO HE COULD BECOME "SPACE BOY!"
AND HE WAS JUST BIDING HIS TIME, READING THE NOTE HE KEPT WRITING TO HIMSELF.
TRYING TO REMEMBER THAT HE *WAS* A BRAVE BOY, NO MATTER *HOW MANY* BULLIES THERE WERE.
IT WAS MY IDEA TO MAKE THE COSTUME.
I TOLD MY MOM IT WAS A SCHOOL PROJECT, SO SHE HELPED ME MAKE IT.
OF COURSE, HE WASN'T SUPPOSED TO WEAR IT IN *PUBLIC*.
IT WAS JUST TO LET HIM KNOW, THAT EVEN IF HE WASN'T A SUPERHERO, HE WAS SUPER TO ME.

129

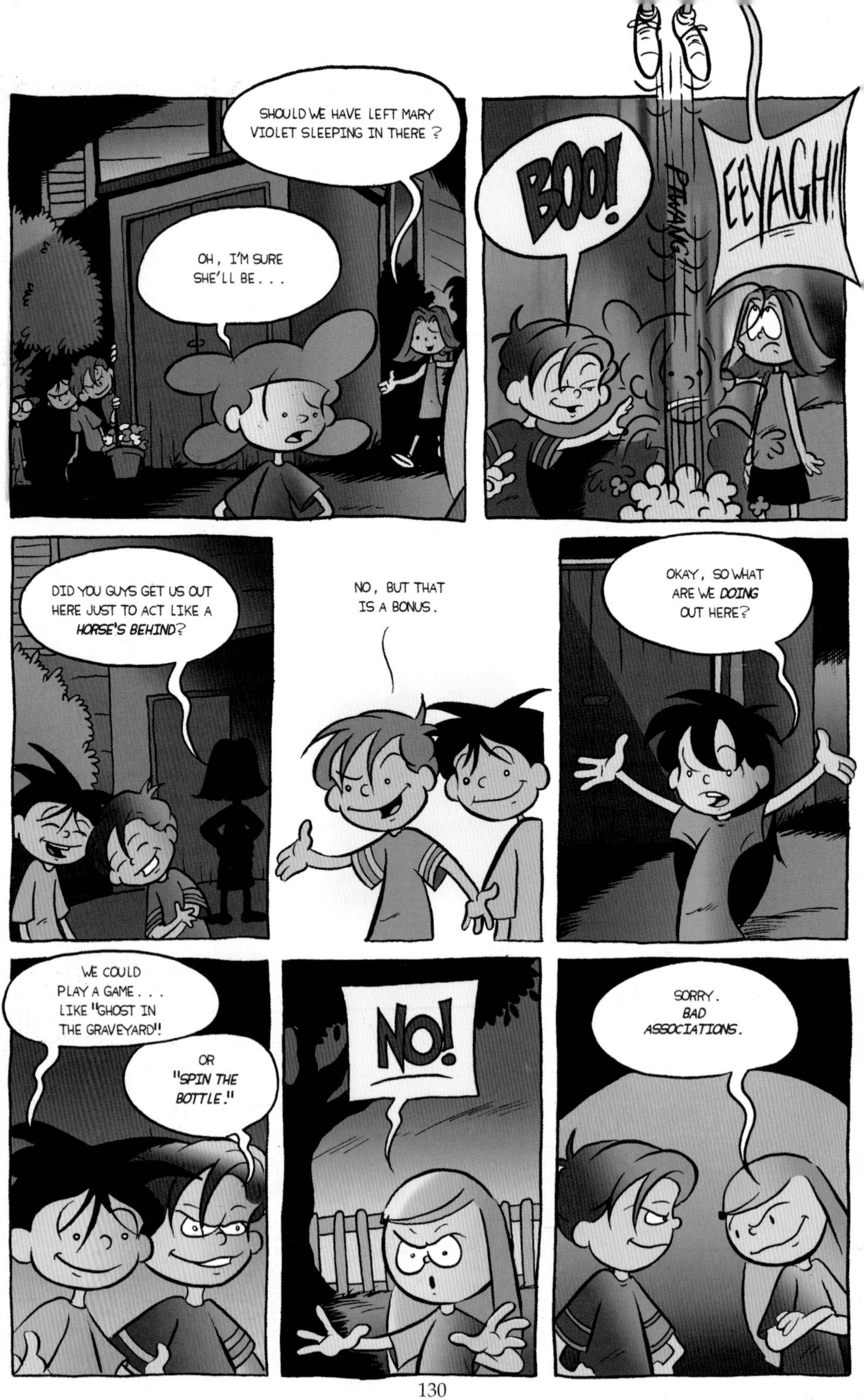
SHOULD WE HAVE LEFT MARY VIOLET SLEEPING IN THERE ?
OH , I'M SURE SHE'LL BE . . .
BOO!
PTWANG!
EEYAGH!!
DID YOU GUYS GET US OUT HERE JUST TO ACT LIKE A *HORSE'S BEHIND*?
NO , BUT THAT IS A BONUS .
OKAY, SO WHAT ARE WE *DOING* OUT HERE?
WE COULD PLAY A GAME . . . LIKE "GHOST IN THE GRAVEYARD"!
OR *"SPIN THE BOTTLE."*
NO!
SORRY. *BAD ASSOCIATIONS.*

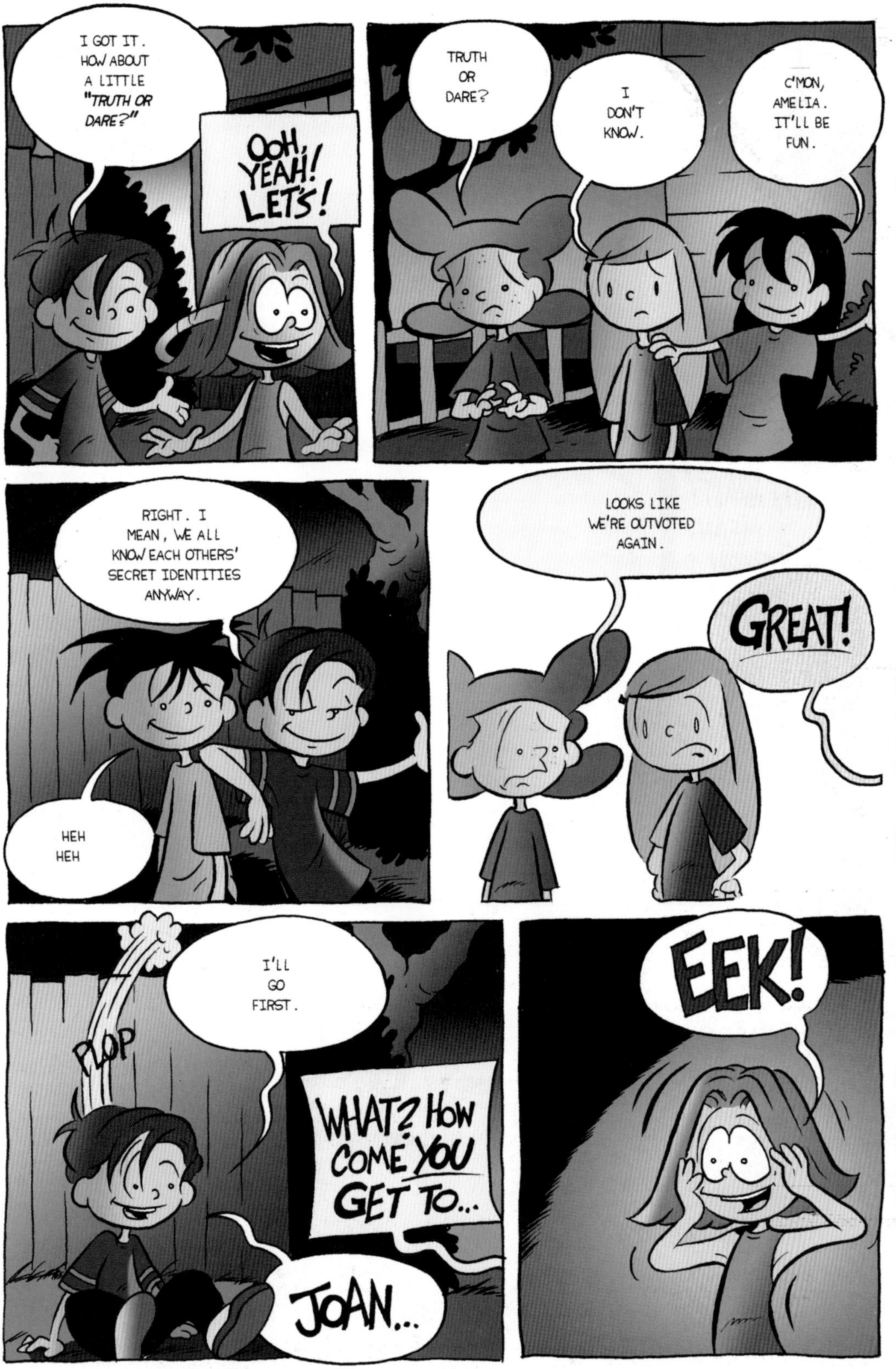

I GOT IT. HOW ABOUT A LITTLE "TRUTH OR DARE?"
OOH, YEAH! LET'S!
TRUTH OR DARE?
I DON'T KNOW.
C'MON, AMELIA. IT'LL BE FUN.
RIGHT. I MEAN, WE ALL KNOW EACH OTHERS' SECRET IDENTITIES ANYWAY.
HEH HEH
LOOKS LIKE WE'RE OUTVOTED AGAIN.
GREAT!
PLOP
I'LL GO FIRST.
WHAT? HOW COME YOU GET TO...
JOAN...
EEK!

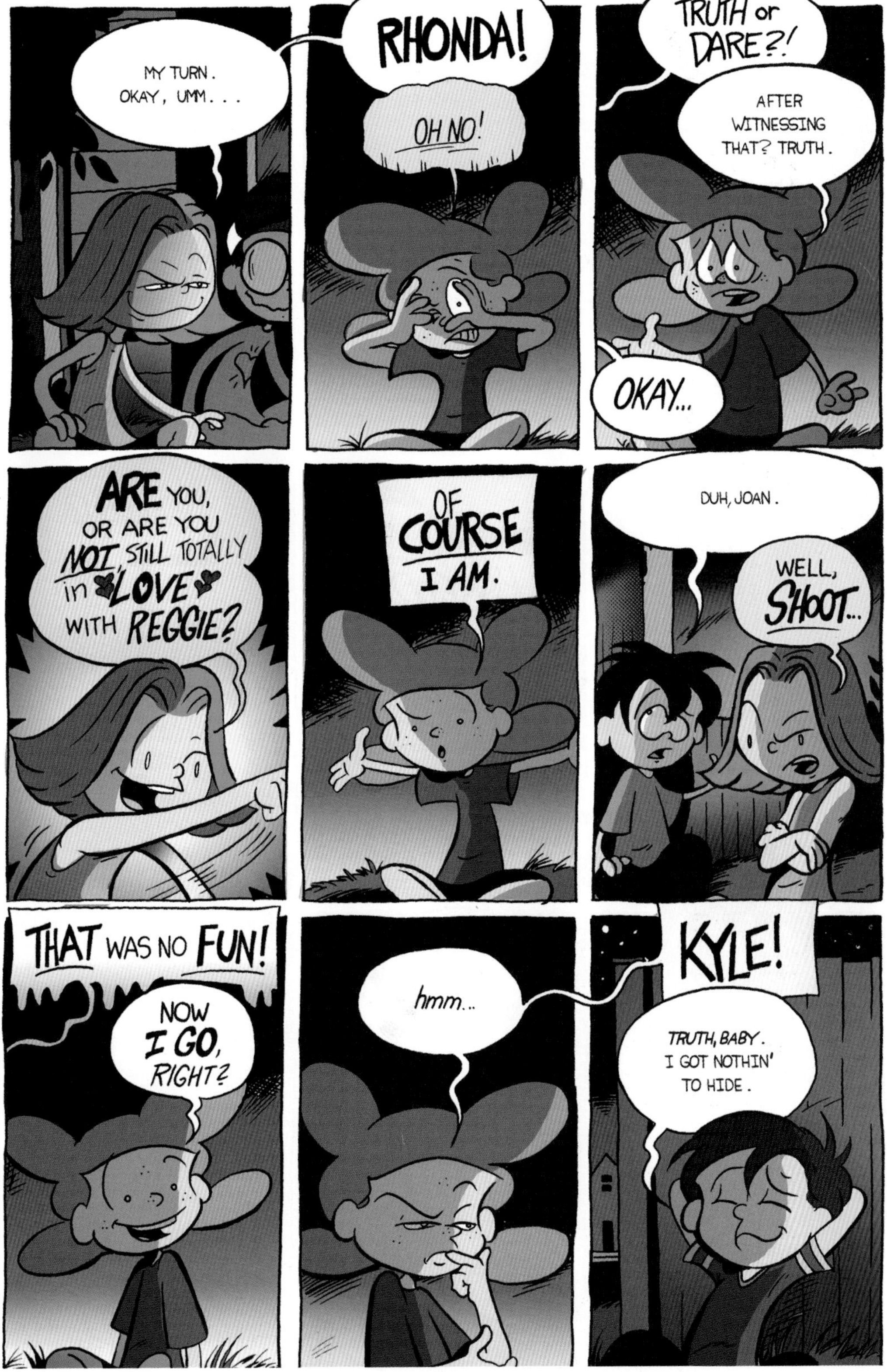
MY TURN. OKAY, UMM...
RHONDA!
OH NO!
TRUTH or DARE?!
AFTER WITNESSING THAT? TRUTH.
OKAY...
ARE YOU, OR ARE YOU NOT, STILL TOTALLY in LOVE WITH REGGIE?
OF COURSE I AM.
DUH, JOAN.
WELL, SHOOT...
THAT WAS NO FUN!
NOW I GO, RIGHT?
hmm...
KYLE!
TRUTH, BABY. I GOT NOTHIN' TO HIDE.

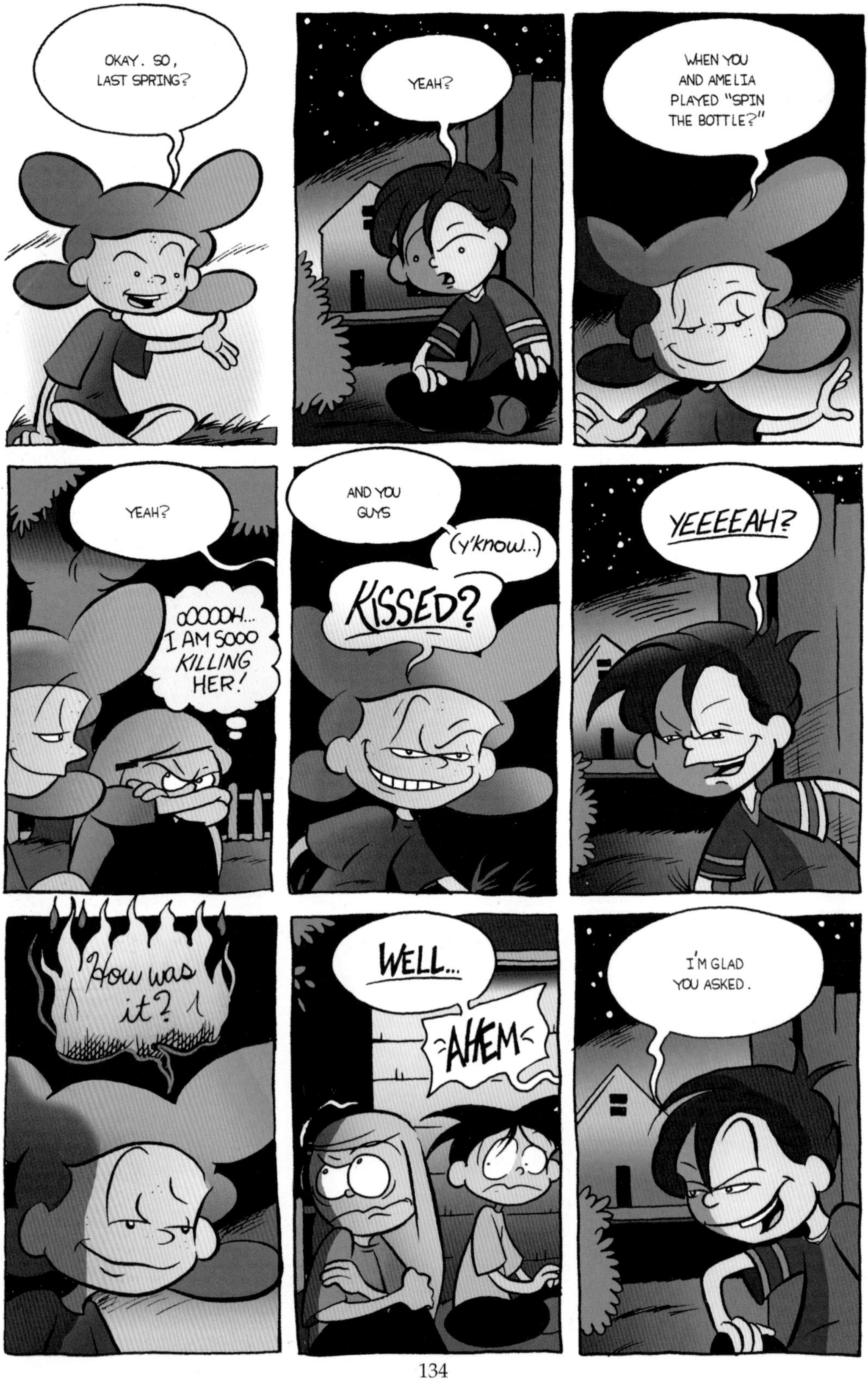
OKAY. SO, LAST SPRING?
YEAH?
WHEN YOU AND AMELIA PLAYED "SPIN THE BOTTLE?"
YEAH?
oOOOOH... I AM SOOO KILLING HER!
AND YOU GUYS
(y'know...)
KISSED?
YEEEEAH?
How was it?
WELL...
AHEM
I'M GLAD YOU ASKED.

135

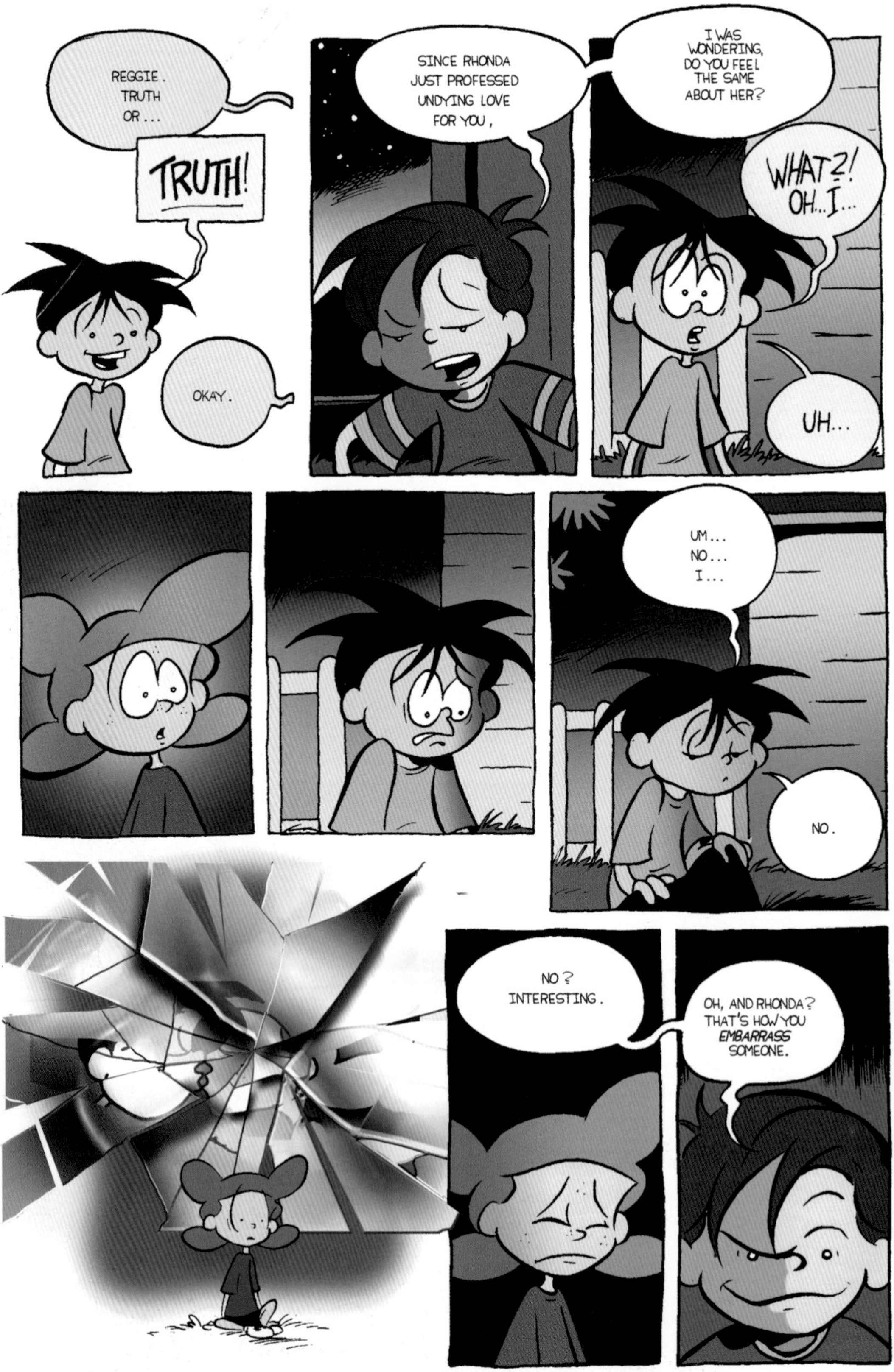
REGGIE. TRUTH OR...
TRUTH!
OKAY.
SINCE RHONDA JUST PROFESSED UNDYING LOVE FOR YOU,
I WAS WONDERING, DO YOU FEEL THE SAME ABOUT HER?
WHAT?! OH...I...
UH...
UM... NO... I...
NO.
NO? INTERESTING.
OH, AND RHONDA? THAT'S HOW YOU EMBARRASS SOMEONE.

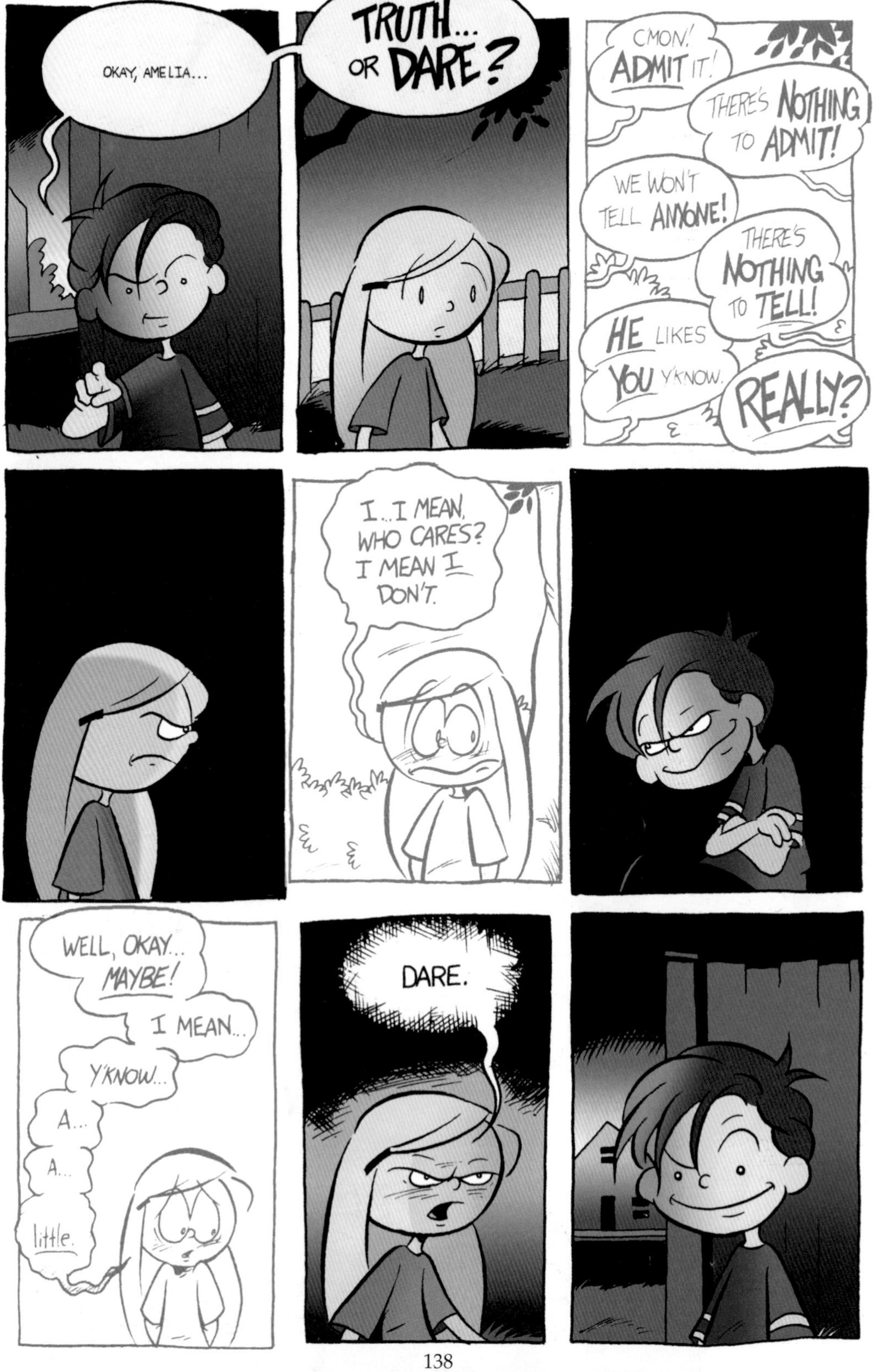
OKAY, AMELIA...
TRUTH... OR DARE?
C'MON! ADMIT IT!
THERE'S NOTHING TO ADMIT!
WE WON'T TELL ANYONE!
THERE'S NOTHING TO TELL!
HE LIKES YOU Y'KNOW.
REALLY?
I...I MEAN, WHO CARES? I MEAN I DON'T.
WELL, OKAY... MAYBE!
I MEAN...
Y'KNOW...
A...
A...
little.
DARE.

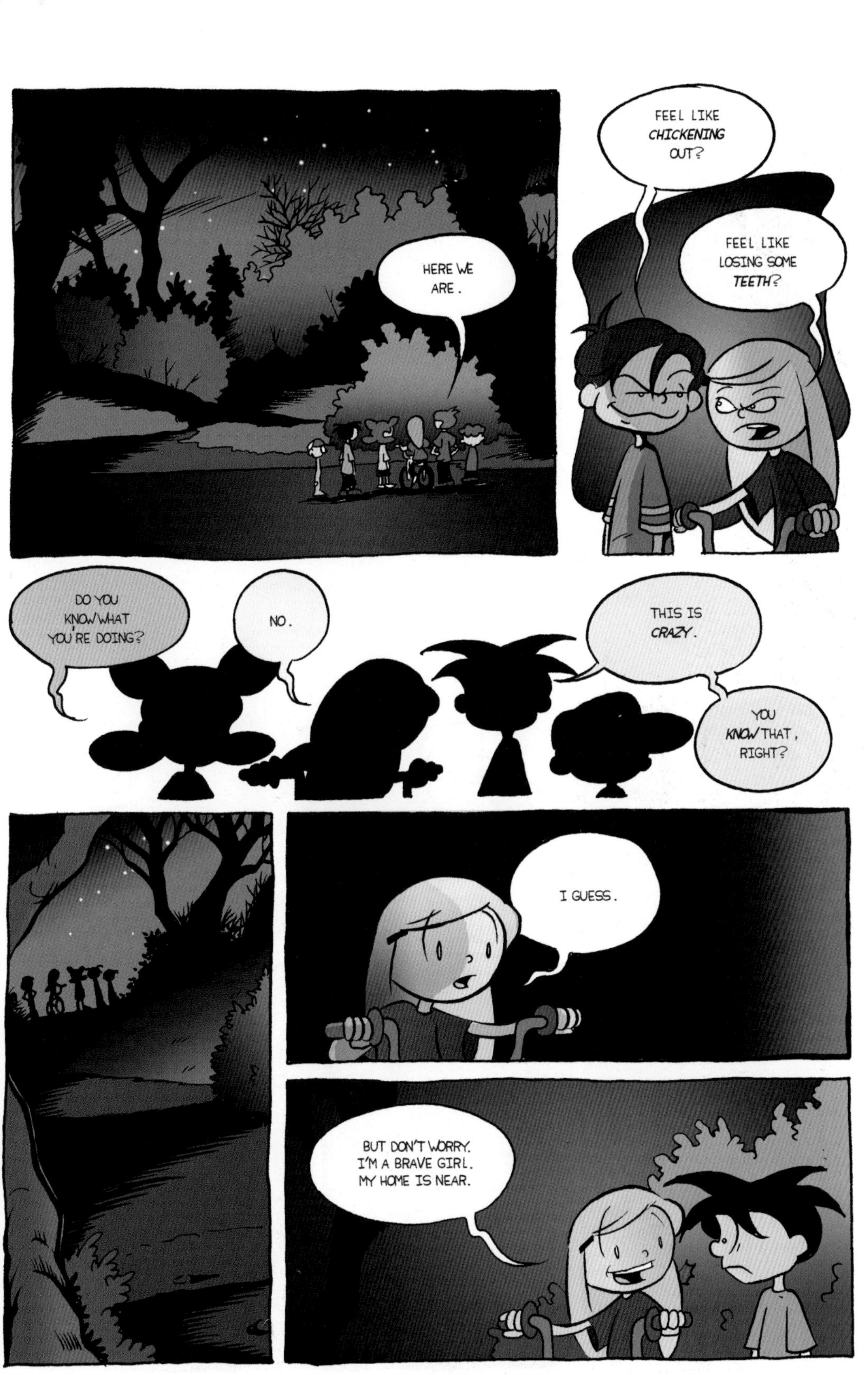
HERE WE ARE.
FEEL LIKE CHICKENING OUT?
FEEL LIKE LOSING SOME TEETH?
DO YOU KNOW WHAT YOU'RE DOING?
NO.
THIS IS CRAZY.
YOU KNOW THAT, RIGHT?
I GUESS.
BUT DON'T WORRY. I'M A BRAVE GIRL. MY HOME IS NEAR.

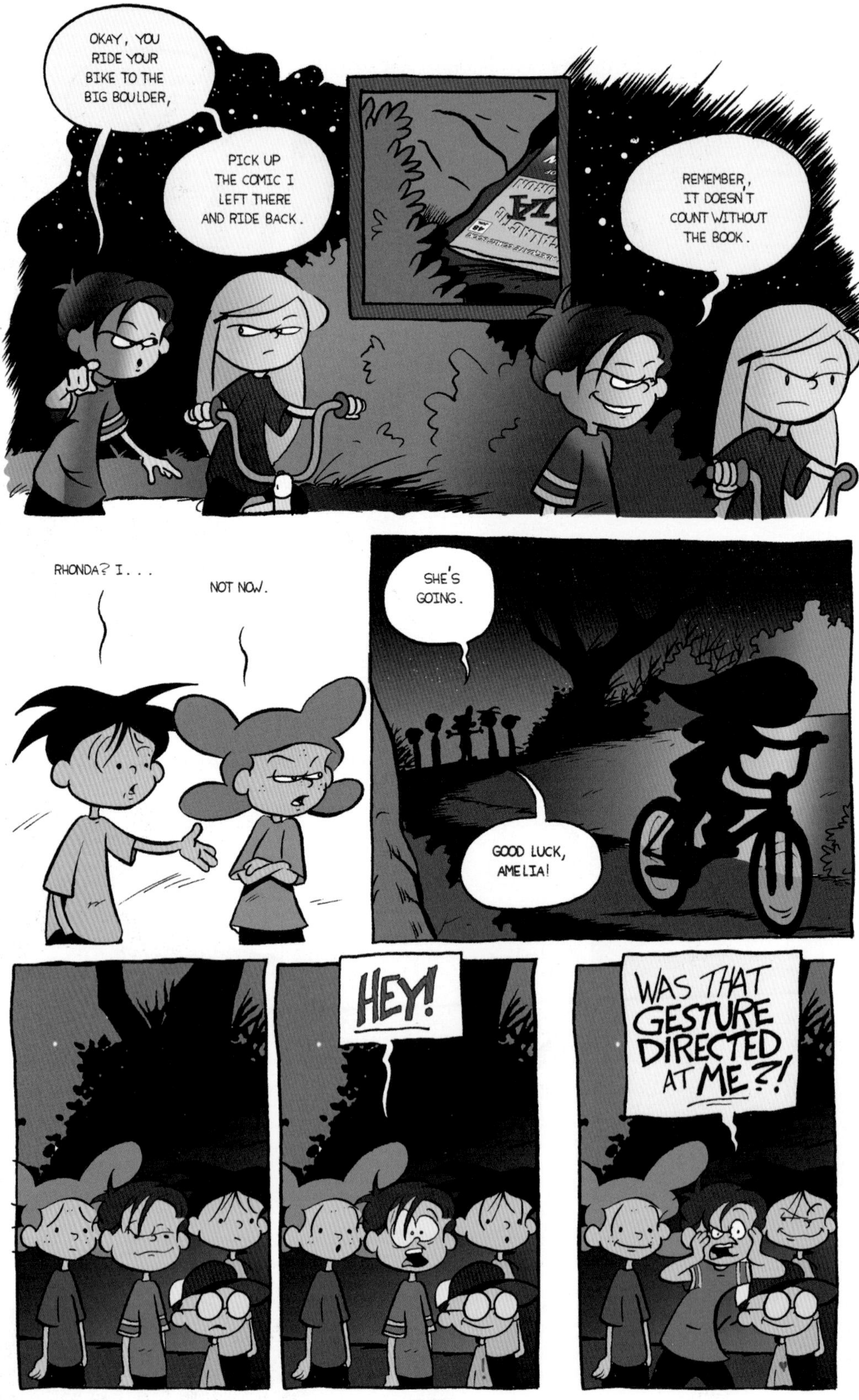

OKAY, YOU RIDE YOUR BIKE TO THE BIG BOULDER,
PICK UP THE COMIC I LEFT THERE AND RIDE BACK.
REMEMBER, IT DOESN'T COUNT WITHOUT THE BOOK.
RHONDA? I. . .
NOT NOW.
SHE'S GOING.
GOOD LUCK, AMELIA!
HEY!
WAS THAT GESTURE DIRECTED AT ME?!

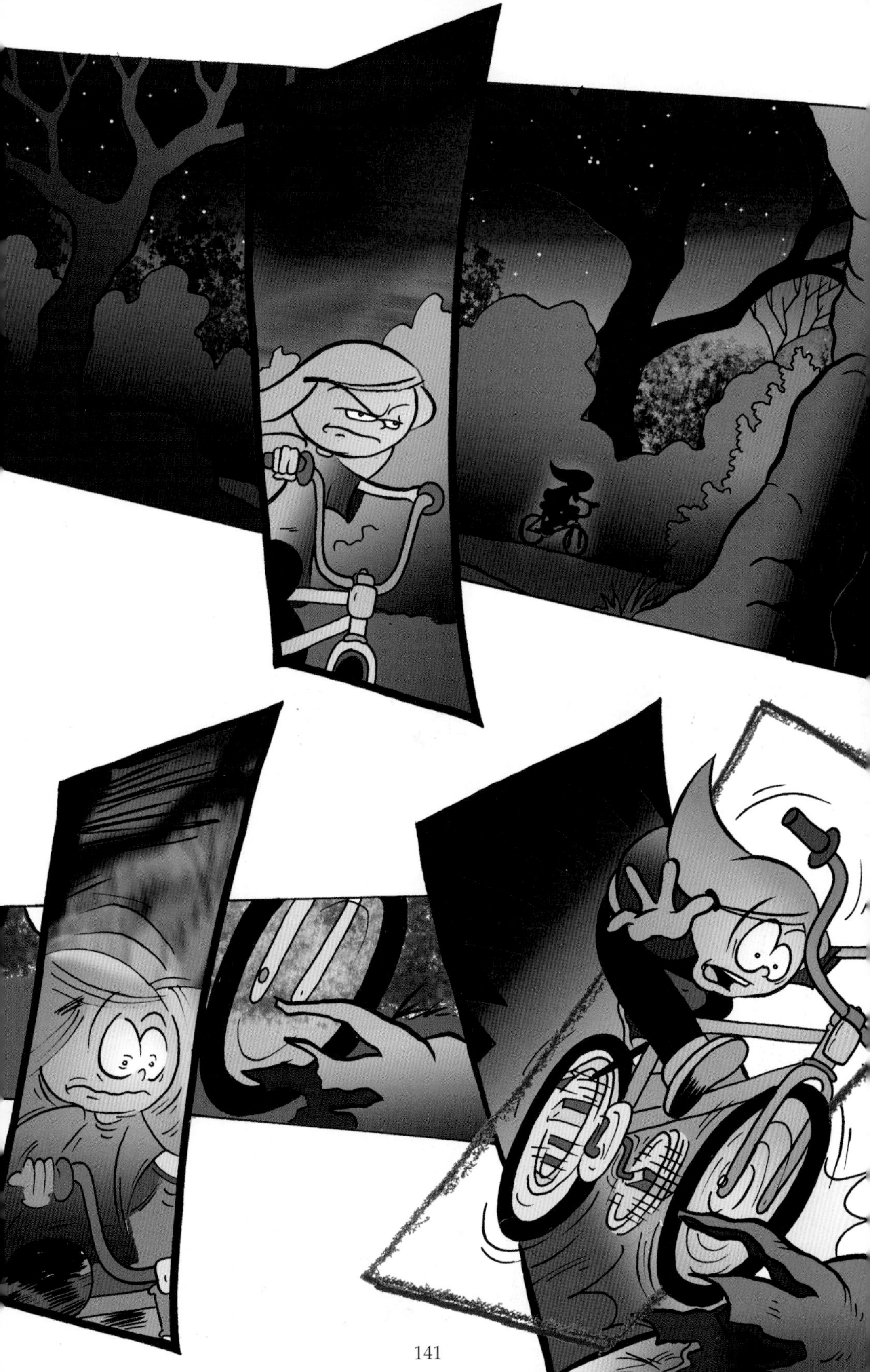

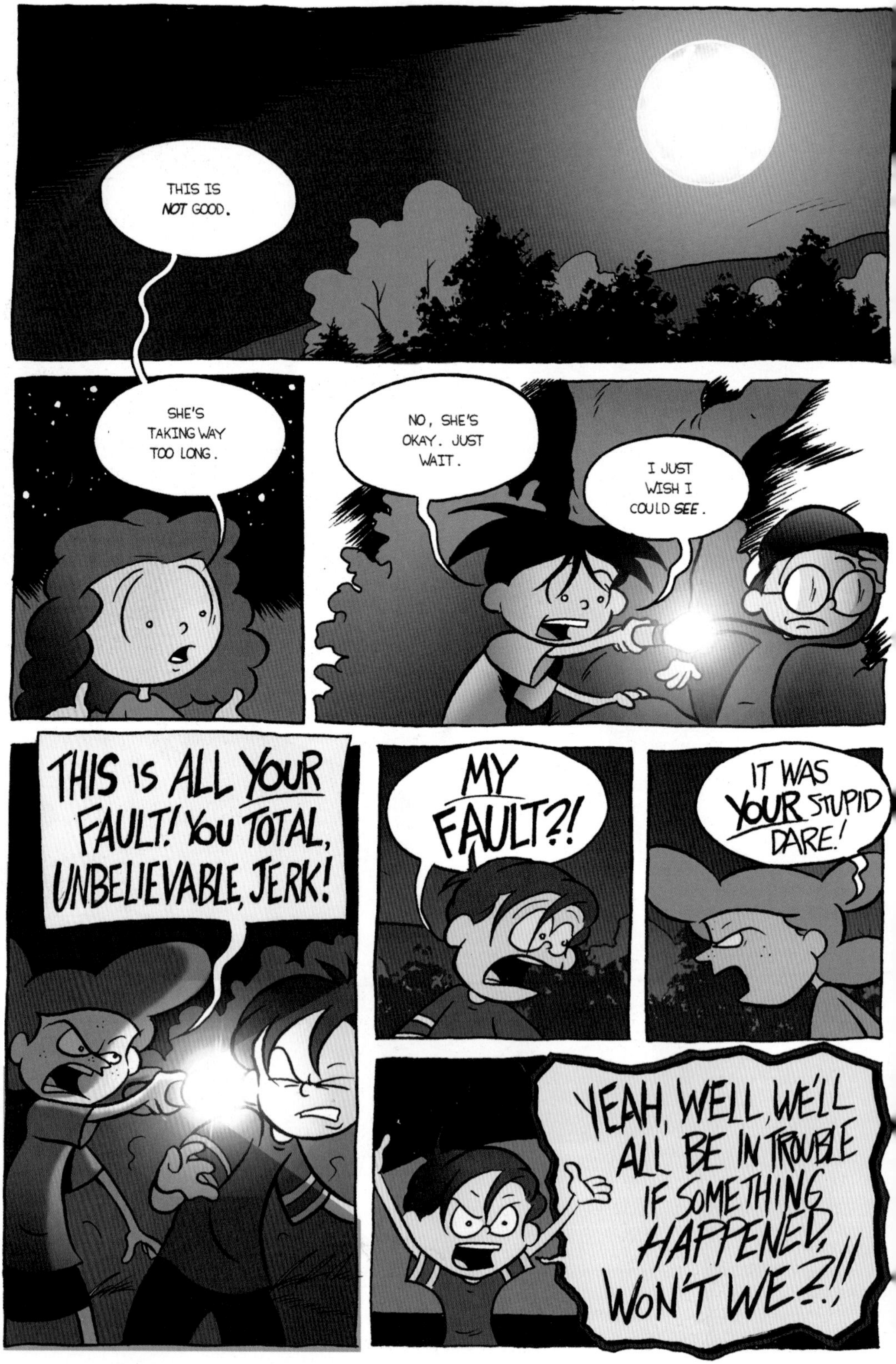
THIS IS *NOT* GOOD.
SHE'S TAKING WAY TOO LONG.
NO, SHE'S OKAY. JUST WAIT.
I JUST WISH I COULD *SEE*.
THIS IS ALL YOUR FAULT! YOU TOTAL, UNBELIEVABLE, JERK!
MY FAULT?!
IT WAS YOUR STUPID DARE!
YEAH, WELL, WE'LL ALL BE IN TROUBLE IF SOMETHING HAPPENED, WON'T WE?!!

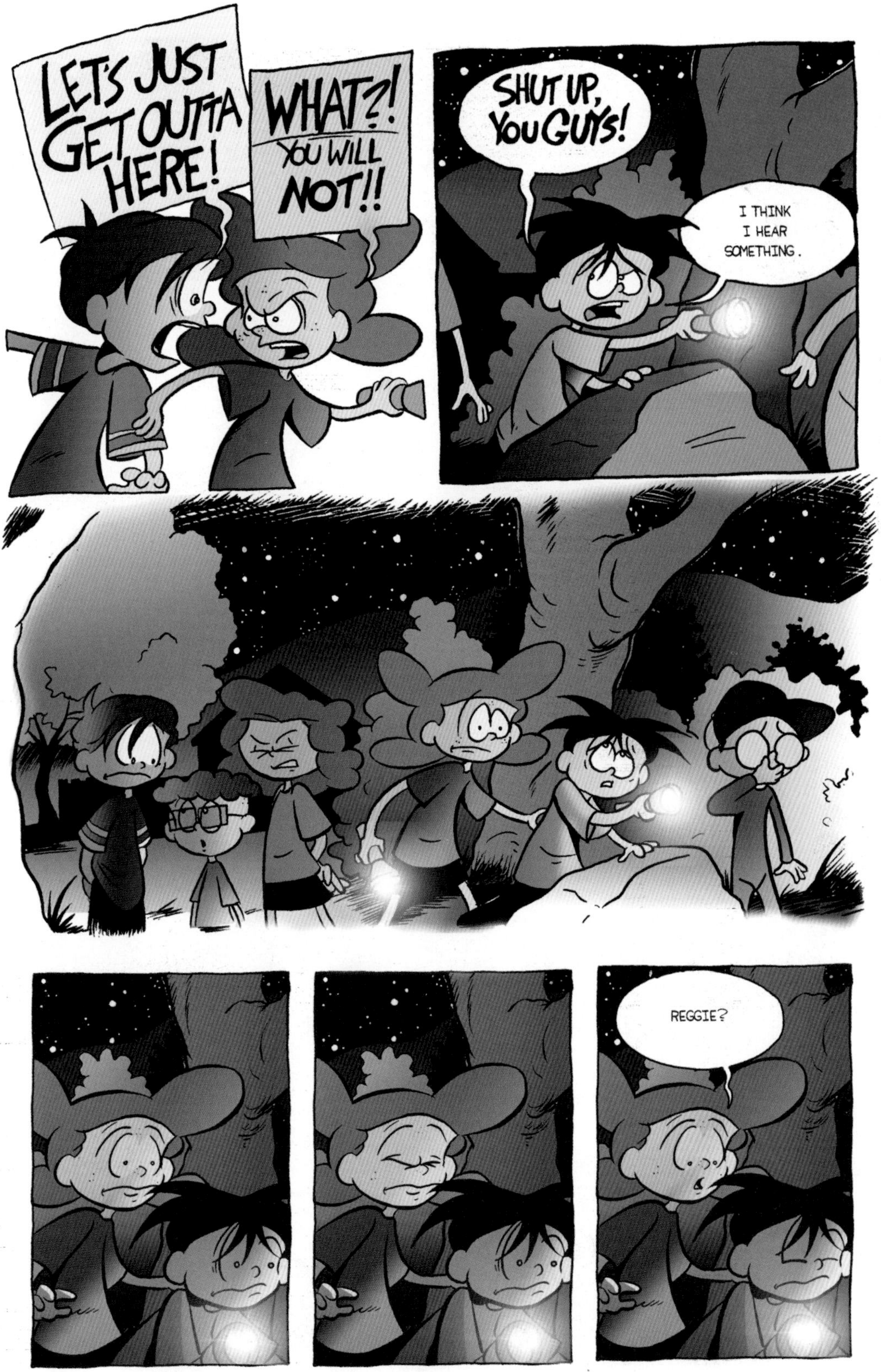
LET'S JUST GET OUTTA HERE!
WHAT?! YOU WILL NOT!!
SHUT UP, YOU GUYS!
I THINK I HEAR SOMETHING.
REGGIE?

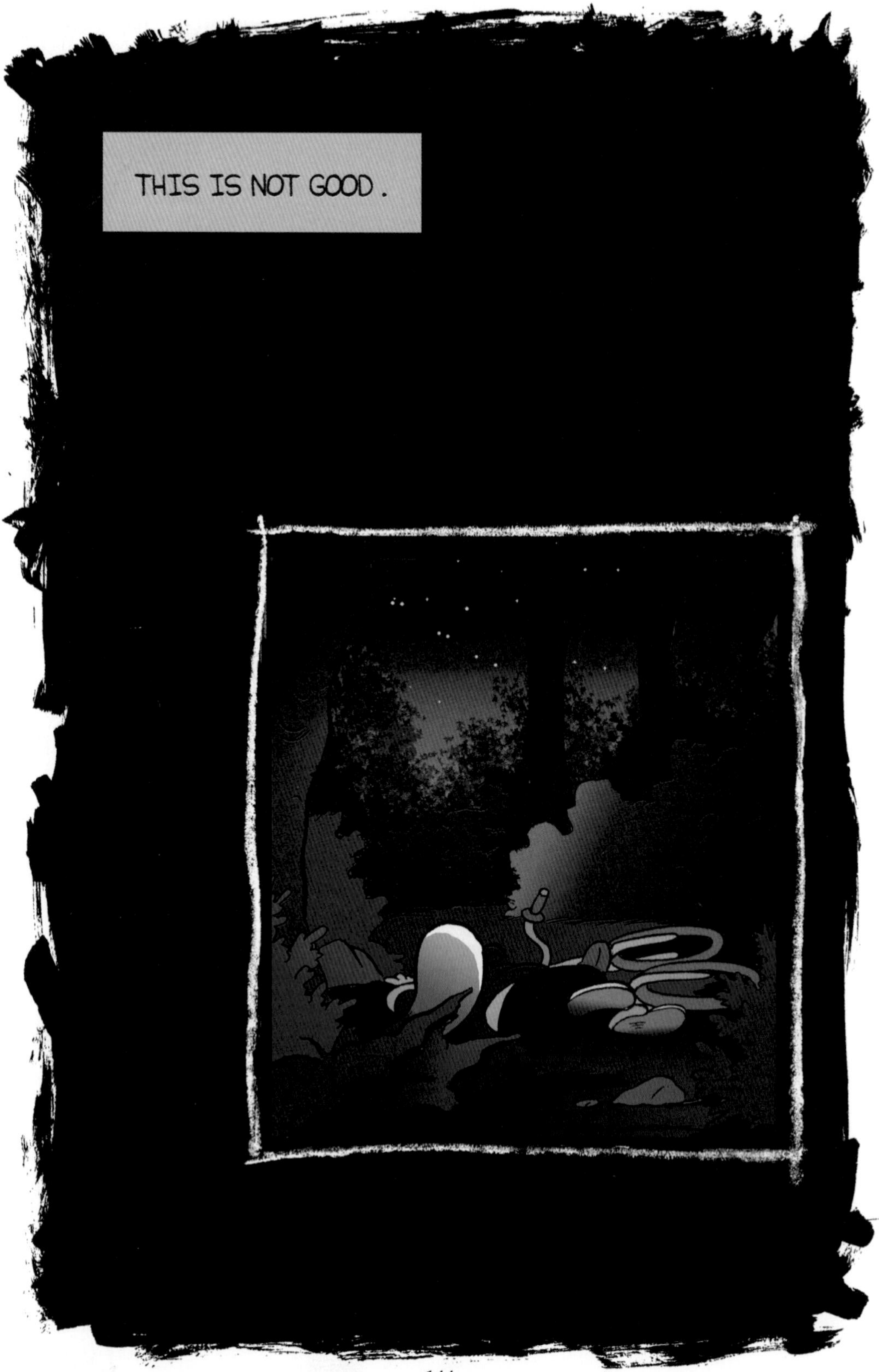
THIS IS NOT GOOD.

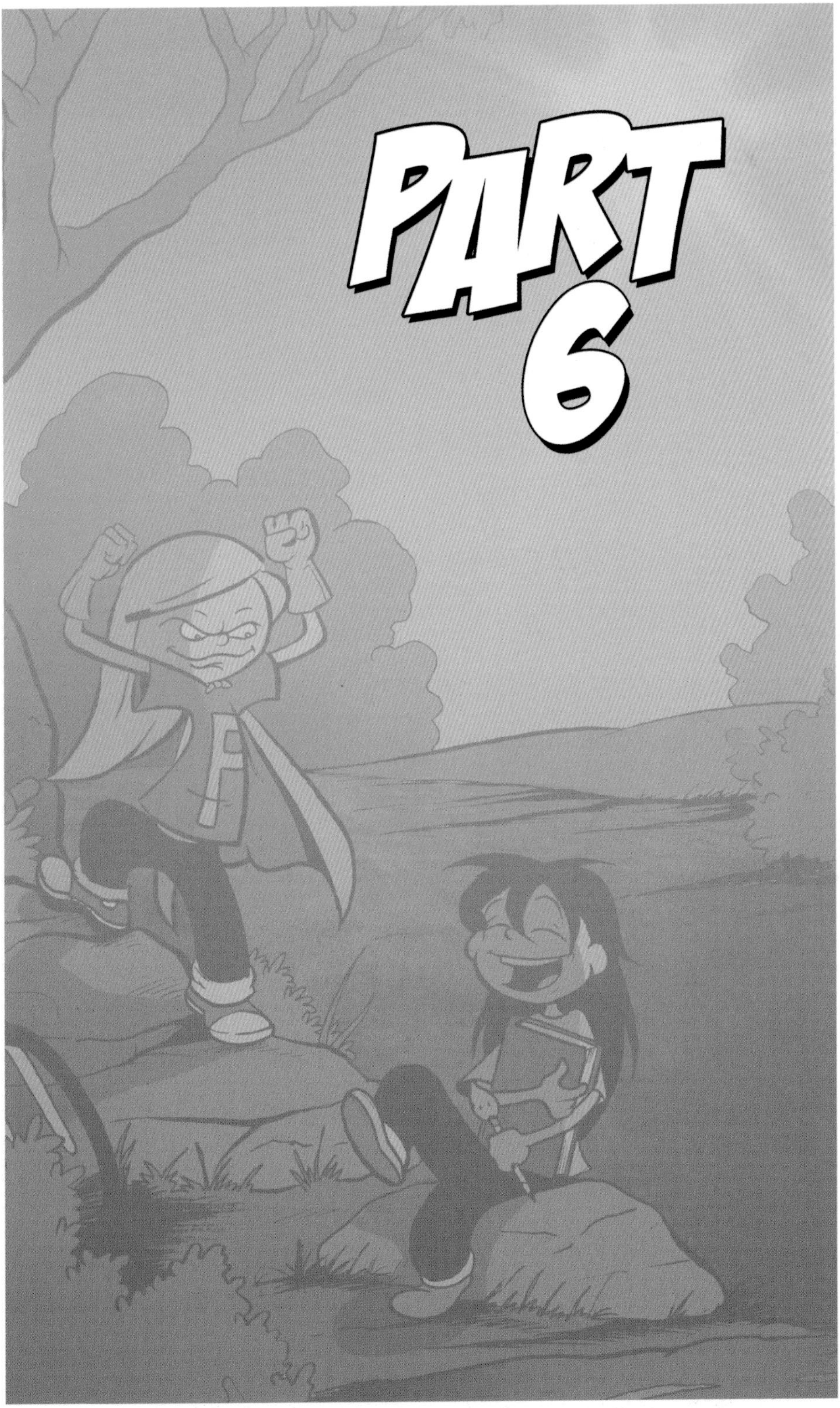
PART 6

Chapter Six:

"Against Unbelievable Odds"

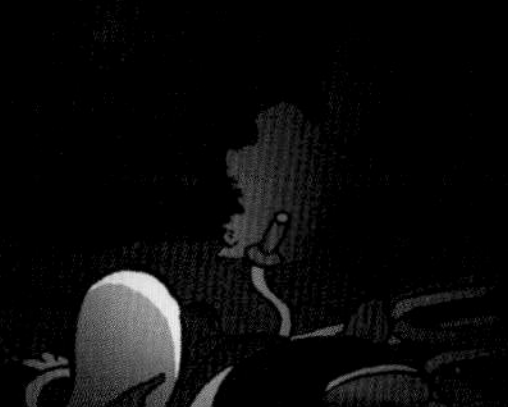

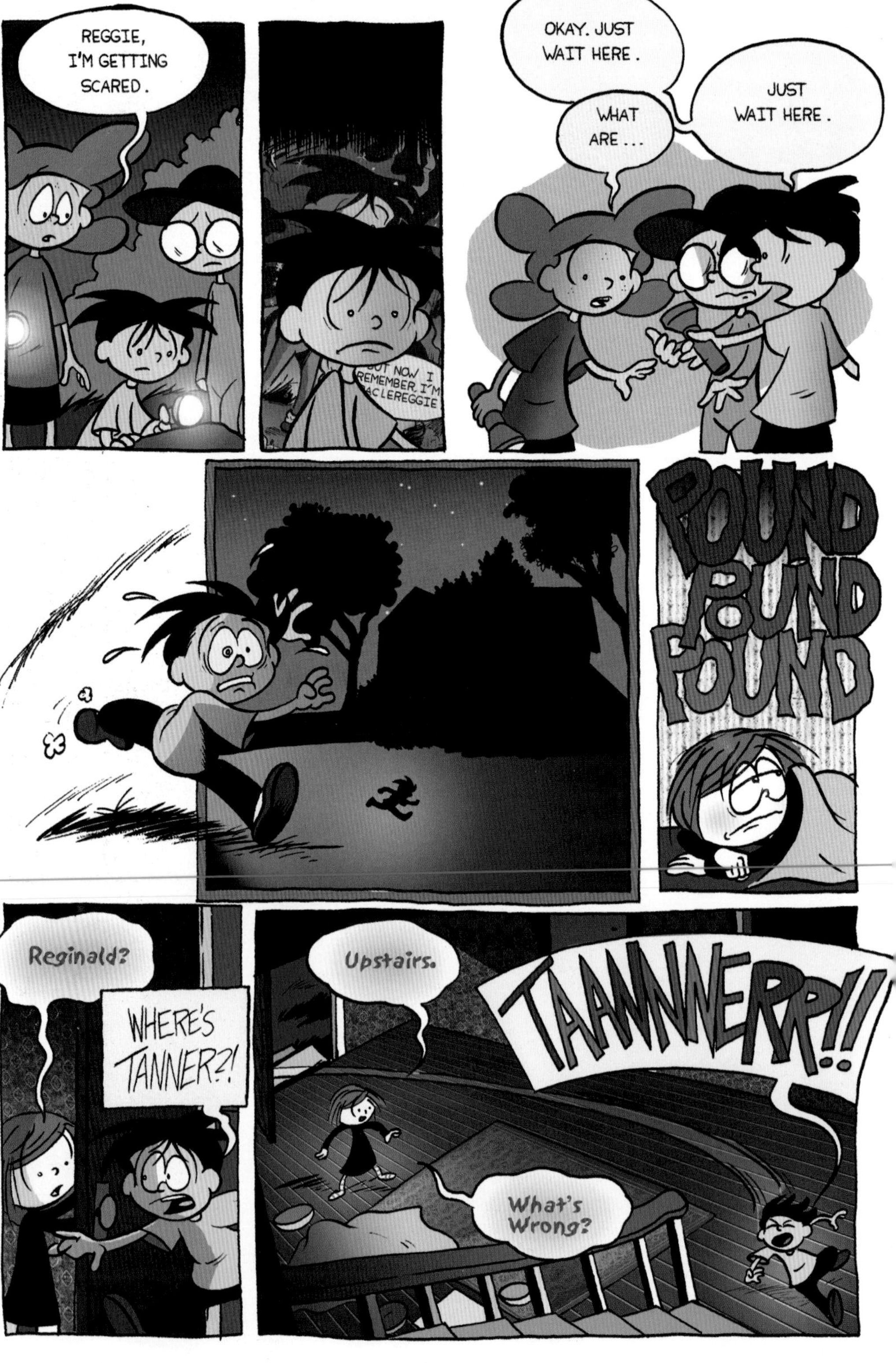

REGGIE, I'M GETTING SCARED.
BUT NOW I REMEMBER, I'M
OKAY. JUST WAIT HERE.
WHAT ARE...
JUST WAIT HERE.
POUND POUND POUND
Reginald?
WHERE'S TANNER?!
Upstairs.
TAANNNERRR!!
What's Wrong?

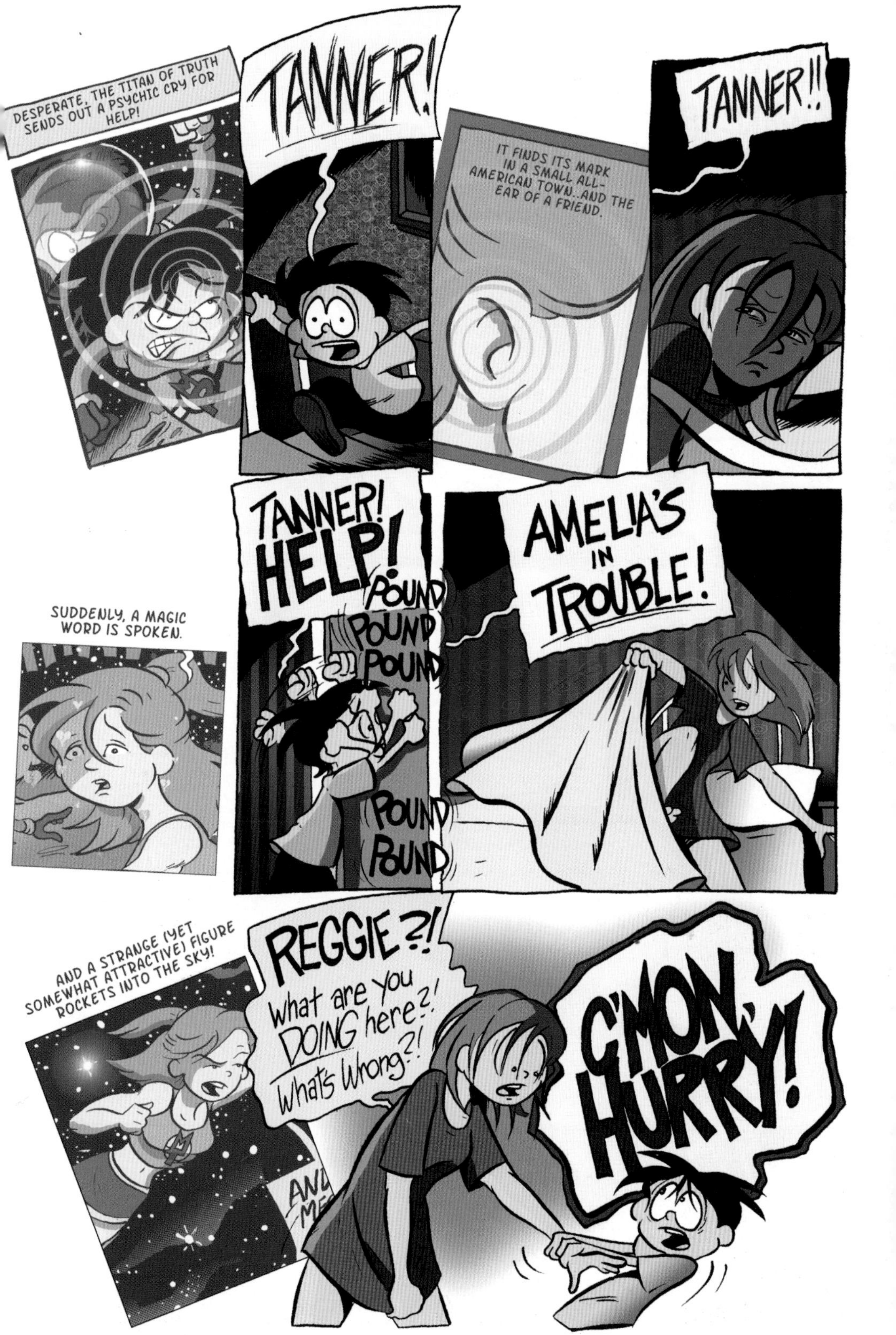

DESPERATE, THE TITAN OF TRUTH SENDS OUT A PSYCHIC CRY FOR HELP!
TANNER!
IT FINDS ITS MARK IN A SMALL ALL-AMERICAN TOWN..AND THE EAR OF A FRIEND.
TANNER!!
TANNER! HELP!
POUND POUND POUND
POUND POUND
AMELIA'S IN TROUBLE!
SUDDENLY, A MAGIC WORD IS SPOKEN.
AND A STRANGE (YET SOMEWHAT ATTRACTIVE) FIGURE ROCKETS INTO THE SKY!
REGGIE?!
What are you DOING here?! What's wrong?!
C'MON, HURRY!

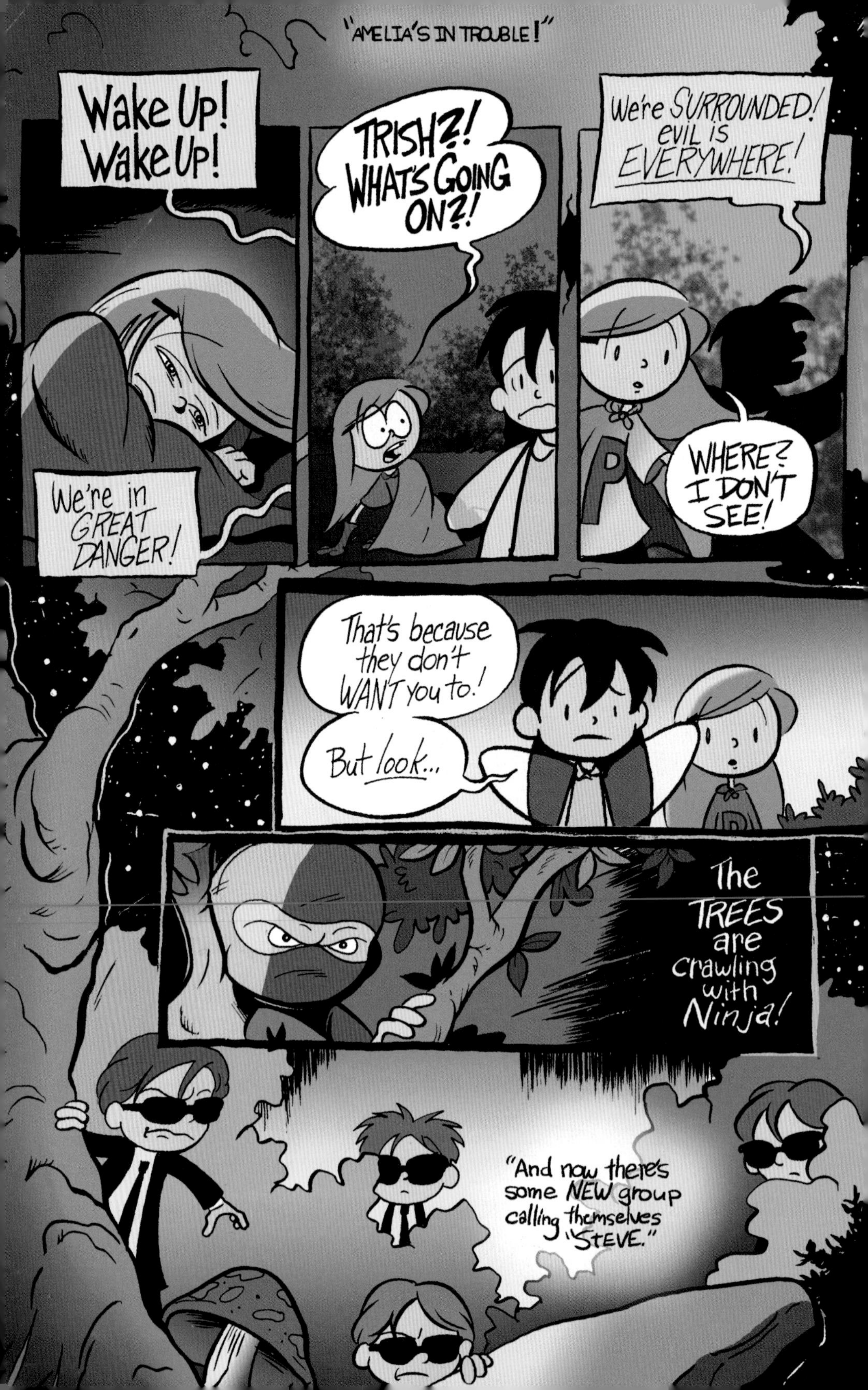
"AMELIA'S IN TROUBLE!"
Wake Up! Wake Up!
We're in GREAT DANGER!
TRISH?! WHAT'S GOING ON?!
We're SURROUNDED! evil is EVERYWHERE!
WHERE? I DON'T SEE!
That's because they don't WANT you to!
But look...
The TREES are crawling with Ninja!
"And now there's some NEW group calling themselves 'STEVE.'"

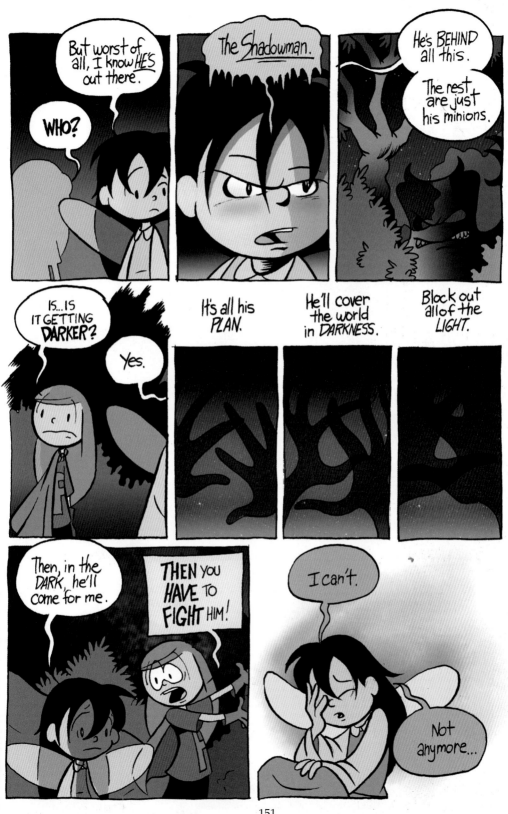

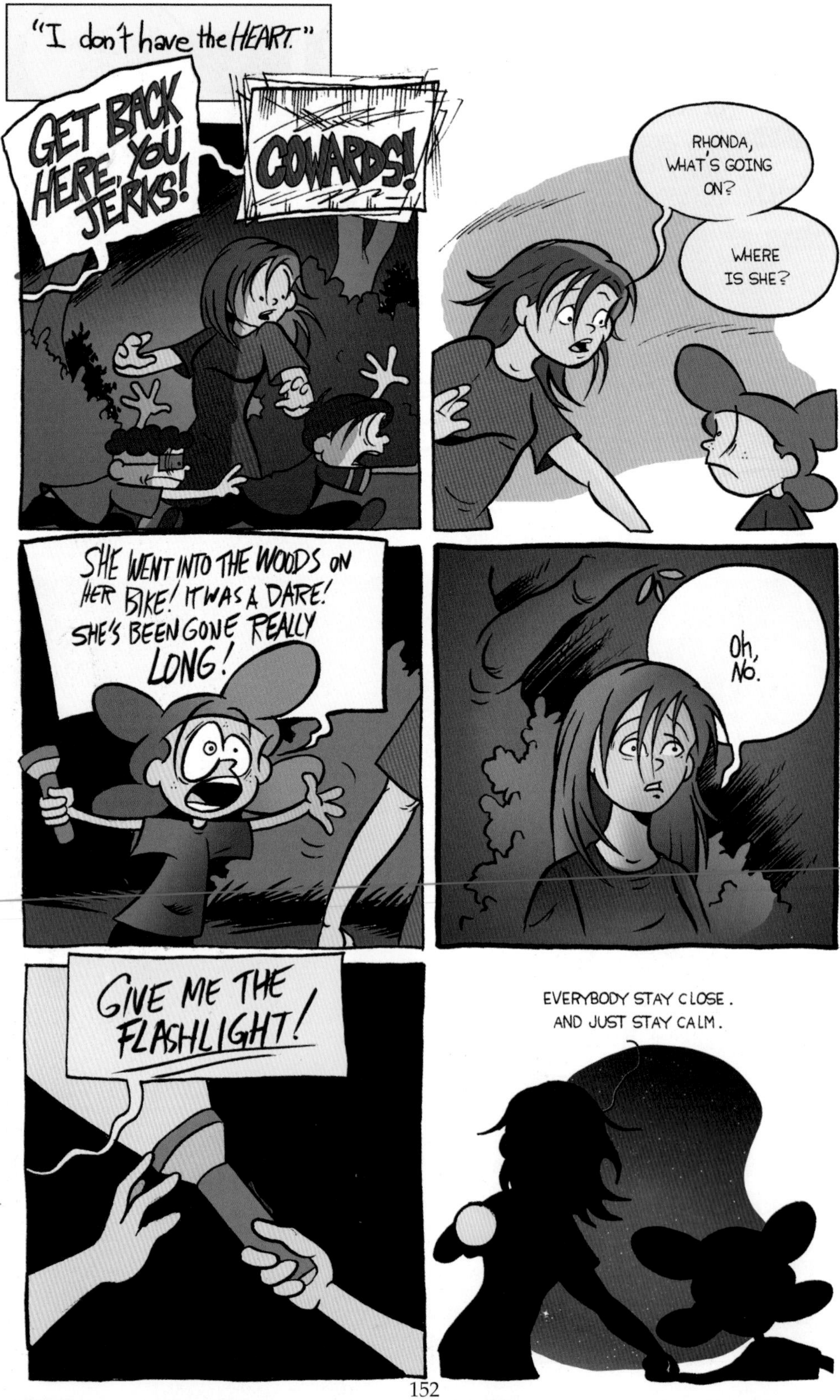
"I don't have the HEART."
GET BACK HERE, YOU JERKS!
COWARDS!
RHONDA, WHAT'S GOING ON?
WHERE IS SHE?
SHE WENT INTO THE WOODS ON HER BIKE! IT WAS A DARE! SHE'S BEEN GONE REALLY LONG!
Oh, No.
GIVE ME THE FLASHLIGHT!
EVERYBODY STAY CLOSE.
AND JUST STAY CALM.

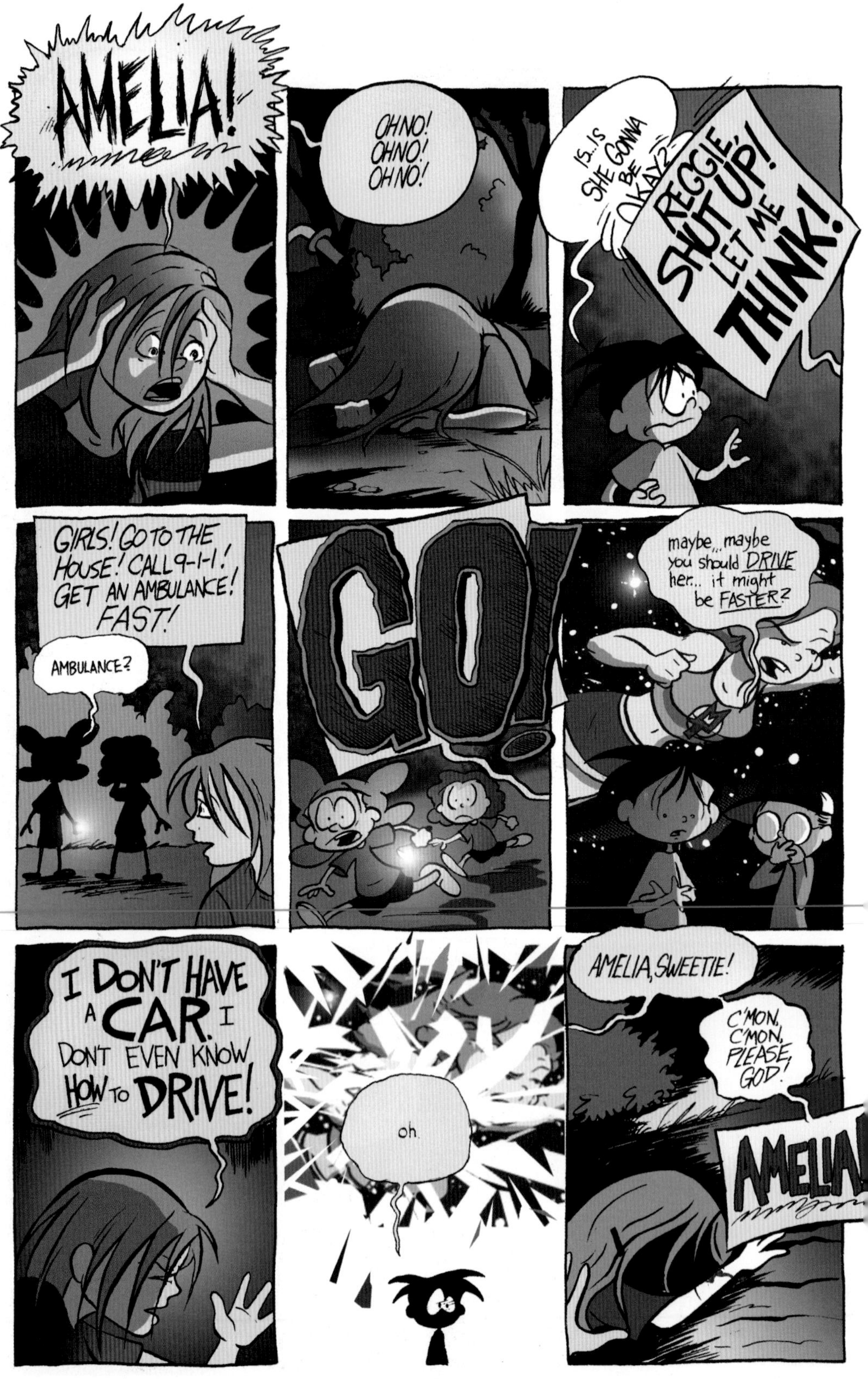
AMELIA!
OH NO! OH NO! OH NO!
IS...IS SHE GONNA BE OKAY?
REGGIE, SHUT UP! LET ME THINK!
GIRLS! GO TO THE HOUSE! CALL 9-1-1! GET AN AMBULANCE! FAST!
AMBULANCE?
GO!
maybe... maybe you should DRIVE her... it might be FASTER?
I DON'T HAVE A CAR. I DON'T EVEN KNOW HOW TO DRIVE!
oh.
AMELIA, SWEETIE!
C'MON, C'MON, PLEASE, GOD!
AMELIA!

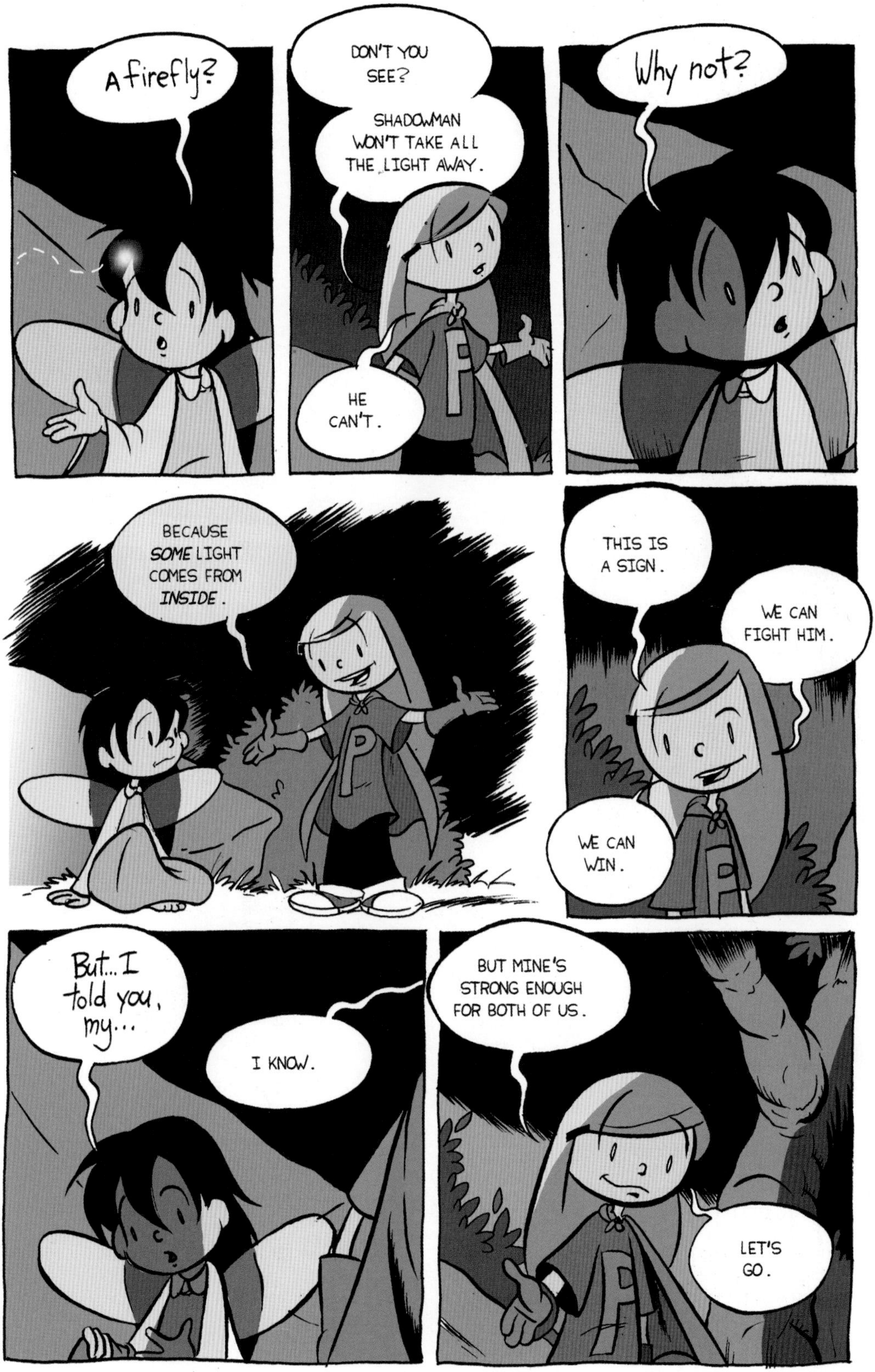
A firefly?
DON'T YOU SEE?
SHADOWMAN WON'T TAKE ALL THE LIGHT AWAY.
HE CAN'T.
Why not?
BECAUSE *SOME* LIGHT COMES FROM *INSIDE*.
THIS IS A SIGN.
WE CAN FIGHT HIM.
WE CAN WIN.
But... I told you, my...
I KNOW.
BUT MINE'S STRONG ENOUGH FOR BOTH OF US.
LET'S GO.

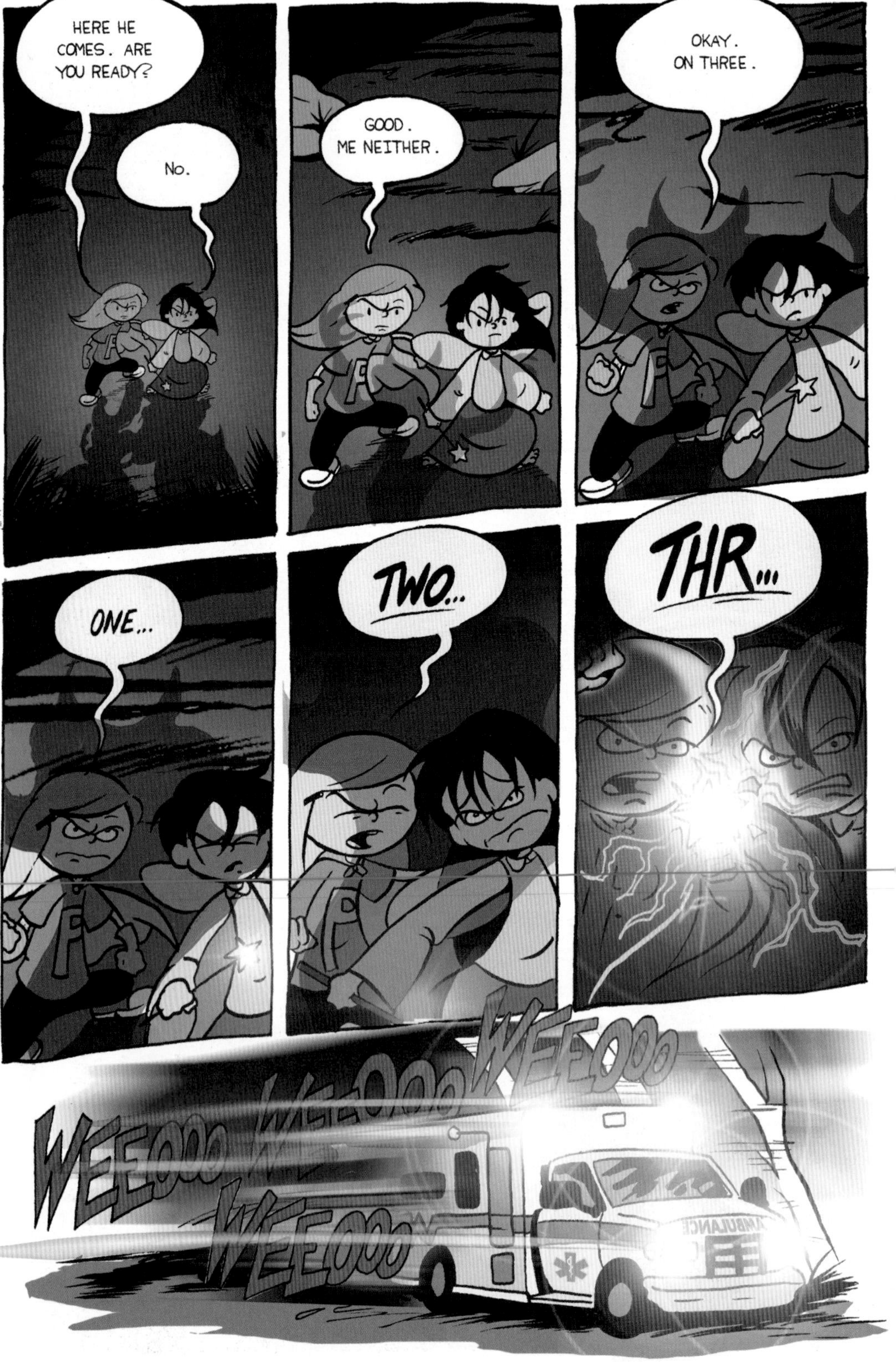
HERE HE COMES. ARE YOU READY?
No.
GOOD. ME NEITHER.
OKAY. ON THREE.
ONE...
TWO...
THR...
WEEOOO
WEEOOO
WEEOOO
WEEOOO
AMBULANCE

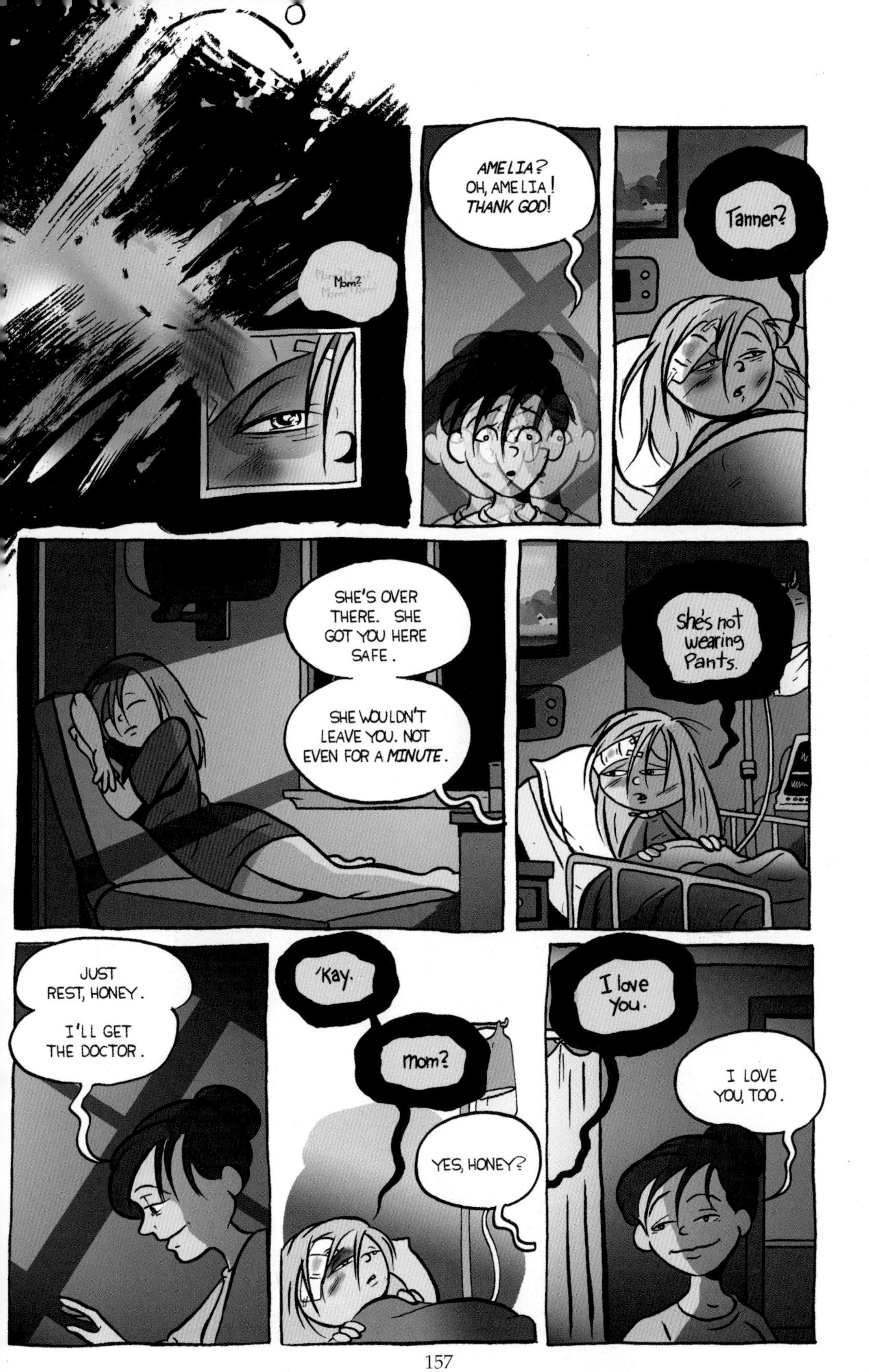
Mom?
AMELIA? OH, AMELIA! *THANK GOD!*
Tanner?
SHE'S OVER THERE. SHE GOT YOU HERE SAFE.
SHE WOULDN'T LEAVE YOU. NOT EVEN FOR A *MINUTE*.
she's not wearing Pants.
JUST REST, HONEY.
I'LL GET THE DOCTOR.
'Kay.
mom?
YES, HONEY?
I love You.
I LOVE YOU, TOO.

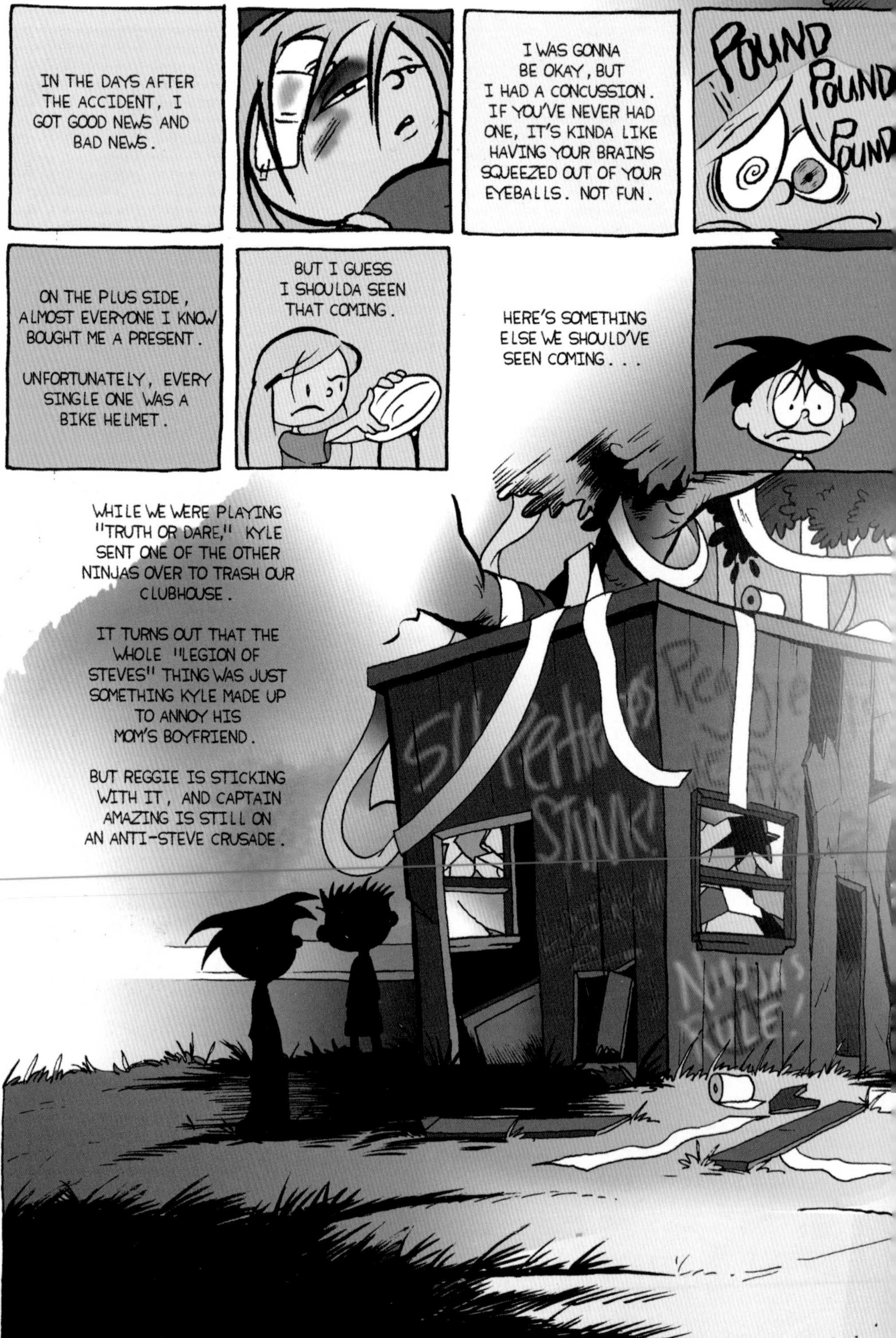
IN THE DAYS AFTER THE ACCIDENT, I GOT GOOD NEWS AND BAD NEWS.
I WAS GONNA BE OKAY, BUT I HAD A CONCUSSION. IF YOU'VE NEVER HAD ONE, IT'S KINDA LIKE HAVING YOUR BRAINS SQUEEZED OUT OF YOUR EYEBALLS. NOT FUN.
POUND POUND POUND
ON THE PLUS SIDE, ALMOST EVERYONE I KNOW BOUGHT ME A PRESENT.
UNFORTUNATELY, EVERY SINGLE ONE WAS A BIKE HELMET.
BUT I GUESS I SHOULDA SEEN THAT COMING.
HERE'S SOMETHING ELSE WE SHOULD'VE SEEN COMING . . .
WHILE WE WERE PLAYING "TRUTH OR DARE," KYLE SENT ONE OF THE OTHER NINJAS OVER TO TRASH OUR CLUBHOUSE.
IT TURNS OUT THAT THE WHOLE "LEGION OF STEVES" THING WAS JUST SOMETHING KYLE MADE UP TO ANNOY HIS MOM'S BOYFRIEND.
BUT REGGIE IS STICKING WITH IT, AND CAPTAIN AMAZING IS STILL ON AN ANTI-STEVE CRUSADE.
STINK!
NINJAS RULE!

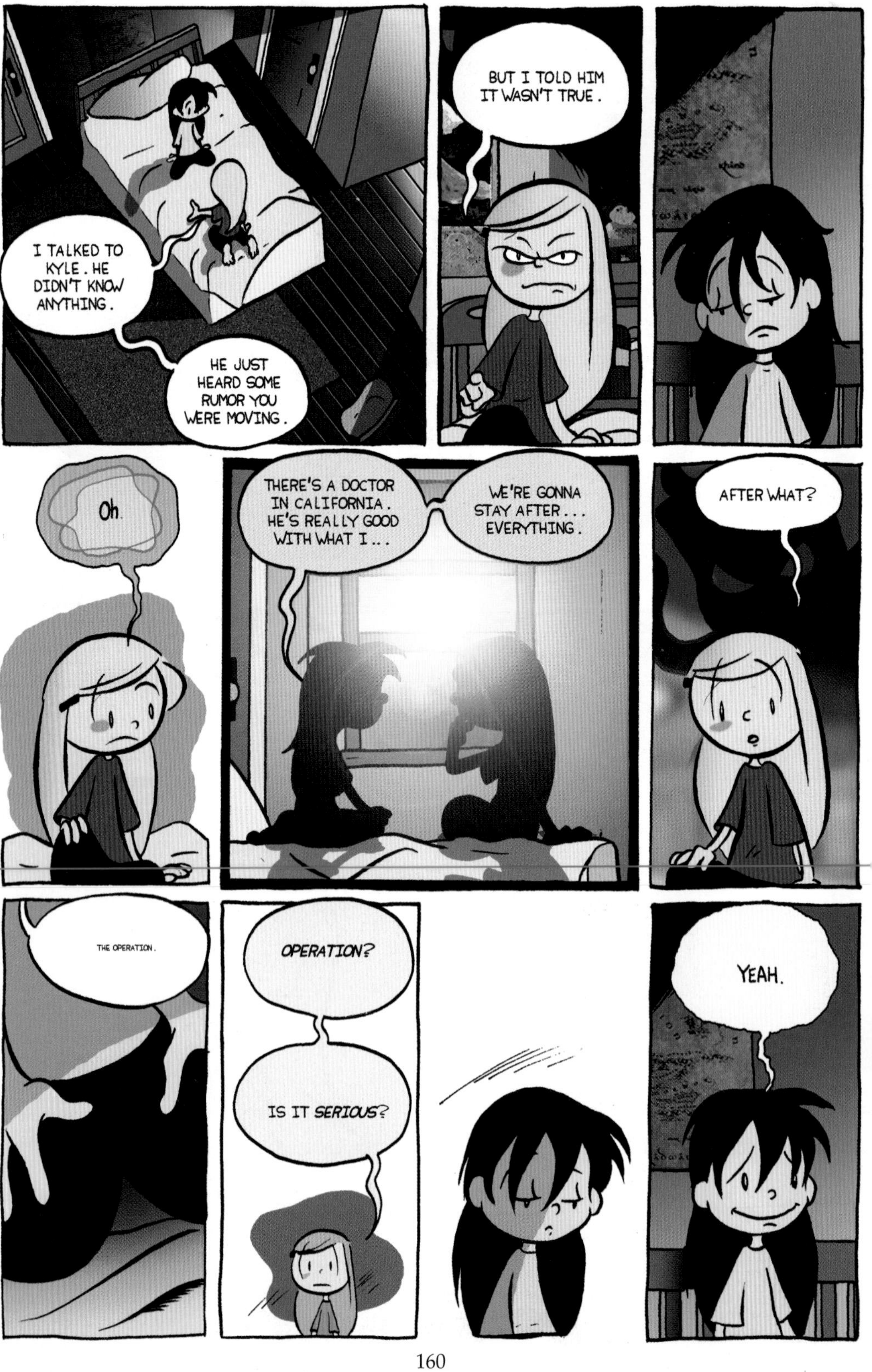
I TALKED TO KYLE. HE DIDN'T KNOW ANYTHING.
HE JUST HEARD SOME RUMOR YOU WERE MOVING.
BUT I TOLD HIM IT WASN'T TRUE.
Oh.
THERE'S A DOCTOR IN CALIFORNIA. HE'S REALLY GOOD WITH WHAT I...
WE'RE GONNA STAY AFTER... EVERYTHING.
AFTER WHAT?
THE OPERATION.
OPERATION?
IS IT SERIOUS?
YEAH.

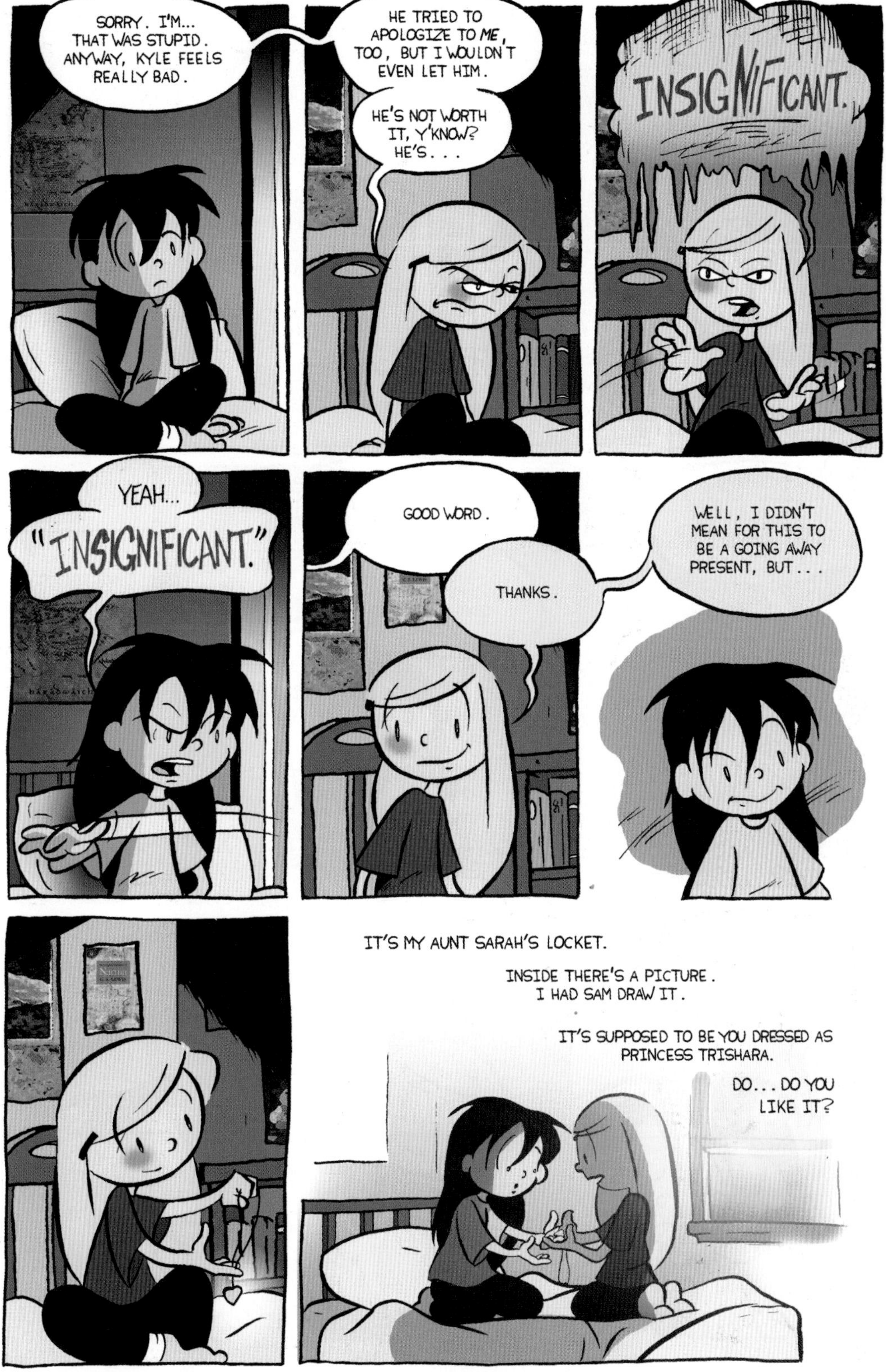

SORRY. I'M... THAT WAS STUPID. ANYWAY, KYLE FEELS REALLY BAD.
HE TRIED TO APOLOGIZE TO *ME*, TOO, BUT I WOULDN'T EVEN LET HIM.
HE'S NOT WORTH IT, Y'KNOW? HE'S. . .
INSIGNIFICANT.
YEAH... "INSIGNIFICANT."
GOOD WORD.
THANKS.
WELL, I DIDN'T MEAN FOR THIS TO BE A GOING AWAY PRESENT, BUT. . .
IT'S MY AUNT SARAH'S LOCKET.
INSIDE THERE'S A PICTURE. I HAD SAM DRAW IT.
IT'S SUPPOSED TO BE YOU DRESSED AS PRINCESS TRISHARA.
DO... DO YOU LIKE IT?

163

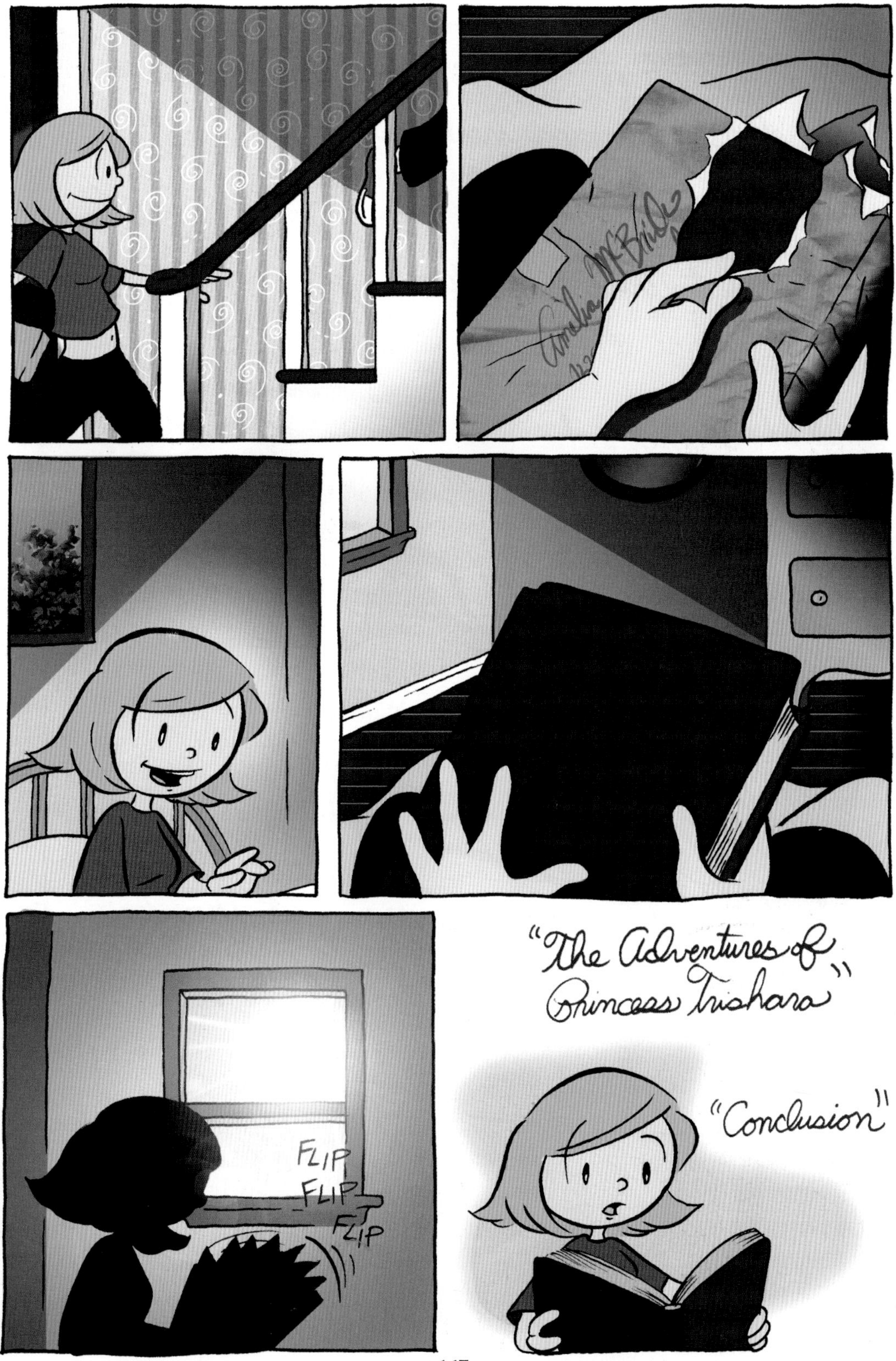
FLIP
FLIP
FLIP
"The Adventures of Princess Trishara"
"Conclusion"

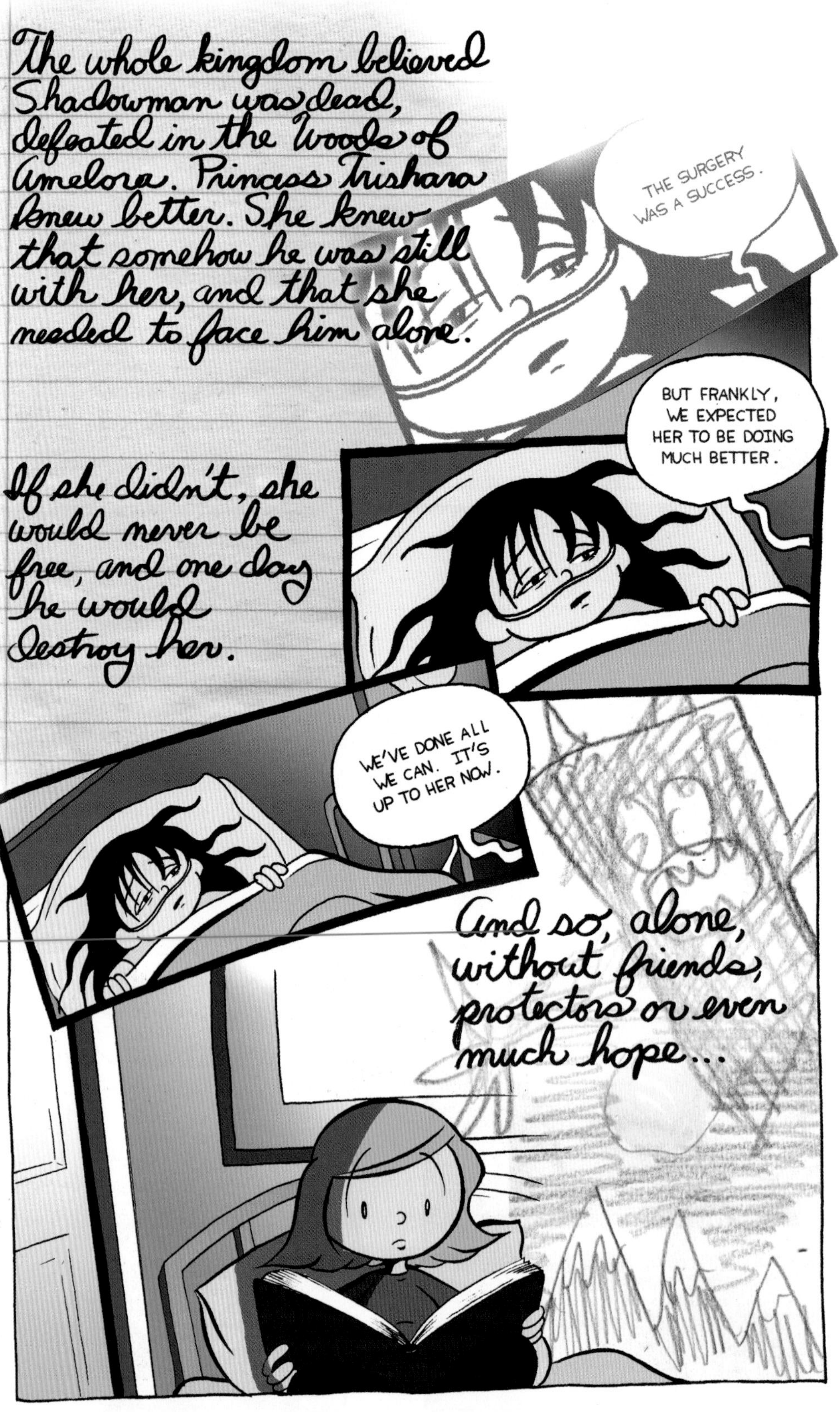
The whole kingdom believed Shadowman was dead, defeated in the Woods of Amelora. Princess Trishara knew better. She knew that somehow he was still with her, and that she needed to face him alone.
THE SURGERY WAS A SUCCESS.
BUT FRANKLY, WE EXPECTED HER TO BE DOING MUCH BETTER.
If she didn't, she would never be free, and one day he would destroy her.
WE'VE DONE ALL WE CAN. IT'S UP TO HER NOW.
And so, alone, without friends, protectors or even much hope...

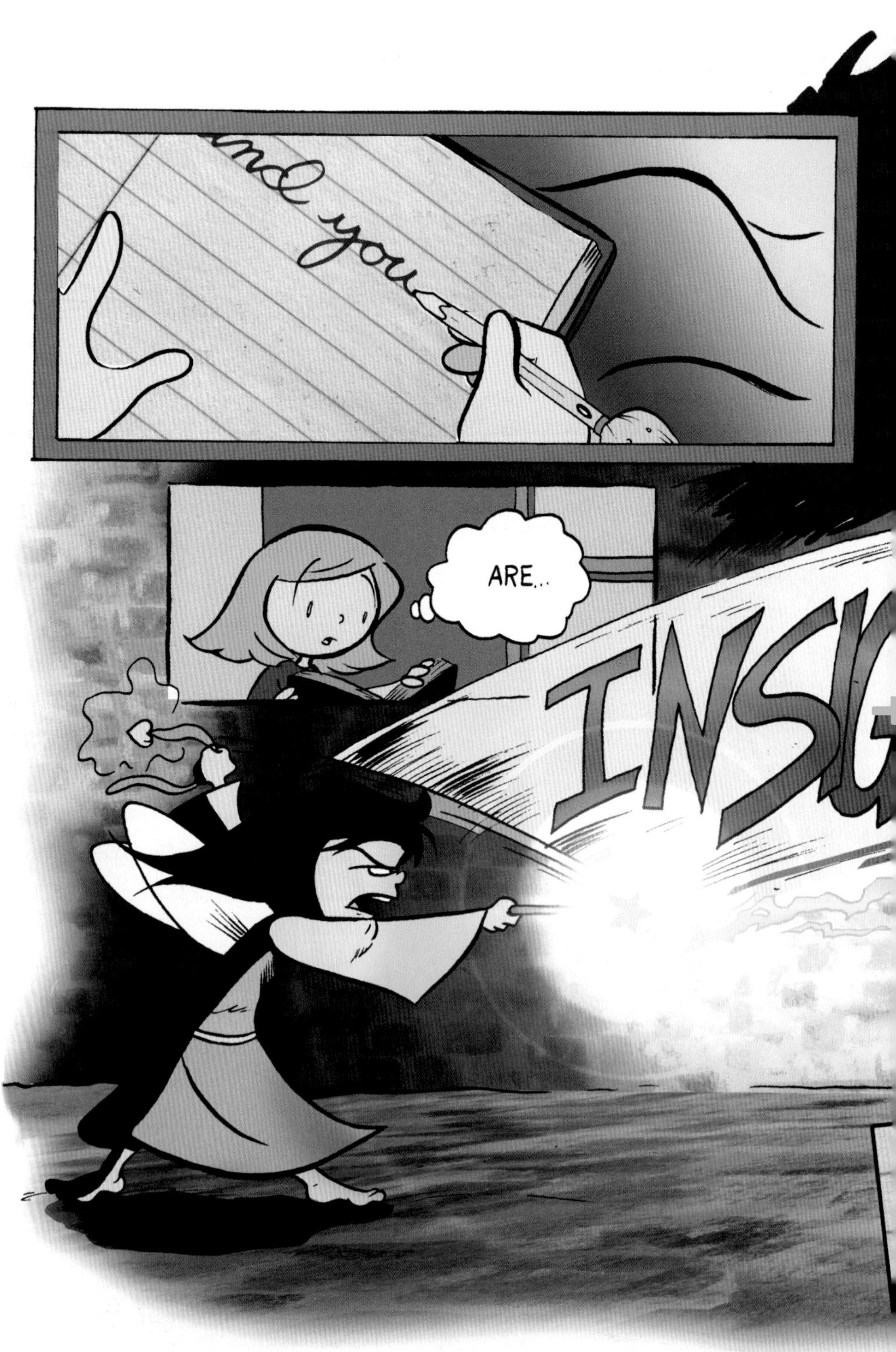
ARE...
INSG

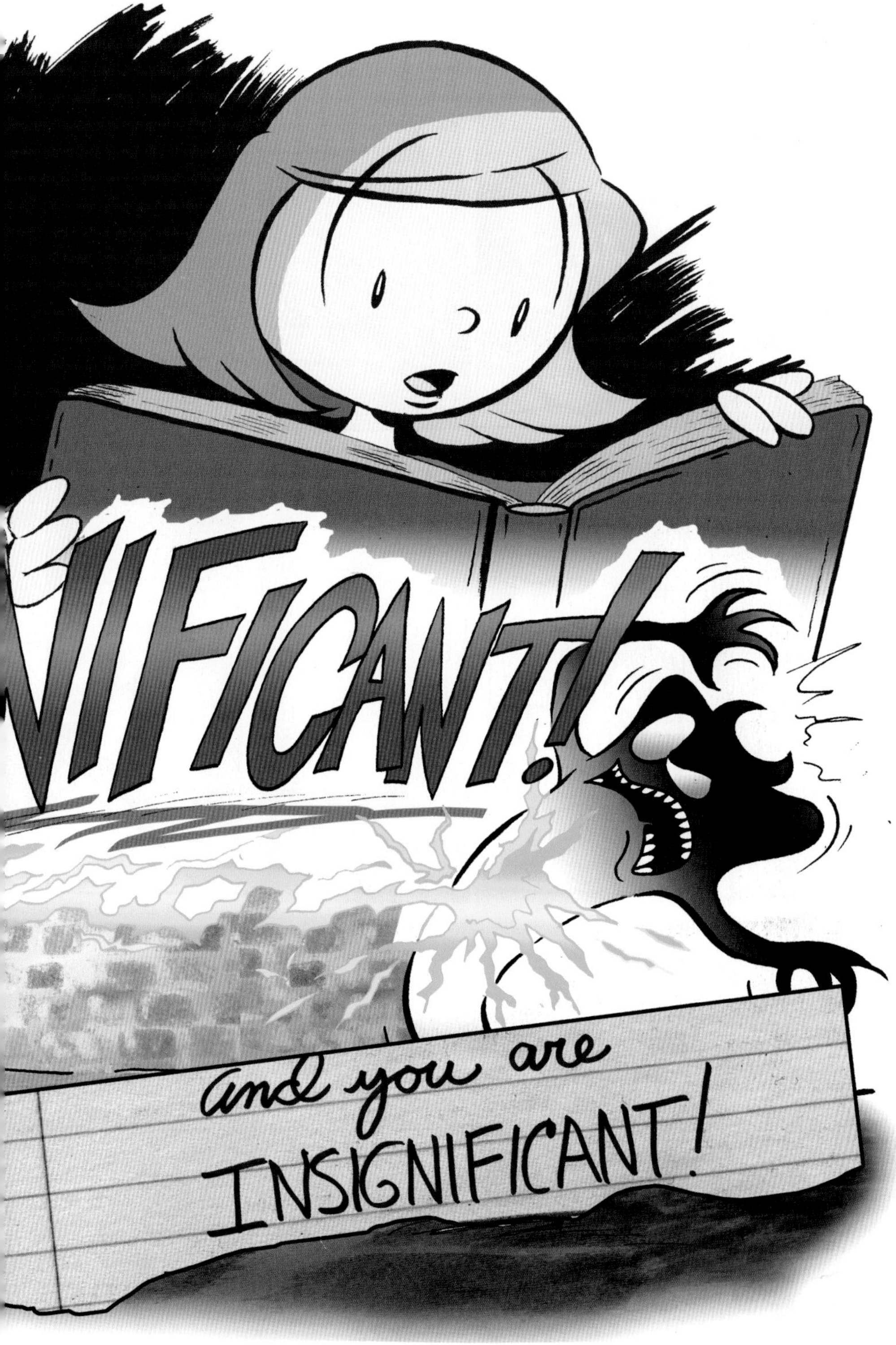
NIFICANT!
and you are
INSIGNIFICANT!

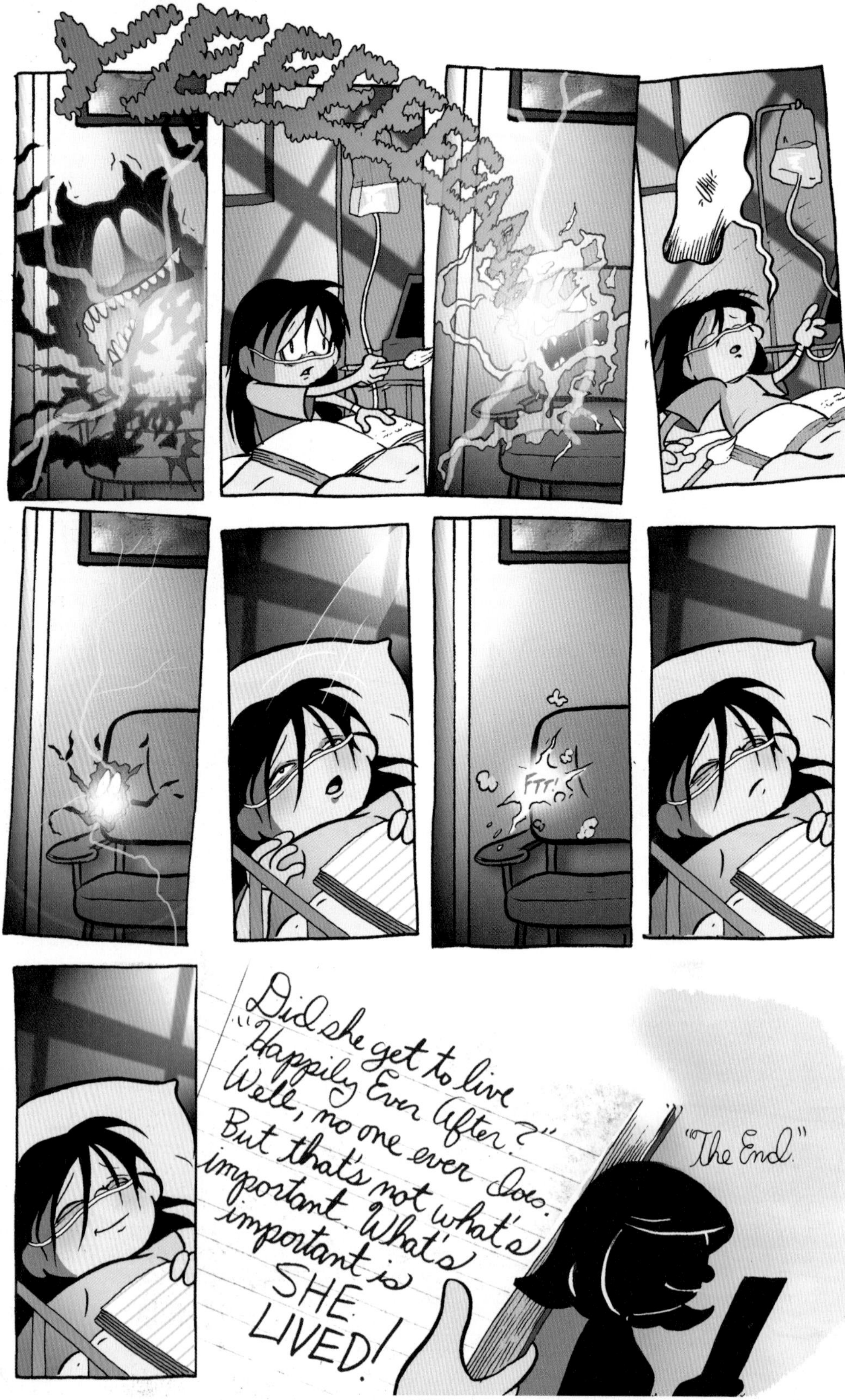
UHH
FTT!
Did she get to live "Happily Ever After?"
Well, no one ever does.
But that's not what's important. What's important is SHE LIVED!
"The End."

"But that's all in the future."

"There's lots between now and then. More school, more play. Lots more laughs, a few more tears."

Cartoonist Jimmy Gownley developed a love of comics at an early age when his mother read *Peanuts* collections to him. Not long after, he discovered comic books (via his dad) and developed a voracious appetite for reading any and all things comic-related.

By the age of 15, Gownley was self-publishing his first book, *Shades of Gray Comics and Stories*. The black & white, slice-of-life series ran 16 issues and was recently collected by *Century Comics*.

The idea for *Amelia Rules!* came about several years ago while Gownley was still working on *Shades of Gray*. The goal was to create a comic book with comic strip sensibilities that both traditional and nontraditional comic book fans could enjoy. He also wanted to provide good, solid entertainment for kids that didn't talk down to them.

Since its debut in June 2001, *Amelia Rules!* has become a critical and fan favorite, and has been nominated for several awards, including the *Howard Eugene Day Memorial Prize*, the *Harvey Award*, and the *Eisner Award*.

34-year-old Gownley lives in Harrisburg, Pennsylvania with his wife Karen and twin daughters Stella and Anna.

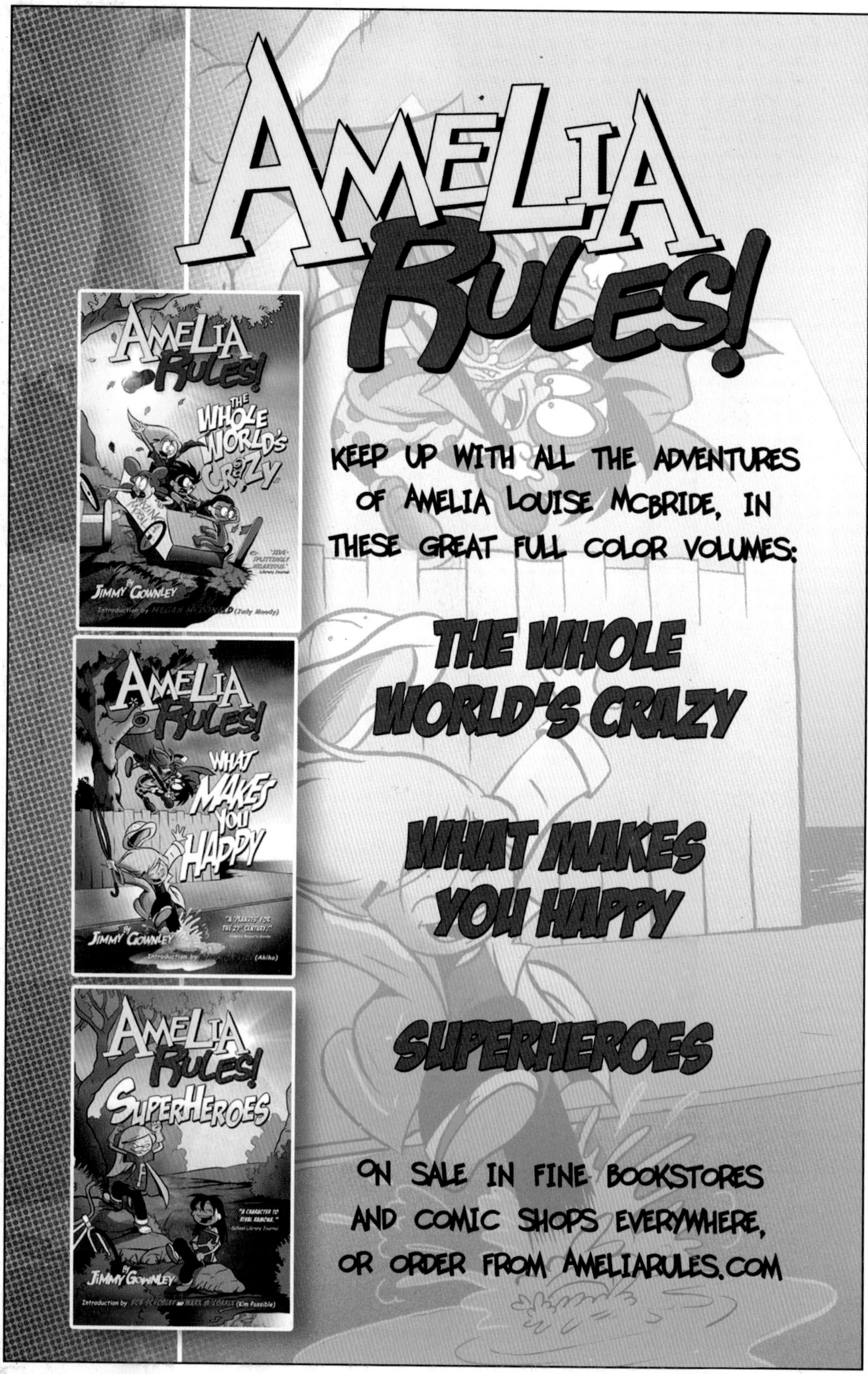
AMELIA RULES!
KEEP UP WITH ALL THE ADVENTURES OF AMELIA LOUISE MCBRIDE, IN THESE GREAT FULL COLOR VOLUMES:
THE WHOLE WORLD'S CRAZY
WHAT MAKES YOU HAPPY
SUPERHEROES
ON SALE IN FINE BOOKSTORES AND COMIC SHOPS EVERYWHERE, OR ORDER FROM AMELIARULES.COM
AMELIA RULES! THE WHOLE WORLD'S CRAZY
BY JIMMY GOWNLEY
AMELIA RULES! WHAT MAKES YOU HAPPY
BY JIMMY GOWNLEY
AMELIA RULES! SUPERHEROES
BY JIMMY GOWNLEY